MON£Y

SIGNS

Astrology, Money
And You

Jane Bowles

Original material by Jane Bowles
Book design and typesetting by David Bowles
Cover illustration by Andrew Forrest. Cover photograph by Ken Hickey
Printed and bound by The Guernsey Press Co Ltd, Channel Islands, UK

Money Signs
© Jane Bowles 1995
(First edition)

ISBN 1-85588-333-3 (Paperback)

The moral right of Jane Bowles to be identified
as the author of this work has been asserted

British Library Cataloguing in Publication Data:
Bowles, Jane. Money Signs. I. Title 133

Additional copies of this book can be purchased both
from bookshops and by mail-order priced at £8.99 each.

UK p&p is *FREE*: overseas please add an additional
£2.00 extra **per book** to cover airmail postage.

Credit card orders welcome: call our order line anytime
on 01803-835593 (or fax 01803-833464). ◼ ⊞ ▭

Please make your cheque/PO/bank draft payable to
'Barton House' in UK pounds sterling.

Please post your order direct to the publisher...

Published by: Barton House
PO Box 6, Dartmouth, Devon, TQ6 9YE, UK
call 01803-835593 or fax 01803-833464
from overseas call (+44) 803-835593, or fax (+44) 803-833464
email address: 100620.3604@compuserve.co

Distributed to the booktrade by *Airlift Book Company*
bookshops only call 0181-804-0400 fax 0181-804-0044

To David and Lucie

and

To the memory of the late Howard Sasportas
"Grace to be born and live as variously as possible"
(Frank O'Hara)

CONTENTS:

A WORD FROM THE PUBLISHERS...

At Barton House we are committed to publishing books which raise the quality of peoples' lives and help to integrate the spiritual with the practical aspects of living in a material world.

If you find this book to be helpful and inspiring we would love to hear from you ...and please recommend *Money Signs* to your friends.

Additional copies can be purchased by mail order — please see the order form at the back of this book — or you can order *Money Signs* from your local bookshop.

ACKNOWLEDGEMENTS

First, I'd like to thank all my teachers of astrology, who helped awaken and sustain my interest and enthusiasm for this fascinating subject over the years — especially Liz Greene, Erin Sullivan, Alan Oken, Darby Costello, Ron Gwynn and Sue Tompkins. Thank you also to the fellow astrologers and experts who introduced me to mundane and financial astrology — Charles Harvey, Daniel Pallant, Nick Campion, Graham Bates and Christeen Skinner. Thanks also to Helena Francis for her enthusiasm and support. A warm and heartfelt thank you also to David Talfryn-Griffiths, for our many useful conversations and his friendship, encouragement and support — and also to Morag Talfryn-Griffiths and Marie-Louise Lacy, whose wisdom, insight and guidance have been a greater source of strength than words can ever express...

A huge thank you also to all who helped to turn *Money Signs* from a dream into reality ...first, to Penny Black for her consistent support with my writing over the years, and to Andy Black, for his humour and generous help with research. To James Bell — without whose unstinting Aquarian enthusiasm, I would have found it hard to get started ...and to Chris Michell, whose spirit helped me bring this project to completion.

Thanks also to James and Salle Redfield, for that special insight that helped me so much, "Never give up!"

Thanks also to Andrew Forrest, for his beautiful cover art, and to Daphne Buckmaster, who helped to edit the text. Thanks to Richard and Gilly Webb, for their help and friendship, and to Peter Rae and Lynne Bateson, for their practical help and advice. A huge thank you also to Eileen Campbell, for her generous friendship and support.

Thank you also to my friends and family, who helped it all happen too ...to Bob and Zara Bowles, and to Mary and Kazik, my parents; to Jenny Britton, Hazel Lewis, Caroline Fay and Bill Hunt, Mandy and John Piggott, Dilys Guildford and Alain, and Debbie and Eddie Shapiro. Thanks also to Sue Wolk, Yvonne Goide and Heather Pinchen — my friends and fellow writers. Thanks also to Ted, Leslie and all at *Café Alf Resco*, in Dartmouth, for making the best cappuccinos in town, and *Cundells Coffee Shop* for providing a congenial space for me to sit and write!

Thanks also to my dear, dear friends and "soul sisters", Janet Ekaette and Jacqueline Stevens, who put up with me so patiently for two long years, and never stopped cheering from the sidelines...

And finally, the biggest thank you of all must go to my husband David, whose love and support means more to me than words can ever say ...thank you so much for "holding it all together", and giving me the space to write ...and for helping make this book become reality... And finally, thank you to my daughter Lucie, who fills my life with such love and joy — and never lets me lose touch with the *really* important things in life!

INTRODUCTION

Astrology, Money and You

In the words of the popular song, "Money makes the world go round", and it's a sentiment that few of us would disagree with. The bottom line is, we all need money. Money keeps our lives moving, and without it, they'd grind to a standstill. We need money to feed ourselves, to keep a roof over our heads, to pay our bills and support our children, and most of us spend a considerable portion of our waking hours either working to earn it or figuring out how to make more of it!

But if money *does* make the world go round, on a material level at least, the fact remains that most of us would dearly love to be on better terms with it. Some years ago, the London Underground carried an advertisement that read, "The two things married couples quarrel about most regularly are sex and money!" I believe that statement could be broadened to include *everyone*, both married and single, for all of us quarrel with someone over money sometime — whether it's with our parents, our lovers, the tax-man, whoever. It's a fact that for around ninety-nine percent of the adult population, money is an inescapable part of our human lives.

But what can we do to make things better? Since the 1980s, we've all grown accustomed to the idea of seeking couples counselling or therapy when the romantic side of our love life hits the rocks. But what do folk do when it's money, instead, that's the problem? Mostly, I'm afraid, they just carry on fighting! Now, however, in the post-recessionary days of the mid-1990s, this state of affairs is at last set to change. The economic slump of the last few years has forced many people to totally re-evaluate their attitudes towards money, work and security, and many are now turning to alternative, less orthodox methods of financial planning. The time has come to take a more enlightened view of money, and that's where astrology − and this book − come in.

One of the most important things to remember about money is that different people view it in very different ways. The prospect of winning £17 million on the National Lottery fills some people with delight, but leaves others feeling distinctly nervous. "Having all that money fall into my lap would worry the daylights out of me", confessed one of my clients the other day. "I wouldn't know what to do with it all, and I wouldn't want the responsibility either. I'd be quite happy with £100,000, though", she added thoughtfully, thus indicating where the boundaries of her own financial 'comfort zone' lay.

On a day-to-day level, some people lie awake at night dreaming how they'll make a million, while others toss and turn, wondering how to make ends meet. Some people get a kick out of hoarding money; others only really feel happy when they're spending it! Some people prefer being paid weekly and in cash; others are happy to get by on sparse, infrequent, but hopefully large cheques. For some members of the human race, six-figure overdrafts and mountainous debts are a fact of life; for others, they are a peril to be avoided like the plague. And have you noticed how some people are always grumbling and complaining about money, even when they've got plenty in the bank — whereas others are content with just the slimmest wage? We all relate to money in endlessly diverse ways, or so it would seem and, at first glance, there's little rhyme or reason to it, let alone any hope of understanding *why* we're all so different! But if you care to delve a little deeper, using astrology as your guide, some interesting facts will begin to emerge.

We're all familiar with the sun-sign columns in national and local newspapers and, for many people, that's where their acquaintance with astrology begins and ends. But the fact is, astrology can also provide the most invaluable and fascinating insights into how we all relate to money, as well as helping to explain those bothersome differences that can cause us so much grief. For the observations of astrologers down the centuries have shown quite conclusively that people born under the same sun sign handle their money in strikingly similar ways.

What that means is that, deep-down, all Ariens relate to money in the same fundamental way, even if their surface behaviour may differ radically at times. That's because they probably have a different moon sign or rising sign — something we'll be touching on in more detail in the fourth section of this introduction. How does this work out in practice? Most Ariens are pretty impatient about having to wait for money and they'll usually view their moneymaking endeavours as one great adventure! The opposite sign of Libra, however, presents a different picture entirely. Librans wouldn't dream of making a fuss about money, even if a bill or debt is long overdue. Indeed, they'll tend to charm, rather than bludgeon, their debtors into paying! Unlike Aries, though, they'll always make a high priority out of spending on their home, for they love to surround themselves with pretty things. Money often runs through a Libran's fingers — unlike Taurus, who attracts it like a honeypot! Taureans get a warm inner glow from having money in the bank and usually manage to pile it high as the years go by.

Their opposite sign of Scorpio loves it too, and will often go to considerable lengths to get it. But you'll also often find that Scorpios and their money are subject to a periodic 'wipeout': Scorpios can make a lot of money in their lives, but they often lose it too, and financially speaking, they'll often rise like the phoenix from the ashes once, twice or even thrice in a lifetime. Take Gemini now: it's a different story again. These quicksilver characters are full of wild, exciting ideas for making lots of money — but when it comes to handling those little financial details, their eyes glaze over with boredom. Nothing could be further from the truth with Cancer, though, who loves to hoard the pennies — and who keeps the firmest possible tabs on each and every cent. Sagittarians have millions of ideas about growing their cash reserves too, though they usually spend their money far quicker than they make it! But every archer has wonderful dreams and once in a while those dreams pay off.

Dreaming wouldn't appeal much to a Capricorn, though, especially when it comes to money. Goats like to build their business empires on a solid financial footing, and they never ever rest till they get to the very top. The top of the mountain appeals to Aquarians, too, though they usually prefer to contemplate the far horizon rather than deal with financial reality. Like their opposite sign of Leo, they can sometimes be very extravagant — though the lions of the zodiac differ in that they regard money in the bank as their god-given birthright, and not something they'd ever stoop to worrying about. Contrast Leo's carefree attitude with the neighbouring sign of Virgo, who is one of the zodiac's great pessimists! Virgoes worry more about money than all the other signs put together ...unlike their opposing sign of Pisces, who always sees the bigger picture, and has a god-given faith that "something will turn up!" Which brings us right back to Aries, and the very point where we started... But first things first. Let's start by looking at *why* we all relate to money in the way that we do.

There's a favourite saying that many astrologers use to explain their art, namely: "Character is destiny". According to our sun sign, we're all born with an innate tendency to react in certain ways to the events in our lives — and that includes financial 'happenings', too. Astrologers are sometimes accused of being fatalistic, but in the case of modern psychological astrology, nothing could be further from the truth. Rather than sentencing you to a predetermined sequence of events, astrology increases your sense of self-knowledge and self-responsibility, which in turn increases your range of choices and, by implication, your personal freedom. If you're a Sagittarian, for example, and you know you're extravagant by nature (which you are!), you can use this knowledge to temper your wild fits of spending. The choice, as I said, is up to you. Forewarned is forearmed, as the saying goes...

Using astrology to understand what makes you 'tick', financially, and thus to become more conscious and self-aware, may well be the most important step you'll ever take towards improving your financial status in a lasting, permanent way. Understanding just *why* you behave the way you do around money is the first step towards making changes and improving your overall financial performance. Getting to know your sun sign can also help you understand what money really means to you on a deeper, psychological level. The chapters that follow will help you to understand your and your partner's inner 'money motives', as well as your inherent financial strengths and weaknesses. We'll also look at the kind of money cycles or financial patterns that some signs seem to experience. So if you were born under a sign like Capricorn, say, where good times and abundance may be slow in coming, astrology can help give you the patience to wait! Astrology simply highlights the issues — how you use that knowledge is up to you.

The other great thing about astrology is that it's a profoundly practical art and provides a wealth of useful knowledge to guide you through the modern money maze. Astrology gives you insights into the spending style of each sign, showing just what they like to spend their money on — and why — so that's something we'll be looking at, too. All of us have our weak spots, no matter how prudent and thrifty we like to think we are, and *Money Signs* will tell you exactly where your financial Achilles heel is! More importantly, it also pinpoints those rare times when no-one, whatever their sun sign, should consider entering into financial agreements, or making major purchases, such as a car or perhaps a new home.

Risk and speculation are two further areas that every sign takes a different approach to, and, using the simple keys and guidelines laid down in this book, you can easily create a savings and investment strategy that's exactly right for you. For some, like Taurus or Cancer, for instance, this involves 'playing it safe' and plumping for property or antiques. Others, like Aries, say, or Leo, will only feel happy when the investment stakes are much higher. Stock-market speculation is mother's milk to these guys — but to many other signs, it's just like drinking poison. A third group of signs, which includes Virgo and Scorpio, tends to fall between two stools, but can develop more financial confidence by learning to take more risks. Investment is a complex subject, though, so whether you tread quickly, like an Aries, or more slowly, like a Taurus, you should *always* tread with care.

You'll note that the investment areas which are potentially profitable for each sign are described here in fairly general terms. That's because I happen to be an astrologer and not a financial advisor, and the law requires me to stick to my area of expertise! *Money Signs* indicates the *style* of investment each sign is happiest with, and the *areas* they like to invest in. So if you want to convert these general guidelines into specific investments, please consult a professional financial advisor or broker.

Since the great majority of us spend a good proportion of our lives engaged in *earning* money, a corresponding percentage of the pages that follow are devoted to a discussion of work. Indeed, untold damage and misery can be caused by choosing the wrong job or career. Leading medical writer Deepak Chopra has expressed the view that lack of job satisfaction is one of the major causes of ill health in the Western world. According to Chopra, more heart attacks take place at 9 a.m. each Monday morning than at any other time in the week!

Choosing our work is something we need to take very seriously indeed. The mass redundancies of the early 1990s may have seemed disastrous at first but for many, the loss of a well-paid but unsatisfying job proved to be the first step towards discovering where their true vocation lay. The solicitor who's fired from her big city practice may realise a long-held dream of running a sailing school. The primary school teacher who can't stand the stress of inner-city teaching any longer may be drawn to move to the country and paint... And the funny thing is that once people start doing what they really love, they often wind up earning far more money than before. So, though it feels scary at first, finding our true vocation is often a sure-fire way of boosting our earning power in the longer term.

Each sign is looking for a subtly different kind of job satisfaction too, and astrology is uniquely suited to show you exactly what that secret ingredient is... In the following pages, we'll explore the work styles and work environment best suited to each sign, as well as their workaday strengths and weaknesses, and reveal what they need to avoid. There's nothing sadder than the sight of a restless Aries tied to a humdrum desk job, or a plodding Taurus whose job requires them to make instant decisions! *Money Signs* tells you who's best at doing what, and why — and backs it all up with some examples of dazzling success stories, both past and present.

Astrology can also help you find your ideal career or 'right livelihood' — even the job that's exactly tailor-made for you. Not only is it one of the most specific sources of career guidance on the planet but science has also substantiated its age-old pronouncements. The research carried out in 1984 by Professor Alan Smithers of Manchester University showed an irrefutable link between astrology and career. For example, a great many well-known showbusiness entertainers are born under Aries, a sign that's well noted for its drive and sense of drama. The survey also showed that more artists and painters were born under Taurus than any other sign, which, aptly enough, is linked with art and beauty. The decades-long research carried out by the late Michel Gauquelin in Paris, France also showed a direct link between astrology and vocation. In other words, *when* you're born most certainly influences *what* you're happiest doing.

Finally, astrology can help you understand not just your *own* financial behaviour, but *other people's* as well. Whether it's your spouse, live-in partner, or your parents, you can use this book as a guide to help you understand not only where you are coming from financially, but also where *they* are coming from as well! *Money Signs* also explains some of the financial pitfalls and problems you may encounter with your children, and suggests some helpful approaches you might adopt. Find out when your boss or business partner's birthday is and you can use this book to shed light on *their* financial behaviour, too. Remember, astrology was the world's first system of human psychology and, at its best, it's a superb tool for helping you to understand the 'significant others' in your life ...as well as those powerful inner forces that shape your own financial reality.

Astrology & Money:
Past and Present

All things considered, astrology is one of the world's great mysteries, for no-one really knows just how it works — or even where it all began... The word 'astrology' means 'speech of the stars' and its origins are shrouded deep in antiquity. We know that man was charting the phases of the moon as early as 15,000 BC and, by 3,000 BC, the priest-astrologers of ancient Babylonia had refined their so-called 'stargazing' into a precise and hallowed art. One thing we do know for certain, though, is that *every* ancient civilisation studied the stars in one form or another and many of their beliefs have survived right up to this day.

Take the moon, for instance, whose ability to affect and intensify human emotions, as well as to swell the ocean tides, has been known and studied for centuries. If you don't think the moon affects people's moods, just ask a policeman, or a nurse down at your local psychiatric unit and see what they think. The

Philadelphia Police Department published a report called "The Effect of Full Moon on Human Behaviour", which clearly showed that crime rises when the moon is at its peak. These findings are simply the latest in a long line of studies that proves the wisdom of the ancients. The movements of the planets *do* correspond to events on earth and in people's lives and, although we may not know exactly *how* astrology works, the fact is it *does* work — so why not use it to your advantage?

Using astrology to improve your financial performance may sound avant-garde, but it actually has a long and very respectable history. The Greek philosopher Aristotle told how Thales of Miletus (636 — 546 BC) used his knowledge of astrology to make a killing on the olive harvest, and streetwise speculators have been following in his footsteps ever since. The great American financier, J.P. Morgan, was an avid devotee of astrology, and once uttered the immortal phrase, "Millionaires don't use astrology, billionaires do!" Such was Morgan's faith in astrology that he had his own personal astrologer, Evangeline Adams, and he never made a major financial move or stock-market investment without first seeking her advice. The Hollywood screen actress Talullah Bankhead also consulted astrologers, as did the legendary Mae West, who used the counsel of the heavens to plot every move of her business and financial career. West was noted for her financial shrewdness every bit as much as her risque one-liners, and she enjoyed considerable wealth to the end of her days.

In our own time, many celebrities and top-ranking businessmen use astrology to light the way to fame and fortune. When the news broke in spring 1988 that

Ronald Reagan, US president of the day, was dictating his daily schedules on the basis of astrology, many officials in the corridors of power were horrified. But if truth be told, Reagan was in good company ...a United Nations survey on the subject revealed that no less than thirteen heads of state also used astrology on a regular basis! The oil tycoon Sheikh Yamani was reputed to call OPEC meetings for times when the planets would be aligned in his favour and the late Indira Gandhi also used astrology extensively. Incidentally, it's also said that Benjamin Franklin and Thomas Jefferson, two of the great founding fathers of the United States, must have used astrology, since they insisted that the Declaration of Independence be ratified on July 4th 1776 — a day when the prevailing planetary line-up augured the foundation of a country with lasting peace and prosperity.

Donald Regan's book about the Reagans, which revealed the President's reliance on astrology, also disclosed the surprising extent to which astrology is used on Wall Street. Regan hinted that a staggering 48 per cent of brokers use astrology in their dealings, though since few will admit this openly, this figure is hard to verify. But the fact remains that the brokers and traders I've discussed this with are so keen to get an edge on their competition that they'll happily consider *any* tool or technique that could tip the odds in their favour — and that most definitely includes astrology. One of the most successful traders in recent years was the late Lt-Cdr David Williams, who was formerly head of purchasing for Consolidated Edison in New York. Williams made millions from stock market speculation between 1982 and 1987, using astrology to tell him when to get into the market and when to get out, finally selling out at the peak just prior to the 1987 crash.

The UK financial astrologer Dan Pallant, another leading figure in the field, has made a comprehensive study of financial cycles based on the Financial Times Index, and now has over twenty large investment trusts on his books, as well as many private investors. The wisdom of the stars can be applied to the property sector too, as well as the stock market. UK astrologer Charles Harvey accurately predicted the collapse of the British housing market many months before the event, advising his clients to sell up in good time and safeguard their investments. As we said before, "Forewarned is forearmed!"

Interestingly, although many Western politicians and businesspeople are reticent about revealing the fact that they use astrology, this ancient art is widely accepted and practised in the East. In India, for instance, there are many businesspeople who wouldn't *dream* of making a major financial decision without first consulting their astrologer. The Chinese business community, too, is well known for its reliance on astrology, as well as its financial acumen. Astrology is also popular in Japan, and Yoko Ono reputedly uses it to help run her multi-million dollar business empire. Many top actors and personalities, such as Anthony Hopkins, Sting and Princess Diana, have also consulted astrologers in their day, so if you take the plunge and 'look to the stars', you'll certainly be in good company!

Sun Signs...

Before we start exploring the money secrets of our sun-signs, we need to understand what 'sun-signs' actually are, and even more importantly, what they can and cannot tell us.

Your sun sign is the most important part of your personal horoscope, and it's the sign of the zodiac the sun was passing through on the day you were born. The zodiac itself is also called the ecliptic, and it follows the sun's *apparent* path around the earth. The ancients believed that the sun travelled round the earth, and although man has known for centuries that it's actually the other way round, astrology is based on how we see things from the earth. Astrologers divide up the circle of the zodiac into twelve equal portions or 'signs' and you can discover your sun sign by finding out where the sun was positioned on the day of your birth. If your birthday falls on the change-over date between consecutive signs — more commonly known as the cusp — you'll need to verify the exact time the sun changed signs, by checking it with an astrologer.

Your sun sign describes your essential nature, and it's the place in life where you're destined to shine. The sun is always the most powerful planet in your personal starscape, and it colours your nature very strongly indeed — more strongly, in fact, than any other factor in your horoscope. Your sun sign also describes what you're striving to *become* and shows your potential as well as your reality. It also says a lot about your financial potential, too. Career-wise, your sun sign describes your innermost essence, and what you'll be happiest both being and doing. For instance, if you're an Aries, and you haven't yet really connected with your true core nature, you may not always resonate with those qualities of drive, initiative and boldness that you keep reading about in the newspapers. You might find yourself stuck in a boring job that offers very few chances to express those qualities — or maybe you're stuck with a partner who says you're just too "brash".

But just allow yourself to daydream for a moment — how would it be if you let all those inner feelings come out; if you spoke and acted in the way you really wanted to? Well, you might suddenly find yourself needing a new job, and maybe even a new partner, but chances are you'd feel a whole lot happier, too. The same applies to the other eleven signs, of course. We may not always feel ourselves to be as persistent as a Taurus, as lively as a Gemini, or as caring as a Cancer — but if we allow our *true* selves to come out, life begins to unfold in a far more interesting and satisfying way. So if you want to start living out your highest potential, there's no better guide than astrology. The ultimate function of sun-signs is to show us what we're really capable of — and isn't that a worthwhile goal?

Studying your sun-sign, as well as those of the significant others in your life, can also give you a wealth of information about your financial future, too. So, Aries, if you're struggling to make the world take notice of you, or to find funding for your latest scheme or project, astrology can help you see just why you're having problems. And it can also highlight your route to success. Had you ever thought of taking other people's opinions and circumstances into consideration, for instance? In your case, the key to improved financial conditions may involve a little compromise and cooperation — and knowing your sun-sign can help you see why!

Another important fact to remember when you're learning about people's 'money signs' is that their sun reveals their deepest, innermost nature — which isn't necessarily the same as the way they behave on the surface. So, if you live or work with an Aries who has a savings account and can be almost frugal at times, please don't be fooled for a moment. Their Aries sun is probably being modified by other factors in their horoscope — like a Virgo ascendant, perhaps. Watch how they behave when they think you're not looking and their actions may be truer to form!

Start learning about sun-signs and you can gradually build on the knowledge you've gained in the newspapers. Not that there's anything *wrong* with those columns — in fact, they are usually about four-fifths correct, which isn't so bad. The main problem is that, by their very nature, they can't help but be general, and so they'll never really tell you all you want to know. Everybody has to start somewhere, though, and the sun-sign columns are probably where most of the professional astrologers you'll ever meet first acquired their interest in the subject.

... & Horoscopes

Many people refer to the sun-sign columns they read as "horoscopes", but strictly speaking, this isn't actually true. Proper horoscopes are the foundation-stone of serious astrology, and they're far more detailed than any newspaper sun-sign column. Horoscopes don't just take into account what the sun is doing, they look at all the other planets as well. Since the position of the planets changes significantly every four minutes and minor changes take place every second, everyone on the planet — even identical twins — has a different horoscope which reflects their totally unique nature. A consultant astrologer can calculate your horoscope by computer in a matter of seconds, but they *will* need to know your date, time and place of birth. Since a birth horoscope is unique to each individual, it naturally reveals quite detailed information, and if you're looking for an in-depth tool which can help you handle your money more wisely, it's a brilliant thing to have.

Your horoscope is essentially a map of the heavens at the moment of your birth and sets out the positions of *all* the planets in the sky, as well as just the sun. A consultant astrologer will look at the position of your Moon to discover your early emotional conditioning and the kind of childhood 'scripts' you acquired about money — which, if you're looking to break free of them, is pretty useful to know! An astrologer will look at your Mercury to see how you communicate, your Mars to see how you assert yourself, and so on. Using the more detailed information available from the horoscope, a financial astrologer will be able to help you with detailed financial planning for the rest of your life. This could involve things like: the timing of major investments; when and how to play the stock market; good times to start a business or take a big financial risk; times to hold back or reduce your debt load; and the very best time to buy your first or second home.

If you're serious about improving your financial performance, I strongly advise you to work with your detailed birth horoscope. You'll can contact a reputable consultant astrologer in your area through one of the professional organizations listed in the 'More About Astrology' section at the end of the book.

Meanwhile, let's start with your sun sign. If you're really serious about improving your finances — I'm sure you are or you wouldn't have bought this book — I strongly recommend that you work with the 'Keys' or exercises at the end of each chapter. There's no need to restrict yourself to the ones I've outlined for your own sign, either. We all have at least a tiny bit of the essence of each sign within us anyway, so why not try some of the other exercises too? Your Ascendant and Moon sign are the next most important factors in your chart, so work with those too, if you know what they are. Reading the relevant chapter will also give you added insight into your real 'money motives' — as well as your financial strengths and weaknesses.

Finally, let me wish you well on your own personal journey of financial discovery. Astrology is a totally fascinating subject and, if you're anything like me, you'll soon be thoroughly hooked! So good luck — and good fortune!

JANE BOWLES

♈

ARIES
March 21st to April 20th

Aries is the first sign in the zodiac and people who are born under its fiery influence love, above all to be first! Enthusiastic, lively and full of get-up-and-go — who could be more fitted to the job of being a leader? Indeed, there's nothing most Aries love more than being in charge — aside, that is, from coming out on top. As the seventeenth-century astrologer William Lilly so eloquently put it, "Aries loveth nothing above a victory!" Or, as a dear Aries friend of mine once said, "The thing we like best of all is winning!"...

Astrologically, Aries is ruled by Mars, the god of war, and a lightning glance through the pages of Greek mythology shows that Mars lived an action-packed life, full of adventure and excitement — and although he landed in hot water at times, his fearless nature always somehow pulled him through. Latter-day Ariens often act in a similar way, for rams need plenty of action to keep them amused and will turn their lives into a battlefield if they get too bored and restless. And though they sometimes have a "devil-may-care" attitude to money, they'll always rise admirably to the challenge of "paying their way".

Aries is the essential child of the zodiac and, like all small children, the ram's energy is boundless. Think of a meadow full of bounding spring lambs in March or April when Aries rules the heavens, or the deafening hubbub of a kindergarten playroom, and you'll soon get the picture... Like all children, Ariens have a deep, unswaying conviction that *their* needs are paramount and that there's nothing else in the world that could really possibly matter. As babies, Aries offspring waste no time in letting you know that 'they want it, and they want it *now*', and this charming character trait — which, it must be said, is far less endearing in adults — is one which many Ariens persist in all their lives. Happily for the rest of us, though, most of them learn to temper their all-powerful desire nature a mite as they reach maturity. There's always a secret, hidden corner of the Aries soul, however, that will never grow up — nor would wish to. Most Aries children were raised on a staple diet of adventure stories and fairytales, where heroes were heroes and villains got their just deserts, and knights in shining armour were forever rescuing fair damsels in distress ...and this is the stuff that their dreams are still made of. But once they're grown, Aries' heroes may be Indiana Jones,

Bruce Willis or Clint Eastwood, rather than Robin Hood or the brave knight Lancelot, and the dream of triumphing over impossible odds to win fame, fair maiden, and sometimes fortune too, remains the same, and is the moving force that drives Ariens of all ages onward and upward, the whole world over.

These would-be heroes and heroines, born as the sap is rising in the springtime of the year, can easily be spotted in a crowd, thanks to their telltale body-language. Ariens are *always* in a hurry, and people born under this sign often walk with their heads thrust forward, rather like their animal namesake — the ram. Aries rules the head, and you'll often find bumps, bruises or even scars around their cranium, for these impetuous Mars-types are often pretty accident-prone, too! If all else fails, you can easily spot Aries by their friendly, if forceful, manner. This often reveals itself through an unflinchingly direct gaze, super-firm handshake and occasional outbursts of "foot-in-mouth" disease! For Ariens may be honest and therefore constitutionally incapable of lies or subterfuge, but they are, it must be said, rarely noted for their tact! ...unless, of course, there's a strong Libran influence in their horoscope as well, in which case a career as a diplomat wouldn't automatically be ruled out.

As the honorary children of the zodiac, Ariens carry all their childhood enthusiasm, energy and drive along with them into adult life — and all too often, their temper tantrums too. Arien infants are not easy to control, but it's important for them to acquire some sense of discipline so that the rules and restrictions of schooling don't come as too much of a shock. Discipline must be liberally sprinkled with praise and encouragement though, so that Aries children retain all that precious joie de vivre, and don't lose any of their vital creative fire. Ariens of tender years also have a touching faith in mythical figures such as fairy godmothers, so don't dampen their youthful spirits by telling them that there's no such person as Santa Claus too soon. Leave it as long as you possibly can, or else that childhood trust in life may be sadly shattered forever...

The leadership qualities of Aries are evident even in the nursery, and if you have an Aries son or daughter, they'll probably elect themselves 'leader of the gang'. They have wonderfully colourful imaginations too, and will constantly come up with new games and novel ways of leading their playmates into exciting escapades and adventures! The main thing, though, is always to keep them busy. All that restless energy needs to be channelled, or it will start to express itself in negative, destructive ways — like fighting, squabbling, beating up their siblings or wrecking the playroom on a rainy afternoon!

♈ Aries and Money

The fantasy world of the average Aries may be filled with grandiose dreams of achieving mighty deeds against the odds, but accumulating a huge pile of cash rarely ranks high on their list of goals. Most Ariens see money simply as a means to an end — and very seldom as a worthwhile end in itself. The purpose of money, as

Aries sees it, is simply to finance the most important thing in life. Which for rams, is nothing less than their own personal vision or "quest". The Aries quest can vary from starting their own business to fighting for justice in human rights, or founding a new orphanage for Bosnian children. Ariens just love to champion the underdog — remember all those gallant knights of old! Rams are real suckers for a worthy cause, and their warm-hearted, impulsive nature may sometimes lead them to take on projects which, when considered on financial merit alone, they'd perhaps be wiser to avoid. To Ariens, however, "sensible" considerations are immaterial. All that really matters is the quest. For Ariens, the bottom line is really all about self-expression and self-determination, for when all is said and done, these are the only things they respect. Doing things "their way", and having the freedom to follow their spirit of adventure wherever it may lead them, are far more important than having money in the bank. Indeed, most Ariens you'll meet will gladly give up financial security for the chance or opportunity to really follow their dreams.

Since Ariens are motivated far more strongly by fame than fortune, they don't always accumulate money as the months and years go by. You see, if you offered the ram a choice between fame and glory, or money in the bank, they'd choose fame every time, for bulging bank deposits don't impress them one little bit. Nor are they impressed by the so-called "security" gained from investing in property — a very high percentage of rams prefer to rent, not buy, their homes. After all, renting is far more flexible, and Ariens never quite know when they might need to "up sticks" and move on in pursuit of that all-important "quest"...

The fortunes of Ariens often follow a clear-cut pattern, with quite a few ups and downs before they find their financial way. Sadly, the young Aries hero or heroine who's just starting out in life often discovers somewhat abruptly that the rest of the world does not share their dreams and visions — and, for some strange reason, is reluctant to finance them! Since Ariens loathe delay or restriction, youth can often be a pretty frustrating time. The passage of the years, however, usually brings a smattering of realism to all but the stubbornness rams and, with characteristic resourcefulness, they'll find a way of keeping their dreams intact and making a living too. It may not always be the most lavish of incomes, though, for Ariens value praise and acknowledgement far more than a hefty cheque. So rams who wind up in a working environment where the pay is average, but they can do their own thing, and more importantly, be appreciated for it, are as happy as the proverbial sandboy. One particular pitfall that idealistic Ariens of all ages should beware of, though, is looking for a Mr or Ms Fix-it — some magic fairy godparent who's going to turn up and pay all the bills. For sometimes, rams get so consumed with the total "rightness" of their vision, and also so convinced of the immensity of their talents — however unproven these may be — they can come to believe that the world, or perhaps their poor unsuspecting partner, should pay all the bills and support them, leaving them free to get on with their quest. Believing the world owes them a living is a trap which Ariens should especially beware of...

As a general rule, though, most Ariens have a refreshingly optimistic attitude towards money. Rams are usually quite adept at earning money — though they're usually just as good at spending it, too. The typical Aries financial philosophy is summed up in the saying, "There's plenty more where that came from", and it's not uncommon for younger, more impetuous rams to have quite a few lessons in the art of budgeting forced upon them by circumstances — or perhaps by their not-so-friendly bank manager — before they finally begin to appreciate the virtues of a properly-balanced chequebook.

When it comes to handling their day-to-day finances, it has to be said that rams are not the star performers of the zodiac. Ariens rarely succeed in balancing their finances without a good deal of practice and often run out of money before their next payday comes round. And since they're often too impatient to deal with small financial details — like remembering to put cash aside for the bills on a regular basis — many Ariens often live quite close to the financial edge. So, in the cliffhanging years before they master the art of budgeting, rams also get pretty skilled at carrying out last-minute financial "rescues". This is where the classic Aries traits of courage, mixed with pure nerve, come in handy, for they're never afraid to ask for a loan! "Where there's a will, there's a way", is the classic Aries motto, and if anyone can find a way through even the stickiest financial impasse, you're safer betting on an Aries than just about any other sign.

Budgeting, then, is not one of Aries' favourite pastimes. Though if the ram in question is a male, he'll insist on doing it anyway, for when it comes to money,

Aries men can be quite chauvinistic. Controlling the family purse-strings is a matter of male pride, as far as they're concerned — although their spouse is sometimes left to "pick up the pieces" financially, not to mention making ends meet. Even if the Aries man happens to live with an Aries female, he'll probably *still* insist on handling all the cash himself. And woe betide you if you offer any advice on what he should do! So, if you live with an Aries male, and you feel that domestic life is getting a little boring, just try telling him how you think he should spend his money! The ram *always* takes the view that since he's earned that money, he alone will decide how to spend it. So if you take the courageous step of allowing an Aries man to run your financial show, just be prepared for the odd drama and disaster. And save some money too, in case that "rainy day" comes along a bit sooner than you thought.

Paradoxically, the Aries woman, who is so dynamic in all the other areas of her life, will often leave managing the money to the discretion of her mate. Like all Aries females who've been weaned on a diet of myths and fairytales, she expects her man to be a real knight in shining armour, and slay the dragon of financial uncertainty whenever it ventures too close. She's only prone to this kind of thinking where joint finances are concerned, however, for Arien gals who have their own independent income will always insist on calling the shots on how it's spent. And if an Aries lady is let down once too often, she'll seize the reins herself and handle the housekeeping on her own.

Once in a while, you may come across one of those rare creatures — an Aries who lives within their means and actually knows to the last penny how much they've got in the bank. But if this is the case, you can rest assured the horoscope of the ram in question also contains a healthy mix of earthy planets to balance out their impulsive fiery sun — a Virgo or Capricorn ascendant, or perhaps an earthy Venus or Moon. Or perhaps they're one of those Ariens who've received some particularly harsh lessons in the School of Financial Reality and are determined not to repeat the experience! Don't think that Ariens are always financially feckless, though, for even the most carefree rams tend to settle down when their Sun progresses into Taurus, which causes money to loom larger on their list of life's priorities.

Since, as we've seen, most Ariens place a higher premium on fame rather than fortune, many rams wind up making money for others, rather than themselves. But just as with every sign, there are also some startling exceptions to this rule. For some Ariens, the great challenge, adventure or "quest" in their lives may be the task of escaping from their disadvantaged backgrounds, so every so often, you'll find an Aries who bucks the general financial profile of their sign and succeeds in amassing a considerable fortune. Two of the twentieth century's most famous rich Ariens are Charlie Chaplin and Alan Sugar, who both began life in this way — their early financial backgrounds were anything but auspicious.

Widely regarded as the greatest comic of the century, Charlie Chaplin was born into a desperately poor family and spent much of his childhood in the workhouse, due to his mother's frequent bouts of mental illness. As a young man with few assets — except a boundless faith in his own abilities — he struck out, like so many before him, to seek fame and fortune in the USA. He secured his first cinema role with Mack Sennett, and soon established himself as America's leading comic, going on to co-found United Artists Corporation at the age of 30. Chaplin's story is a classic Aries tale of "rags to riches", for before long he had become the highest-paid star in Hollywood, having gloriously succeeded in his youthful dream of overcoming the poverty of his early years. Chaplin's success was virtually unparalleled, but he was also quite good at making enemies. Just as his early life was a struggle against poverty, his later years were characterised by battles with authority, and he was finally branded a Communist and banned from the USA.

The Arien electronics tycoon Alan Sugar, once described as "Britain's greatest entrepreneur", also had a pretty humble start in life. Born into a poor Jewish family in London's East End, Sugar began his business career at the tender age of 16, when he began renovating old TV sets and selling them out of the bedroom of his parents' flat. By the age of 21 he had established his own company, Amstrad, despite his mother's continued refrain of, "Alan, when are you going to get a *proper* job?" In keeping with the classic Aries trait of ensuring that all their endeavours are emblazoned with their trademark, Sugar created his company name from his initials — A M S (Trading), and owing to his superb ability to sense intuitively exactly where consumer trends in electronics were likely to turn next, Amstrad became one of the great business success stories of the 1980s. And by 1988, Sugar's personal fortune stood at £597 million, a far cry indeed from his teenage years, when his prospective father-in-law had declared his prospects to be unpromising! But then, what greater spur to action could a true-blue Aries desire? Alan Sugar is an Aries who succeeded in the daunting challenge of winning fame, fortune *and* fair lady and is thus the epitome of the Arien dream.

More commonly, however, many Aries run into financial problems owing to their overwhelming habit of living totally in the present. To an Aries, yesterday (along with all its expenditures) is dead and gone and the future hasn't happened yet. Tomorrow never comes — for today is where the action is, and that's all an Aries ever cares about. This means that they can often be quite forgetful about the bills and expenses they incurred last month, when they were busy doing something else entirely. For although most rams are honest souls are heart, and do greatly prefer to pay their bills and debts on time, if you happen to have lent them money, you may have to work hard to get it back — and do quite a bit of prompting and reminding in the meantime! If you need money, though, it's quite a different matter, for most rams will gladly lend it — if, indeed, they've any to lend.

The phrase "Live now, pay later" is pure Aries, and it's actually the reason why Ariens are sometimes seen as spendthrifts — a tag which seems strangely at odds with their typically spartan lifestyle. Being such natural optimists at heart, Ariens usually take it for granted that the future will be sunny, and that all their dreams will come to fruition — so why on earth should they worry? Ariens possess a powerful trust in life and, like Dickens' Mr Micawber, they're always confident that "something will turn up" — even when financial disaster is staring them squarely in the face. Indeed, they often substitute trust for more formal financial planning. The axiom "Expect a miracle" is a classic Arien saying, for rams don't just believe in miracles, they depend on them! What the other more practical signs of the zodiac find particularly annoying, however, is the fact that miracles frequently *do* happen to rams — who happen to expect them! In the meantime, however, Ariens will do well to take some practical steps too — like curbing their basic impulsiveness, and practising the art of budgeting.

As the quintessential "children" of the zodiac, Ariens can sometimes have a somewhat irresponsible attitude to money, and it rarely turns out that they're the bank manager's top loan prospect. Their credit rating may leave something to be desired, but to even out the balance-sheet, please don't forget that the ram is delightfully generous. Ariens will never skimp on gifts or presents, particularly if they care about you. But be sure to show your appreciation for those gifts very warmly, or they'll be cut to the very quick. Do them a good turn, though, and you can count on being richly rewarded, just as soon as their bank balance permits. And if the ram has chosen you as a friend or partner, they'll lavish you with money, presents and all the favours you could possibly require, for as long as their fancy dictates — which could be forever, or simply till tomorrow. It really all depends on where that "quest" will take them next!

♈ The Spending Style of Aries

If you need to go shopping in a hurry, take an Aries along for company. You'll get the job done in record time, for no-one spends faster than the ram! Mars-ruled people are the most decisive shoppers in the zodiac. They know what they want and they know where to get it, and they rarely waste time in window-shopping or dithering. Depending on how their horoscope as a whole happens to be, Ariens see shopping as a necessity rather than a pleasure — but they can often clock up record bills in record time as well! The downside of their snappy shopping style can easily be spotted, though, for Ariens are the great "impulse buyers" of the zodiac, and they often meet their downfall at the "point-of-sale" display...

Typical rams often spend way beyond their means, tending to eke out their cash-flow by using lots of charge cards and credit. It's important that they learn to use credit wisely, however, and never take on more than they can handle. On the plus side, though, Ariens always have an eye for a bargain — and having glimpsed a prize buy or "snip", they'll never, ever let it go. Arien actress Ruby Wax portrays a thoroughly spendthrift lady in her latest auto advert — and though she's only acting, the character is true to the Aries type!

So what does the typical Arien like to spend their money on? Just about every Arien under the sun loves sport, and most rams see money spent on fitness as money well spent indeed. Expensive trainers, running gear and tracksuits — all are grist to the Arien's mill, for it's vitally important to look the part, too. They'll also probably subscribe to the local gym, health club or sports resort, as they like to keep in shape and burn up some of that boundless energy!

Ariens love speed, so when it comes to buying a car, a bright red sports model is naturally their first choice. But even the ram who's constrained by the transportation needs of the family, or the sober range of company cars they're obliged to choose from, will always choose the one with the fastest acceleration and snazziest style possible. Preferably in the colour red! The Arien's love of speed is also reflected by their fondness for labour-saving gadgets. Time spent in the kitchen could be more profitably spent elsewhere, thinks Aries, and anything that speeds up the process must surely be good news. The Aries kitchen is therefore usually choc-a-bloc with timesaving gizmoes and microwaves.

Ariens love to eat out, and they like their food just the way they like everything else in life — fast, hot and exciting! So if you're dining out with an Arien, they'll usually head for the local curry house, or the new Mexican place that does the spiciest chilli in town. The meal will also no doubt be washed down with liberal volumes of alcohol, for Ariens often prefer quantity to quality, though they often go for fine wine when they arrive at middle age. And when an Arien takes you out on the town, keep your fingers crossed that the eaterie is up to scratch, for they certainly won't shrink from complaining if the service isn't up to par. I still have vivid memories of a lunchtime rendezvous with a dear Aries friend who became vexed to the point of exploding when five full minutes had elapsed and still no-one had taken her order. Raising her hands above her head, she clapped them loudly, instantaneously reducing the entire room to silence. She then demanded to be served in no uncertain terms. Not surprisingly, a bevy of red-faced waiters instantly flocked to our table and our meal was produced in record time!

If your Arien friend is entertaining you at home, you'll probably notice that the decor is quite spartan, for rams don't usually spend much money on their homes. They rarely notice that the chairs are hard and uncomfortable, that the sofa springs gave up their last breath several years ago, and that they've still forgotten to lay that stair carpet they bought in the sales last January. To the Arien, home is simply the place where they hang their hat and plan their next move — and since they always like to think they're en route to pastures greener, doing up their house can often seem like a waste of money.

What rams *do* like to spend on, though, is anything and everything that will help them make headway in their chosen career or profession. So although the Arien's home may not qualify for "Homes and Gardens", they'll usually cut a pretty dashing figure at work. "Fake it till you make it" is a classic Aries motto and rams always look like they're really going places, which, of course, they undoubtedly are! Their clothes will always be smart and stylish, even if they aren't from the top designers, and they'll carry their papers to the office in a stylish leather case. Arien women will lavish the greater part of their clothes budget on smart outfits, jewellery and shoes for work, usually in bright vibrant colours that ensure they look "dressed for success" — whilst at home, they'll slop around in comfy sweatshirts, joggers and trainers.

Finally, although most Ariens are generous to a fault and love giving presents to their nearest and dearest, they also enjoy spending money on themselves. An Aries man will be happy to buy that kid leather handbag for his wife, and expensive new riding gear for his daughter — provided he can afford it after he's bought himself that new sports holdall. Having said that, it's always a delight to receive a gift from the ram. Rest assured it will be chosen with your pleasure firmly in mind, and disarmingly bestowed with all the warmth of their fiery heart. So just be sure to say thank you, won't you?

♈ Aries: Saving and Investing

It's often said that money burns a hole in Aries' pocket but although that's true, you shouldn't assume that rams can't save. For although the typical Aries would far rather spend their money than save it, when the chips are down, they can hoard it almost as cleverly as the next sign — which just happens to be Taurus, the champion saver of the zodiac.

Ariens never save for mere "security" though. The idea of sinking all their liquid assets into bricks and mortar rarely gets them excited, and many Ariens will rent a home for decades before getting "tied down" by a mortgage. No, the only motive that ever really inspires the ram to save rather than spend, is — you guessed it

— that all-important quest! Ariens have no difficulty whatsoever in cutting their spending to the bone, provided they're saving for a treasured creative project or a goal that truly fires them. Like a once-in-a-lifetime trip up the Amazon, or a week-long intensive in a new career skill or sport. So if you're aiming to encourage the Ariens in your life to improve their skill at saving, just suggest a goal that excites them — and sit back and wait for results.

When it comes to investment, too, most Ariens have a short-term focus. Their restless nature makes them impatient for quick results, and since they live so strongly in the present, long-term investments hold little appeal. When it comes to making money, typical Ariens like to get in fast, do their thing, and then get out quickly, while they're still ahead. This approach to investment, allied with their keen intuition and love of adventure, means they're ideally suited to all forms of speculation. The adrenaline-filled buzz of the stock, futures and commodity markets, coupled with the potential for speedy returns, is usually a thrill they can seldom resist — though many Ariens are far more attracted by the "high" of winning rather than the actual financial gains, though naturally these are great, since they allow them to carry on playing.

The Arien love of risk-taking might easily be mistaken for gambling, were it not for the fact that their investment moves are always highly intuitive. Rams usually have a very strong sense as to which particular stocks will bear fruit, and they'll never put their money down unless they're positive they have at least a 50% chance of winning. Ariens are brave, but they're not foolhardy — and they usually have the sense to get out while they're still ahead. There's one major fly in the ointment, though, and that's the ram's reluctance to take any advice but their own. Brokers and financial advisors can suggest away till they're blue in the face, but as far as rams are concerned, they alone know best...

The Arien urge for quick returns can also prove something of a liability when they seek to broaden their investments beyond the narrow field of the markets. Rams are great at seeing and seizing opportunities, but in order to take advantage of longer-term investments, like property or business, they need to develop the staying power that's required to see things through. One way round this problem is for Ariens to concentrate on investment projects where they can be in on the action right at the outset, and thus be seen as pioneers. Remember, to an Aries, the praise and acknowledgement they receive for a project are almost more important than the straight financial return. So if they get involved in projects right at the earliest stages — like researching and developing a new drug, launching the prototype of a car, or planning a new property development, their interest is less likely to flag.

The other investment pitfall that Ariens often encounter is their tendency to take on just too many projects at once. Rather than scattering their creative and financial energies too widely, it's better for rams to choose two or three major projects and wait for them to bear fruit before moving on to the next.

Areas of investment which Ariens are likely to find profitable include the following: medical companies (especially research and development), dentistry, hairdressing, any sports-related businesses, cars and motor accessories, publishing and schools. Property development related to any of the above could also prove lucrative. If these kinds of businesses do not appeal, then Ariens should simply look for a venture where they can help to innovate and bring about the birth of a new product or organization. Or better still, start a brand-new project themselves!

♈ The Earning Power of Aries

The creative, dynamic and forceful energy of Aries naturally stands them in good stead when it comes to making a living and they usually genuinely relish the tests and trials of the workplace. With their deep-seated love of challenge and adventure, their wisest career choice is one that involves plenty of action and lets them make their mark on the world in a pretty definite way. Job-security and pension prospects don't figure high on the Arien list of priorities — and unlike many other signs, they positively revel in unpredictability and change. Rams need to compete, and they don't mind a brush with adversity. So a routine that's fixed day after day, with no room for spontaneity, will truly stifle their soul and lead them to break out and rebel — thereby ensuring their prompt resignation or dismissal!

Young Ariens who are just starting out on the great adventure of life are frequently unaware of their true vocational needs. So by the time they hit thirty, their resumés may well reveal a breathtaking turnover of jobs. Despite their tender age, most young rams baulk at the prospect of "working their way up the ladder", and their biggest problem is often their tendency to believe the only place that's worth aiming for is the top. They want success, and they want it now, and the prospect of having to wait leaves them champing at the bit! But as the years go by, they slowly come to see that patience and staying power can be virtues after all ...or then again, they may not! Ariens have a marked dislike of listening to advice or learning from experience, so they usually graduate with flying colours from the School of Hard Knocks by the time they leave their twenties. Chances are, they may also look a bit older than they really are, for Ariens work hard and play hard and, sooner or later, it begins to show.

Ariens have a lot to offer and they're certainly well aware of it! They love to test themselves and stretch things to the limit, and they'll often take on challenges at work that would leave other signs feeling daunted. Since they love to launch new ventures, and mastermind team efforts, most rams have real leadership ability — and they'll usually be the first to admit it. Let's be blunt here — along with tact and diplomacy, modesty is a quality that's often conspicuously absent from the roll-call of Arien virtues. This can manifest as a confident, cocky manner that Aries' workmates may believe to be unassailable. But beneath that invincible facade beats a vulnerable, childlike heart — and ego — that need constant reassurance. Ariens need to be told loudly and often that they're really doing a great job fighting all those dragons and rescuing all those maidens. They take success and failure at work very personally indeed, and if, for some reason, the necessary paeans of praise aren't forthcoming, they'll do the unthinkable and lapse into depression. But it won't last for long. Besides, our Arien warrior will probably have done the right thing and married a suitable partner, like solicitous Virgo or caring Cancer, who will support them emotionally and morally so that they can fight the good fight at work...

Like all fire signs, Ariens care deeply about things, and when they're faced with a workaday challenge, they'll always know just what needs to be done. The main problem they generally run into is the fact that not everybody sees things just the way that they do. And if the person who sees the world differently happens to be their boss, then trouble — in buckets — is likely to ensue. Compromise is a concept that most Ariens have trouble accepting, and adjusting to the will of others is usually one of their hardest lessons. Flexibility is a quality all rams would do well to cultivate! Ariens also love starting new projects, but often lack the staying power to see them through — and that's why they desperately need their co-workers — though they don't always see it that way.

It's hard for Aries to overcome their innate belief that the shortest distance between two points is a straight line, but sooner or later they get the message that behaving like a human battering-ram is not always smiled upon by their colleagues and superiors. The dividing line between assertiveness and aggression is a fine one indeed, and with their warriorlike nature never far from the surface, rams can cross the line with quite startling regularity. You can see this happening quite easily — for when things are not going their way, most rams get ratty and rude. Skilfully harnessed, however, that Arien directness enables the ram to get straight to the heart of any problem and find out exactly what needs to be done. So if the sure-fire instincts and insights of Aries can be tamed and put to good use, they can be a tremendous working asset, instead of a problem or liability.

The ideal working environment for Ariens is one which offers them plenty of excitement and the opportunity to strive for their goals in an atmosphere of competition, or even plain old strife. Ariens thrive on dealing with "difficult" customers or clients, and can become a huge asset in this department of any business — particularly if they're called upon to sell something, too. Ariens are ace communicators, and love to tell everyone about the things they really believe in — so they often turn out to be the all-star promoters of the zodiac. Ariens are excellent salespeople, and if they believe in their product, they can persuade even the most reluctant customer to buy. They need to work at demanding projects they can pour all their energies into and should preferably be allowed to work flexible hours. They also need to have their efforts constantly acknowledged — or they'll feel they're making no headway, and will sooner or later lose interest.

Since Ariens are such great self-starters, they're brilliantly suited to running their own businesses and masterminding their own careers. Indeed, their innate urge to carve their own path in life and make their own decisions often means they have a problem with deferring to authority . This can become a major drawback when rams find themselves working in a large organization where managers and superiors must always be consulted and there's a bureaucratic structure that's constantly slowing them down. For this reason, rams are often far happier when they leave and "do their own thing" — either by running their own business or becoming self-employed. At the end of the day, if life is to have any real meaning or happiness, the role of leader must always fall to Aries. As a leading financial consultant remarked to me once in true Arien fashion, "I'd rather starve at my own game than work for someone else!"

Another reason why Ariens often succeed so spectacularly in business is their buoyant self-confidence, which never leaves them, even in the very midst of difficult times. "Fake it till you make it" is a favoured Aries saying, and it can carry them safely through the bad days when business is sparse and their bank balance even sparser! Their overwhelming conviction that things are going to work out just fine will probably ensure that they will — even if there *are* a few cliffhanging moments along the way. But for Aries, no true quest would be complete without its sorties into the darkened forests of financial adversity, and they tend to see it all as just part of life's great adventure.

Rams can make a business venture succeed almost by dint of willpower alone, and their ability to execute daring financial "rescue operations" and handle a crisis smoothly is unparalleled in the zodiac. So when things look black, think of Alan Sugar who rescued Amstrad from certain disaster back in 1989, clawing back debts of over £100 million or so at a dizzying pace and confounding all the critics who had consigned his business to the scrapheap! Another Arien "knight triumphant" is Jeffrey Archer, who braved near-bankruptcy, social ignominy and political disgrace in the 1970s to pen not just one, but several blockbusters, and become an internationally renowned best-selling author and millionaire.

♈ The Aries Boss

In an ideal world, rams will always be the boss — but the fact that they love to lead doesn't always mean that they're easy to work for. Rams drive their workers every bit as hard as they drive themselves, so people who are seeking an easy day job while they write that novel, or cut that demo tape they've been dreaming about, would be advised to look elsewhere. Working life with an Aries boss will always be unpredictable — that's because Aries executives rarely have the faintest idea of how new projects will work out in practice — they simply *know* that they will. Ariens aren't noted for being great team-workers either, but if they're the head of the team, then that's a different matter entirely.

Arien bosses demand unswerving loyalty, but they'll always reward like with like. If they're pleased with your performance, the Aries boss will be generous to a fault, and you needn't be nervous about asking for a pay rise. You'll probably get it, along with the healthiest Christmas bonus you ever saw, if the ram feels your performance is up to scratch. And if they don't, well you'll be the first to hear about it, in their customary upfront style.

Arien bosses can also be quick-tempered and sharp-tongued, and you may have to protect them from the results of their blunt repartee! In case this all sounds just too daunting, however, remember that Arien bosses are wonderfully enthusiastic and the chances are they'll get you just as fired up about things as they are. So if you're blessed with an Aries boss, there's perhaps only one thing you can ever really count on — your working life will certainly never be dull!

♈ The Aries Employee

Youthful Aries employees are likely to change jobs with astonishing regularity, because their threshold of boredom is so notoriously low. So if your business needs a sturdy, dependable soul to carry out routine, regular tasks, then forget about hiring Aries for the post. But if, on the other hand, you need a tirelessly committed troubleshooter, who thrives on change and will jump on a plane or train at a moment's notice, then look no further — for bold, feisty Aries is perfect for the job.

That's the good news. The not-so-good-news is, Ariens also have a disconcerting propensity to make up the rules as they go along, so they operate best in small organizations with a flexible bureaucratic structure, rather than huge corporations where there are just too many people to upset. For Ariens *do* upset people. Their tactics may be bold, fresh and exciting to some, but they can also seem thoroughly out of line to more conservative minded souls. And if there isn't enough action, rams will soon rebel, resign and head off in search of a new challenge — if their exasperating behaviour hasn't led them to get fired first!

Aries employees always want to be paid the going rate for the job, but since they rarely think that "money is everything", they'll take a temporary pay cut if circumstances demand. And if you've succeeded in capturing their enthusiasm and loyalty, your Aries employees will soon become the jewels in your company's crown — provided you let them be "top dog", of course!

♈ Aries and Career

Aries men and women are the real "doers" of the zodiac, and they have the capacity to excel in just any career that they choose, provided they can take the lead and hopefully stand out from the crowd. One of *the* most important things for Ariens is to feel that their work allows space for self-expression, and they'll put up with a very great deal if they're simply allowed to do their own thing. Leonardo Da Vinci and Vincent Van Gogh are just two of the famous painters born under the sign of the ram, and many latter-day Ariens take up the tough, testing challenge of a career in the creative arts.

Ariens are extremely ambitious people, and they often shine in careers that less spirited signs reject as being too arduous, too difficult, or simply too exhausting. Politics is a place where many Ariens find a natural home, and surveys have revealed that the ram outnumbers most other signs in the corridors of power. Ariens' ebullient self-confidence stands them in good stead, especially in the early stages of a political career, where defeat and discouragement are so commonly encountered. UK Prime Minister John Major is one ram who battled his way to the top at an impressively early age. Other famous Arien politicians include Michael Heseltine, Anthony Wedgwood Benn and David Steel.

Acting — both on stage and screen — is another career that attracts many Ariens, for their fighting spirit sees them through times of rejection and joblessness. Forceful Aries personalities like Marlon Brando and Warren Beatty have barged their way to the top with ease, along with feisty female superstars like Bette Davies and Joan Crawford. The world of TV has its fair share of Arien personalities too. Arien comedienne Ruby Wax has built a dazzling career on her forthright interview style and her gift for asking the right question — at precisely the wrong time. Another TV star who leaves his interviewees quaking in their boots is David Frost — and then there's veteran performer Peter Ustinov, adored the world over for his gentle, comic wit.

Ariens also excel in showbusiness, where their stamina and zest give them a fighting edge — think of Arien showbiz queen Diana Ross, or other star singers, such as Elton John. And then there's composer Andrew Lloyd Webber, whose musicals are unstoppable, producing smash hit after smash, every single time.

Journalism is another career where Ariens excel — although their prose may be a trifle terse at times! Some Ariens like to go right where the action is and work as reporters and broadcasters in the hottest war zones of the world. Other Mars-ruled men and women confine their communication skills to selling. All the selling professions, in fact, from advertising to PR, are great career choices for Aries — and their drive and boundless energy give them a fairly considerable advantage. Think of Lynne Franks, an Arien businesswoman par excellence who built a thriving empire in fashion PR.

Mars is the god of war, so many Ariens are drawn to the military — though naturally, they prefer to work as officers and generals. Adventure-minded Ariens often find their niche by working in the rescue services — snatching mountaineers or shipwrecked sailors from the very jaws of death. The police force is another great place for action-minded Ariens — along with the ambulance service, or a career as a para-medic. And since they rarely flinch at the sight of blood, many Ariens opt to work as dentists or surgeons, both typical Mars vocations.

Ariens are often keen sportspeople in their spare time, so sport is a field where they can really aim for the top, and maybe turn a hobby into a career. Back in the 1950s, Arien athlete Roger Bannister was the first person ever to run the four-minute mile and there are thousands of fellow rams who've enthralled the world with their sporting skills. Think of yachtswomen Claire Francis, tennis star Gabriela Sabatini, or golfer Sevvy Ballasteros — to name but three.

The world of business is often the place where quick-witted Ariens can usually be seen at their best, and it's one of the most satisfying outlets for their natural drive and zeal. Business-minded Ariens often flock to merchant banking and venture capital — the high-flying world of risky speculation, where vast sums of money change hands! Rams love nothing more than to exercise their intuitive skills and moneymaking "hunches", and their brilliance in this area is often unsurpassed. The famous banker J.P. Morgan, one of the richest men of his generation, had not just his Sun, but three other planets in Aries, and his investments were uncannily sound. Incidentally, he also employed an astrologer, one Evangeline Adams, to advise him, and was once heard to utter the immortal phrase,

"Millionaires don't use astrology — billionaires do!" Closer to home, the split-second decision-making and lightning deals of the stock market make it a place where action-oriented rams are happy to work, for the prospect of making millions is just too good to ever pass by. Think of the kind of explosive energy that's expended in the dealing rooms whenever the stock market swings up or down — that's pure Aries energy, and the world of business would be lost without it!

♈ Aries: Keys to Financial Success

- DO learn to take your time before making important financial decisions. Stand back and analyse the consequences first. And don't say Yes to anything, unless you have a *really* strong sense that it will work — does it qualify as one of your famous "hunches"?

- DO be honest with yourself about how you're happiest earning your living. Try and do your own thing wherever possible and, best of all, aim to be your own boss.

- DO curb your "impulse buying". Try and cultivate the habit of planning all important purchases in advance, rather than rushing out and buying the very first thing that takes your eye.

- DO cultivate the art of setting financial goals. If the word "budget" sounds just too boring to hold your attention, then why not see it as a *challenge* to try and meet savings targets, pay your bills on time and live within your monthly income?!

- DO try and cultivate the habit of saving on a regular basis. Just think — those savings may one day mean you can start up in business on your own or help you finance a career move that would otherwise be impossible.

♈ Rich & Famous Ariens

Lucretia Borgia
Leonardo Da Vinci
Tennessee Williams
J S Bach
Nikita Kruschev
John Major
Frank Woolworth
Hugh Hefner
Gloria Steinem
Arthur Hailey
Stephen Sondheim
Aretha Franklin
Eric Clapton
Charlie Chaplin
Gregory Peck
Richard Chamberlain
Sir Alec Guinness
Spencer Tracy
Eddie Murphy
James Caan
Gloria Swanson
Julie Christie
Ali McGraw
Hannah Gordon
David Frost
Linda Goodman

Casanova
Vincent Van Gogh
William Wordsworth
Eugene McCarthy
Jeffrey Archer
J.P. Morgan
Florenz Ziegfeld
Paloma Picasso
John Fowles
Andrew Lloyd Webber
Andre Previn
Diana Ross
Elton John
Francis Ford Coppola
Sir John Gielgud
Dudley Moore
Rod Steiger
Dirk Bogarde
Paul Michael Glaser
Mary Pickford
Debbie Reynolds
Doris Day
Jane Asher
Ruby Wax
Peter Ustinov

♉

TAURUS
April 21st to May 21st

After the breakneck exploits and derring-do of Aries, the pace slows down considerably when we come to Taurus, the sign traditionally associated with that favourite farmyard animal, the bull. Just like their animal namesakes, most Taureans tend to amble through life at a steady pace, keeping their feet firmly planted on terra firma all the while. And just like the bull, most Taureans are predominantly gentle, peace-loving creatures although they're also famed for their occasional outbursts of mighty rage, which bear more than a passing resemblance to an eruption of Vesuvius! They are also, generally speaking, the financial whizzes of the zodiac, and their skill in handling money must be counted as second to none. Money means a lot to Taurus, and most people born under this sign end up enjoying a considerable measure of financial success at some point or other in their adult lives.

Taurus is ruled by Venus, the planet of love and beauty, and as befits the children of such a pleasure-loving goddess, Taureans adore the good life. They revel in all the sensuous pleasures that life has to offer — good wine and food, fine perfumes and massage — and they're also great devotees of the arts, especially painting and music. The typical Taurean idea of heaven is a fabulous home-cooked meal, accompanied by superb vintage wines, enjoyed in the company of friends, or better still, one's loved one, in front of a blazing log fire. Taureans hate to be lonely, and since life means little to them without a mate, they often marry young and stay married, too — no mean feat in this day and age. Since they're also highly practical too, most Taureans are prepared to spend the greater part of their time and energy accumulating the wherewithal that will allow them to live in comfort. Please note, I said comfort. Not style, or luxury — but pure and simple comfort. Few things in life matter more to Taureans than having sufficient money to create a comfortable lifestyle for themselves and their family, and they'll work extremely hard to achieve it. Then they will relax — and they'll often relax so successfully that they'll rarely stir again, unless an unkind twist of fate or circumstance dishes them up a helping of what they loathe most in the world — which happens to be change. Having said that, the art of relaxation is generally one that most Taureans have refined to an art form, and this makes them the most soothing companions that anyone could wish for. They also have a natural gift for enjoying the simple everyday pleasures of life, a gift that's delightfully infectious. So if you're feeling a touch jaded by the "slings and arrows of outrageous fortune", as Shakespeare once put it, get yourself invited to dinner with a Taurean, preferably a dinner that they're cooking themselves, for they're also true artists in the kitchen. The pure delight that a Taurus takes in a rainbow, a sunset, the pungent smell of burning woodsmoke, or the simple pleasure of roasting chestnuts over an open fire will soon restore your faith in life, and, by the end of the evening, you'll have completely forgotten what made you so uptight in the first place...

Green is the colour of Venus, as well as the colour of money, and when they take a hard-earned rest from their labours, Venus-ruled Taureans find their greatest tranquillity and peace of mind in the countryside, where all the shades and hues of the colour green hold sway in Nature's palette. Sun sign Taureans, and also people with a Taurus Moon or Ascendant, will often gravitate to the countryside, and even when their work keeps them in the city for long stretches, they'll spend as much time outdoors as possible. It's a wise course of action, too, for if deprived of fresh air and rolling green meadows for too long a spell, they'll more than likely fall prey to some passing malaise.

Taurus is an earth sign, and bulls are earthy beings in every sense of the word. A wise astrologer once remarked that what Taureans really want out of life is "good food, good sex and a nice place to live", and to a great extent that's absolutely true! For those born under the sign of Taurus the bull, it's absolutely essential to feel a sense of connection to the earth, and experiencing life through food, money and sex — as well as all the other things they can see, hear, smell, taste and touch — is the best way they know of doing just that. The other way that Taureans like to feel connected to the earth is by owning a piece of it — preferably a large piece! For most Taureans, acquiring their own chunk of real estate or land is a prime motivating factor in life and a spur to overcoming their natural inertia. In common with Cancerians, Taureans see their home as very much a refuge from the uncertainty of the outside world, and bulls will work hard indeed to secure their very own bit of pasture. For, whilst Taurus can sometimes be a slightly lazy sign, Taureans are also the great realists of this world. They know that you can't get very far without money and they're prepared to work damned hard to get it.

Physically, the goddess Venus leaves her telltale mark on Taurean men and women alike, who tend to be dark, well-built and sensuously good-looking. Venus had a policy of passively attracting the people and things she desired through her beauty and personal charm — and latter-day Venusians tend to follow her example. Taureans are good at attracting both people and money to them, for the simple basic reason that they're naturally very attractive! Bulls are usually well-groomed and well-dressed, and tend to amble through life at a slow, steady pace. But don't ever make the mistake of thinking that because they're slow, they're also slow-witted. Remember the fable of the tortoise and the hare? Well, Taureans are a bit like tortoises — and once they've decided on a goal, whether it's to do with finance, business, or affairs of the heart, they always, but *always* seem to get there in the end...

Taurean men tend to be the strong, silent type — the taciturn movie star Clint Eastwood is a good example, both on-screen and off. Gary Cooper too, had the same kind of sensual appeal. Taureans are also renowned for their lusty manner, bawdy sense of humour and voracious appetites, both in bed and in the kitchen, and it's the latter that gives many Taurus women their distinctly "earth mother" image. Top fashion designer Mary Quant once said that a woman must choose between clothes and food, and there'd surely be little doubt which a Taurus lady would choose. Sadly, some Taureans allow themselves to sink into lassitude and spend night after night lolling in front of the TV like the proverbial "couch potato", forgetting to take exercise and to keep themselves in shape. But Taureans don't always succumb to weight problems as a matter of course. There's also another kind of Taurean female, the more Venusian, goddess-like type, whose stunning good looks can pave the way to a high-flying career in show business or the movies. The fragile porcelain-like ballerina Margot Fonteyn, was born under Taurus, as was the gamin film star Audrey Hepburn. Top model-turned-actress Joanna Lumley is another Taurean stunner, along with raven-haired Maureen Lipman, the versatile actress and author.

The boons and blessings that Venus bestows on the typical Taurean are seemingly never-ending, but there's a downside to those virtues too, and it can be spotted quite early in childhood. Little Taureans may look disarmingly sweet and good-natured, but they're also very stubborn. If you want to see their flip side, just try getting them to do something you know they won't want to — like eating their greens or taking a nap. A Taurean child can reduce its parents to a state of total exasperation when Mother or Dad see things differently, and though the easiest course of action would be to let them have their own way, it's not a good idea to give in too often. Otherwise, the not-so-attractive Taurean trait of stubbornness (that's the polite word for it) will become oh-so-firmly entrenched. Having said that, it's questionable whether Taurus's obstinate streak can ever really be tamed. In childhood, as in adult life, the best way to handle a Taurean who's bent on following a different route from the one you had in mind is to appeal to their Venusian capacity for harmony. Another less agreeable Taurean trait is their legendary temper — something that even their partners only glimpse on rare occasions. For Taureans tend to endure a great deal until, one day, something snaps — and then all that pent-up rage and fury is unleashed in a mighty torrent. If you've ever been unfortunate enough to provoke a Taurean outburst, the phrase "like a bull in a china shop" will surely come to mind. For when they've lost their rag, Taureans like to throw things. Plates preferably. So if you live or work with a Taurean and they're pawing the ground and spoiling for a fight, please don't provoke them in the kitchen — not if you value your precious china, that is!

♉ Taurus and Money

It's no coincidence that astrologers down the ages have waxed lyrical about the financial expertise of Taurus, for it's here that most bulls really come into their own. To put it simply, Taureans love money — they revel in it, feel totally relaxed around it, and tend to view it as their natural birthright. Most Taureans have a real talent for dealing with the nuts and bolts of everyday finance that drives other, less earthy signs into paroxysms of envy. Typical Taureans often have a real Midas touch, and they love acquiring and handling money, just as Ferdinand the Bull enjoyed munching those golden buttercups. To Taurus, all these things are the pure and simple expression of life's bounty, the goodness that earth has to offer, and they see no reason whatsoever why they shouldn't have as much of everything — money, buttercups, whatever — as they please.

The goddess Venus rules money and pleasure alike, and it's a rare Taurean indeed who gets suckered by that hoary old chestnut, "Money is the root of all evil". No poker-faced, puritanical platitudes for them. On the contrary, most Taureans are far more likely to affirm that "The *lack* of money is the root of all evil", for, of all the signs in the zodiac, they have perhaps the best understanding of how money really works, along with the surest instincts for acquiring it. Taurus rules the second house in the natural zodiac, which is the house of material resources, both physical and financial. Most bulls, therefore, have a keen sense of how best to utilise and apply their earthly resources, both inner and outer.

For although Taurus loves money, the bull is rarely extravagant or a spendthrift — not unless there's also an afflicted Jupiter in their chart, or they happen to have a great many planets placed in fire !

For Taureans, money is very much an end in itself, and to them it spells security — something they deem indispensable for their happiness and wellbeing. Above all else, Taureans are driven by the urge to build a secure base for themselves and their family, and their overwhelming desire to earn and accumulate money is inextricably linked to the need for a solid foundation on which to build and grow. Bulls also like life to be structured, and they usually set about building their basic life-structures as soon as they possibly can. Financial security is one of *the* prime motivating factors for Taurus, along with the need for a secure and lasting relationship. And because they tend to live very strongly in the realm of the physical senses, most bulls base their security on things they can see and touch — like gold, for instance, or property or antiques. Taureans don't particularly care for intangible assets, like stocks and shares. They like solid things, things that will stand the test of time, — and that's another clue to what makes most bulls tick financially. They always tend to take the long view and they like to invest for life. So whether it's a building, a painting or a business, they only like things that will last. Most bulls view the accumulation of money as a worthwhile end in itself — and having money in the bank makes them feel good about themselves, too. And because these Venus-ruled people love beauty, they use money to acquire lovely things, which provide further pleasure for the senses. But although the classical Taurean love of money usually goes hand in hand with their ability to make it and keep it, experience shows that there can sometimes be a distinct disadvantage to having one's sense of identity and self-worth so profoundly tied up with money.

Just as Taureans' faith in life is directly related to how much money they have in the bank, their sense of self-esteem is also directly linked to their cash. The sad example of Taurean Orson Welles, who virtually drank himself to death because he failed to reap the financial rewards that his early success had suggested, is a salutary case in point. Moreover, with the heavy, disruptive influence of Pluto in Scorpio opposing their natal Sun in recent years, many latter-day bulls have also discovered that money isn't always everything. For it's a sad fact that when things go awry in the financial sector, as they can and often do, bulls stand to lose far more than just their shirt: life can actually seem not worth living at all. The recent property crash and lingering recession of the early 1990s hit many Taurean bankers and property developers very badly, and it's interesting to speculate whether a higher than average proportion of those who jumped to their deaths in Wall Street following the Great Crash of 1929 were also born under Taurus! In any case, it's certainly true that bulls become extremely angry and insecure when anyone or anything comes between them and their money — even when they've just mislaid their chequebook or their billfold. The simple truth is, bulls just *hate* to be parted from their cash. The best opportunity for observing this little Taurean quirk is to find a bull who's going through a divorce and see how far they'll go to keep it. Taureans, especially female

Taureans, will fight tooth and nail to hang on to the house and the car, as well as a healthy chunk of maintenance, and they're prepared to resort to quite unsavoury tactics if necessary. One man I know who was going through an acrimonious separation from a Taurean female found himself being literally beaten over the head on a nightly basis because he refused to hand over what she felt was her rightful share of *his* property. In this case, the lady bull was insisting on a full half-share of his house which he'd bought many years previously — despite the fact that she'd only been contributing to the mortgage for a year or so!

On a day-to-day financial level, Taurus's performance can rarely be bettered and it's no overstatement to say that their money skills are superb. It's a subject that's seldom far from their thoughts as well — for along with food and sex, most bulls spend a lot of time thinking about cash: Taureans *like* money, and they love growing it and managing it, too. Most bulls have a gut-level instinct about finance that rarely fails them, and their judgements about saving and investing are usually extremely sound.

Totting up the bankbalance is an activity that's as natural to a Taurean as eating or sleeping, and they usually know down to the very last penny just how much they have in the bank. The Taurean approach to moneymaking is slow, deliberate and measured: this is not one of the fastest signs of the zodiac at making money, but it's one of the most reliable. Taureans also hate being rushed into important financial decisions, like buying a house or taking out a pension. They like to consider all the possible options, then sleep on it, then ruminate and sleep on it some more, before making up their minds. Trying to hustle bulls into parting with their money quickly is a sure-fire way of upsetting them, and those who live or work with Taureans would be wise to bear this in mind. But although they like to hang on to their money, Taureans are rarely mean or stingy. And they usually leave their heirs a pretty generous inheritance.

When it comes to handling the housekeeping, most Taureans prefer to be in charge. Typical Taurean men are often financial chauvinists at heart — though since they like to project a positive image to the world, they're rarely ever likely to admit it. The fact remains, though, that they infinitely prefer to control the family coffers themselves. They're quite happy to pay all the bills — they love to provide for the family, remember? — but they're also far happier and more relaxed if *they're* the only one that's signing the cheques. The partner of a Taurean certainly won't want for anything, and because the bull enjoys seeing his mate look well-groomed and well-dressed, he won't complain when the charge-card statements arrive. After all, he appreciates the very best in life, so why shouldn't she treat herself to a few new outfits? The Taurean male likes his "little treats" too — but only after he's dealt with the basics, like paying the mortgage and stashing away some money for the kids.

Taurean women have a similar penchant for controlling the domestic finances — even if their partner should put up any resistance, they'll soon succeed in seizing hold of the family purse-strings — which is no bad thing, really, since they usually manage them so well! Most Taureans take their financial commitments seriously and they're the kind of people who like to pay their bills on time. But although they're kind-hearted to a fault, few bulls will lend money if they've even the faintest suspicion it would leave them short of cash. And with the possible exception of close family members, they'll never, ever lend if they don't think the loan will be repaid. When it comes to borrowing money, too, the bottom line is, they don't like to... With the exception, perhaps, of housing loans and mortgages, debt is something that most Taureans find profoundly alarming and they'll go to considerable lengths to avoid it. Many Taureans steer clear of using credit cards and store cards completely, and if they *do* use them, they'll be sure to pay the balance off each month. And if perchance bulls should find themselves in temporary financial difficulties — perhaps as a result of excessive pleasure-seeking — they'll be quick to tighten their belt and take steps to cut back on expenses. If all else fails, though, and a full-blown cash crunch ensues, Taureans are more likely to seek a loan from the bank, rather than friends or family. After all, the bank manager is more than likely to be a good friend already, and there are few other signs in the zodiac so skilled as a Taurus at persuading a bank to give them exactly what they want.

Taureans also rise admirably to the challenge of coping on a limited budget, especially when they're sacrificing short-term gratification in favour of a long-term financial goal — such as buying a home or investment property. So if they're obliged to dine on liver or lentil casserole rather than filet mignon for a limited period — or even for several years — they really won't mind a bit. Besides, it's a great excuse to indulge in that other great Taurean hobby — bargain-hunting!

Taureans are past masters at financial planning and providing for the future. The only problem is, some Taureans get so preoccupied with building long-term financial security that they overlook the need to live in the present. For some poor Taureans, financial success may come a little too late in life to enjoy it! A dear Taurean fifty-something friend of mine insisted on driving around town in a draughty, unreliable car, and kept postponing plans to refurbish her house and buy herself a little holiday place in Spain — something she'd long dreamed of. All her friends, myself included, naturally assumed she was short of funds, so when poor Veronica suddenly died of a brain haemorrhage, we were thoroughly staggered to learn she'd left a cool million pounds in the bank! How nice for her son, we all thought — but how much nicer it would have been if she could have relaxed about her money sufficiently to enjoy it a bit more in her lifetime! For Taureans *do* worry about money, and they find it hard to relax until they feel totally secure. But how much is enough? And for the typical Taurus, is enough ever really enough?

This leads us on to the shadow side of Taurus's financial behaviour. Accumulating enough to provide for yourself and your family is all well and good, but some poor bulls just never know when to stop. All Taureans have a well-developed desire nature, but sometimes this can get slightly out of hand, and they then fall victims to greed and over-acquisitiveness. For those who live for their possessions, enough is never enough, especially when there happen to be Aries planets in the birthchart, too. This can lead an otherwise calm and gentle bull to pursue the never-ending thrill of new challenges and conquests. Think, for instance, of Adolf Hitler: a Sun Taurus whose appetite for land was seemingly inexhaustible.

The other thing about Taurus that's rarely mentioned in polite astrological circles is that their desire for money can become so strong, if they can't make money legally, they'll resort to fringe activities — like dealing in drugs, for instance, or even prostitution. And if all else fails, Taureans will sometimes marry for money — although they'll always marry for love if it seems the practical thing to do! If not, then good old financial security will do very nicely, thank you...

In a sense, Taurus is *the* sign, above all others, that lives to make money — and generally speaking, money is rarely a problem for the bull. The minority of Taureans who *do* experience recurring financial problems in this area would do well to invest in a detailed astrological analysis, so that they can really get to grips with the issues that are holding them back. Chances are, they may need to take the painful, but necessary, course of reviewing their childhood and unravelling their scripts about money — which are invariably derived from their early models. For if you run across a Taurus who's insecure or in a mess about money, you can be pretty sure that they suffer from low self-esteem. That makes them feel they don't *deserve* what they surely desire. But if they gain some insight into those early money patterns, then they can chose to rewrite their "money-script" just about any way they like!

♉ The Spending Style of Taurus

Taurus is one of the zodiac's star performers when it comes to making and accumulating money. When it comes to spending it, however, they always begin by asking three questions: First, is it practical? Second, will it last? And third, is it good value? If, on reflection, the purchase doesn't measure up, Taurus will simply hang on to the money and wait, wait, wait till something better comes along. Or at least until the sales, when they can get the same quality items at a handsome discount. For although bulls enjoy spending money, they'll rarely do so just for the sake of it — unlike Leos, say, for whom shopping is like therapy! Taureans like to think before they spend, so window-shopping is also a favourite pastime...

An astrologer friend of mine likes to jibe that Taureans only do their supermarket shopping just before closing-time, when all the bread and vegetables are marked-down — and there's certainly no denying that Taureans are brilliant bargain-hunters. But they rarely allow their natural prudence to degenerate into miserliness, for the simple reason that they like the good life far too much. They may well track down day-old bread for their toast — but they're equally likely to splash out by giving one of the most lavish dinner-parties you've ever attended! One thing Taurus rarely does, however, is buy major items on credit. Bulls positively enjoy saving up to buy things, and they view interest payments on credit card purchases as "money down the drain".

Being such sensuous creatures at heart, bulls will go for anything that makes them feel good in themselves. Food comes high on their list of priorities and a Taurus will *never* squeeze the grocery budget: if they need to save money, they'll cut corners elsewhere. Bulls like good food and plenty of it, and entertaining at home is one of their very favourite pastimes. On the rare occasions that they can be persuaded to eat out, their chosen eaterie will be a place where the food is superb, but the decor may be variable. Taureans are happy to pay for a good dinner, but not for fancy wallpaper — leave that to the Librans! They'll head for places like that little wine bar in North London where the bread and cheeses are air-freighted from Paris, but the shopfront looks like a tacky takeaway ...or an Indian restaurant on the wrong side of the tracks, which has the best tandoori marsala ever. Good food, no frills — that's the Taurus idea of fun.

Bulls also like to spend money on their homes — though generally speaking, they don't go overboard. Taureans tend to have nice, comfortable houses that convey a sense of solid, reliable wealth, rather than ritzy apartments stuffed with antique chairs that you can't sit down on. They go for comfortable, well-made furniture that's built to last, and they're prepared to fork out for a good-quality sofa — well, after all, they need somewhere really comfy for that afternoon nap or siesta. Decor-wise, Taureans usually opt for a chintzy country look rather than a chic, city image and they favour classic, conservative styles that aren't likely to date. When something strikes their fancy, however, be it Limoges china, or pottery ducks, Taureans can be obsessive collectors, and their homes may soon get cluttered with the evidence of their latest passion.

Taureans rarely stint themselves when it come to spending on clothes, because all bulls like to look their best. The men go for classic, well-cut suits in top-quality fabrics, and Taurean females are nicely-groomed, too — though they'll rarely be fashion leaders. Lady bulls dress largely for comfort, favouring sportswear and separates for casual wear; for business and social occasions, they'll wear well-tailored clothes in top-quality fabrics — wool, silk and other natural fibres; never, ever synthetics. Lady Taureans usually like to dress in strong, vibrant jewel colours — jade, amethyst, turquoise and fuchsia — although dark-haired bulls look stunning in pastels, too. At sale time, you'll naturally find them ransacking the rails of the very best stores, looking for designer items at a substantial discount. They're also fond of haunting factory shops and designer discount outlets. Jewellery is another passion, and Taureans love to buy gold.

Taureans also like to indulge their sense of smell, and won't hold back on buying toiletries. The bathrooms of lady Taureans are usually well-stocked with essential oils, luxurious bubble baths and lavish unguents and moisturisers, and they enjoy giving and receiving a regular massage, too. Fragrant-smelling cut flowers are another Taurus extravagance, and they love to fill their homes with colourful plants like azaleas and orchids.

Although bulls generally avoid spending money on gadgets, they're often great music-lovers and will happily lash out for a stylish top-of-the-range hi-fi. When it comes to cars, bulls tend to favour reliable,

quality models like a Range Rover, say. They'll buy a
Bentley, if they've "made it" — never a flashy Porsche
or Ferrari. And they rarely spend heavily on leisure,
often preferring to spend holidays at home. The bulls
that do travel often choose trips with a cultural theme,
like a holiday in Florence or a watercolour painting
course. But they'll only be tempted to leave home if
they're positive the food will be good. And their
favourite holiday reading matter? Biographies of the
rich and famous, of course!

♉ Taurus: Saving and Investing

Taureans are great creatures of habit, and most bulls
acquire the habit of saving well before they're old
enough to have their own bank account. Taureans are
strongly attuned to the cyclical rhythms of nature, and
every bull loves to tuck their pennies away, just like
squirrels hoard nuts in winter!

Taureans are aware of the importance of money
from an early age, and little bulls will usually be salting
away pennies in a jar long before you've got round to
buying them a piggy box or opening their first savings
account. Well before adolescence, most Taureans have
learned that having money around the place just makes
them feel good, and they get a real kick out of saving
up for that new bicycle they've been coveting.

Planning for the future is second nature to a Taurean
and it's rarely something they'll need to be coaxed into
doing. Bulls always take a long-term view of their

finances, and often set up a pension savings plan the week they start their first job. But they also adore those little five-year annuities they can invest in along the way: little caches and stashes that will grow into juicy nest-eggs, the way acorns become mighty oaks. For Taureans like their investments the same way they like everything else in life: slow and steady, rock-solid and predictable.

The investments that Taureans like most are those that hold a minimum of risk, and they're not at all fussed if the payoff takes a bit longer. Many a bull opts to leave their savings in a building society account (where they can get their hands on it quickly), rather than a higher-yielding, but less accessible account: this preference also reflects the classic Taurean love of property. The expression "safe as houses" was surely coined by a Sun Taurean, and bulls usually invest in their own home at the earliest possible opportunity, preferably one with its own back yard, where they can watch the flowers grow! To the Taurean, home is the ultimate security blanket, and the bull will work hard to secure it, working overtime and weekends if necessary. They'll probably try and pay off the mortgage well ahead of time, and then look around for property they can renovate and sell for profit... For many Taureans are natural property developers, and this is a field where they really excel. And despite the real estate crash of the early 1990s, the average Taurean's faith in the value of property is still often quite unshakeable.

To the degree that most bulls love property — which they tend to view as synonymous with security — so, too, do they distrust the high-risk speculation of the stock market. Bulls who speculate at all are likely to invest in only the safest of institutions, such as public utilities — water, electric and gas. Their instincts usually urge them to steer clear of flashier investments, which is a pretty wise move really, or they'd have too many sleepless nights.

When it comes to saving and investing, Taureans have few shortcomings — with the possible single exception that they sometimes hesitate too long. Their overly-cautious attitude and habit of chewing everything over a hundred times before making a move can sometimes mean that they miss out on good opportunities. As the saying goes, "He who hesitates is lost!", and Taureans certainly do a great deal of hesitating. Bulls also have a profoundly conservative streak and often get very set in their ways — unless they hitch up with an Aries or Gemini, say. Bulls of all ages should beware of their tendency to get stuck in a financial rut and need to keep their minds open to new financial products and approaches.

The bull's natural long-term perspective, allied to their patience, staying power and ability to weather temporary business setbacks, means that many Taureans are instinctively drawn to industry, where seeing a project through can take a decade or even two. Taureans are the real merchants of the zodiac and do best when investing in mass-market products. They instinctively know that only by selling to the widest public can they ever really build themselves a solid base of wealth.

Good investments for Taurus include furniture, gold, financial products and institutions, antique cars, art and antiques. Business-wise, bulls can prosper by investing in all forms of retailing connected with the arts, such as the music business, prints or painting. Good business opportunities may also exist in the perfumery trade, cosmetics and beauty culture, floristry, millinery, fashion design, the jewellery trade, interior design and Feng Shui. The bull's natural affinity with the soil means that landscape gardening, farming and nursery gardening may also prove fruitful for investment or setting up a business. Taureans often do well in hotels, the wine trade, catering, food retailing and baking.

♉ The Earning Power of Taurus

Taureans are the great "builders" of the zodiac, and their powerful drives towards consolidation and accumulation can seldom be better observed than in the workplace. Taurus is the second sign of the zodiac, and the bull likes to grow and nurture the primal seed that Aries has planted. Which is another way of saying that when it comes to work and business, Taureans are usually better at keeping enterprises going than at starting them in the first place...

Placid, passive Taurus isn't a wildly ambitious sign, but Taureans often succeed in acquiring considerable financial muscle by the time they reach middle-age. And at the very least, they'll usually have built themselves a thoroughly comfortable lifestyle. In keeping with their general approach to life, Taureans like to build their empires slowly. A prime example is media tycoon William Randolph Hearst, whose life story was depicted in Orson Welles' "Citizen Kane". Hearst had no less than four planets in Taurus, and was the forerunner of contemporary media moguls like Rupert Murdoch and the late Robert Maxwell: he virtually invented the tabloid press as we've come to know it today. His populist style, with its bold headlines, racy style and lavish illustrations, was widely criticised by his contemporaries, but Hearst was adept at giving his public what they wanted, and under his super-canny aegis, the *New York Journal* trebled its sales. In the course of his 60-year career, Hearst amassed a multi-million dollar fortune that allowed him to build his own "kingdom" — the ultimate Taurean fantasy — the extravagant San Simeon Towers on California's Pacific coast. A true Venusian at heart, Hearst made regular trips to Europe where he would spend vast sums on art and antiques to furnish his "palace" in classic Taurus style.

Along with their instinctive urge to accumulate money and wealth, most Taureans have a deep-seated need to be liked. Giving people what they want is a sure-fire way of gaining their approval, so the bull often opts for strongly practical vocations, which involve meeting people's needs on a fairly basic level — like running a supermarket, say, or even a neighbourhood bakery. Taureans always ask the question, "What do people need?", and they plump for popular products, that will reach the greatest number of customers. People born under the sign of Taurus are often deeply creative and artistic people, but will often sacrifice these abilities in deference to "making a living". Like Virgos and Capricorns, their fellow earth signs, Taureans find it hard to relax until the mortgage has been paid and their savings account is full. They often develop their gifts for painting, music or crafts later in life, however, when they've amassed some financial security and money is no longer an issue.

Unlike Aries, the bull's success in business isn't based on a love of competition, but on a deep-rooted need to build structure and security. Taureans positively thrive on routine. It gives them a warm, inner glow to know that coffee comes at 11 a.m. prompt, lunch is always from 1 − 2p.m. (or preferably 2.30, since they hate to rush their food) and that board meetings happen on Fridays, as regular as clockwork. Their love of fixed schedules means that Taureans are seldom suited to the haphazard, unpredictable world of freelance work, and they're usually far happier working as salaried employees, or as a manager or executive in a long established family business. They *need* that routine too, for the discipline of a fixed schedule is the best way to combat inertia. Balancing work and play, discipline and pleasure, is the best way for Taurus to build anything of lasting value and to find lasting happiness in life. Britain's highest-paid woman, best-selling Taurean author, Barbara Taylor-Bradford, is a lady of awe-inspiring habit. Despite the fact that her income now tops $12 million per annum and she long ago passed the point of ever needing to work again, she sticks to a rigid routine of writing, day after day and year after year ...that's the Taurean approach to work for you, and it certainly produces results. Once they've found their working niche, a Taurean will quite happily stick to the same schedule, year in, year out until, for some unfortunate reason, they're obliged to change their habits. Taureans are hard, industrious workers, and they usually make a good job of everything they tackle, but there's little that they loathe as much as change or spontaneity — a fact which their colleagues would do well to remember.

The average Taurean has little taste for office politics either. They'd rather get where they're going slowly and surely without having to step on people, for they know they'll surely get there in the end! The bull is generally a straightforward, patient and tolerant co-worker, which makes the office a nicer place to be — provided, of course, that everything's going their way. Taureans are great team players, and since they're also happy to shoulder responsibility and commitments, they make excellent business managers. Bulls are ill-suited to the precarious, high-risk life of an entrepreneur, however, and are far happier playing the role of second-in-command, holding the reins of financial power just one step behind the throne. They are keener on managing a business that's already up and running rather than starting their own. Indeed, becoming an executive in a family business that's been running steadily for decades would be the bull's idea of paradise! But should they decide to start their own business from scratch, they're certain to start small and build up slowly. A Taurean just venturing out into the clothing business, for instance, would begin by selling cheaper clothes from modest premises, rather than jumping straight in and opening an expensive boutique financed by huge borrowings from the bank.

With their love of job security, many Taureans were formerly drawn to large organizations with a highly structured workstyle: places like the big banks and local government. But since the recent recession, these institutions have shed staff too — and that hallowed "job security" has become very much a thing of the past. Some Taureans were hit very hard. Wiser bulls seized the chance to pursue a more creative calling — and also to find inner security, as distinct from their job and bankbalance!

Taureans are best placed as financial managers or supervisors within a large business, as this is the kind of position where they generally excel. Marketing and selling are *not* good areas for Taureans, as a rule. Their plain speech and forthright ways will rarely fit the bill, unless, of course, they're selling something they love — like houses, buildings or financial products. Once they've set their direction, Taureans find it very hard to change — so it's important that they spend time considering where their true vocation lies. Otherwise they'll waste many valuable years just drifting from job to job. Young Taureans who haven't connected with what they really want to do in life can lack focus and direction, and often seem somewhat lazy. Taureans can sometimes lack confidence, too, and need to work somewhere their talents will be recognised. Taureans also need to find joy in their work. Once they've found their niche, though, and the work that really inspires them, they'll plough ahead like steamrollers, pursuing a tireless path to success.

♉ The Taurus Boss

In the early days of my media career, I once worked for a Taurean film director who exemplified many characteristics of the breed. The centrepiece of his office was a huge, well-padded sofa, where he'd spend many a happy hour reading film scripts and puffing a cigar. If you wished to bend his ear on some pressing matter, it was always a good idea to knock in case he was taking a nap, for although it was common knowledge that he enjoyed his siesta, he also liked to "keep up appearances"! By and large, my Taurus boss was delightful to work for — apart from the time when I asked for a pay rise. He looked totally stunned, as though he couldn't believe his ears — but several days later, he agreed to my request — grunting just a little, to signal his displeasure.

My boss also displayed the typical Taurean reaction when I told him I was training to be an astrologer, for bulls are universally renowned for their contemptuous attitude to the stars. Fewer Taureans than any other star sign enrol for astrology classes, and you'll rarely find a Taurean boss who uses it for personnel recruitment. They're deeply sceptical of all things esoteric, so if you're studying astrology or healing, you're best advised to keep it to yourself. Having said that, the Taurean boss often has a kind of psychic "sixth sense" about money matters. And since bulls are interested in *anything* that helps them make money, you'll probably find them reading this book on the quiet, when they think that nobody's looking!

When they're faced with making decisions, Taurean bosses can hold everything up for days, for they like to do everything *slowly*. They don't like surprises, either, so if you're planning a trip or sabbatical, do give them plenty of notice. On the plus side, however, Taurean bosses are supremely loyal, and they'll certainly be supportive if you're going through personal problems. Their shoulders are among the broadest in the cosmos, and all Taurean employers are pillars of strength in a crisis. And if, like them, you value job security, they're probably the best boss you could ever possibly choose!

♉ The Taurean Employee

Just like Taurean managers, Taurus employees place a premium on security, routine and set patterns of work. And since the more security they have, the better they work, it's a good idea to see that they get it. Taurean employees need time to work things out: it isn't that they're unintelligent — just that they like to do things thoroughly — and that takes a little longer. They pay attention to detail, too, and their natural Venusian artistry gives them a flair for presentation.

Since Taureans have a deep respect for tradition and authority, they're good at taking orders. They also excel at helping businesses to run smoothly and generally "minding the store" — but they'll be totally, utterly miserable if you ask them to work on commission. Taureans always like to know *exactly* how much is coming in at the end of the month, so that they can budget, plan and save.

Taureans employees also need tangible proof that they're doing a good job — or in other words, regular pay raises! The annual increments don't need to be dazzling, but they do need to keep on coming. Otherwise, the typical Taurean will look for pastures greener — the ones where nice, green banknotes are in more plentiful supply!

♉ Taurus and Career

Their legendary love of money provides the basis for many Taurus careers, and so you'll find a high percentage of bulls who work in banking and finance. Not only is your local neighbourhood bank manager likely to be a Taurean, but so is your life insurance consultant, and your financial planner too. So, too, are the rather comfortable-looking ladies who sit behind the glass and cash your cheques. They look calm and contented, and naturally of course they are, for the bull who handles money for a living is as happy as the day is long. Queen Elizabeth II, the richest woman in England, has the sun in the sign of Taurus, and there is an amusing story of how, as a young woman, she dissolved into raptures of delight when she won £17 (about $28) playing cribbage — and was quick to count her winnings, and stash them away in her handbag! Many top financiers, entrepreneurs and millionaires are born with the Sun in Taurus, but since they prefer to keep a low profile, they are rarely "household names". Since the Taurean's financial instincts are second to none, and they're brilliant at sensing the deals that will or won't work out, many excel in business. They'll be especially successful if they venture into any kind of business that has a Venusian theme or emphasis, such as a music store, a hair salon, or even a hat boutique!

The Taurean's second favourite career, after money, is real estate — be it commercial, residential or rural — for there's little the bull loves more than selling property, land and buildings. Farming is another great career for Taurus: bulls are often "country squires" at heart and get a real thrill from striding their muddy green acres, wellington boots and all. Failing that, you'll often find nature-loving Taureans working as vetinarians, for they're usually great animal-lovers, with a gift for healing, too.

Beauty-loving Taureans are often drawn to work with antiques and, since they have a great eye for colour, they also excel at interior design. And with their eagle eye for the pennies, they're more than likely to complete the job on budget! Taureans also love ceramics, and I know one Taurean lady who's built a thriving business out of restoring china! Since Taurus rules the throat, most bulls have good voices too: just think of Cher, Stevie Wonder and Barbra Streisand — all of whom are Taureans. Many bulls also make good TV and radio announcers. Those stunning Taurean good looks can often turn the bull into a movie star — think of Ryan O'Neal and Ann-Margret, not to mention Rudolph Valentino — and not forgetting Jack Nicholson, or sultry Al Pacino. Taureans often make great dancers, too — think of Martha Graham, Fred Astaire and the indomitable Shirley MacLaine.

Sensual, pleasure-loving Taureans have a real skill for tending to the body, and three of the best masseuses I know have Taurus strong in their chart. The combination of strong, firm arm movements, and selecting just the right blend of healing, perfumed oils to relax, soothe and nurture their clients is an art at which they uniquely excel, and the patron saint of massage must surely have been a Taurus!

Still in the realm of the body, many other Taureans are drawn to work with food, as restaurateurs, hoteliers or grocers. Other Taureans work with the body in a different way, for a surprisingly high percentage grow up to be doctors or nurses. So if you're unfortunate enough to find yourself in hospital, that boundless Taurean commonsense could be a welcome boon indeed.

♉ Taurus: Keys to Financial Success

- DO acknowledge and develop your skills at financial management, because they are among the best in the zodiac. You're a genuine whizz with money — give yourself credit for that and use it to your advantage!

- DO recognise that you need structure, routine and financial security, and choose a career path that offers these qualities. You'll prosper more readily when you're able to plan ahead. But...

- DON'T get so bogged down in planning for the long-term future that you forget to allocate some money for enjoying life right now. Open a Current Spending Account today!

- DO aim to develop a sense of detachment about money. Remember it will always be there for you when you want it, so lighten up a little and do *stop worrying*!

- DON'T identify with your possessions, and try not to be too materialistic, for everything we have is really on leasehold from the cosmos. Give away some of your favourite things from time to time — for we all have to let go of everything in the end.

♉ Rich & Famous Taureans

William Shakespeare
Charlotte Bronte
Johannes Brahms
Dr Benjamin Spock
Daphne du Maurier
Margot Fonteyn
Queen Elizabeth II
Joseph Heller
Yehudi Menuhin
Liberace
Duke Ellington
Keith Jarrett
Brian Eno
David Byrne
Grace Jones
Henry Fonda
Ryan O'Neal
Al Pacino
Nora Ephron
Shirley MacLaine
Glenda Jackson
Jessica Lange
Annette Bening
Maureen Lipman
Susan Hampshire
Pope John Paul II

Anthony Trollope
Orson Welles
Salvador Dali
Sigmund Freud
Fred Astaire
Audrey Hepburn
Angela Carter
Randolph Hearst
Barbara Taylor Bradford
Ella Fitzgerald
Stevie Wonder
Mike Oldfield
Bono
Cher
Tammy Wynette
Jack Nicholson
David Attenborough
Ben Elton
Barbra Streisand
Kathleen Turner
Michelle Pfeiffer
Jill Clayburgh
Joanna Lumley
Victoria Wood
Caroline Charles

♊

GEMINI
May 22nd to June 21st

Who *was* that handsome young man, so tastefully attired in stylish chartreuse, who dazzled you with his smile at the cocktail party last night? It's a shame you didn't get a chance to talk, because you overheard he was taking out shares in the new nightclub downtown, and it sounded like such an interesting proposition... The problem was, he spent most of the evening flitting around and talking on his mobile phone. Ask an astrologer, though, and they'll tell you the *real* reason you couldn't pin him down long enough to have a proper conversation was because he's a Gemini — and that's just the way they are. Always. Well, nearly always... For sometimes they'll turn turtle and do just what you didn't expect...

Changeable, volatile and always on the move, get to know a Gemini, and you've got three friends for the price of one! The mutable nature of the sign means they're guaranteed to surprise you in matters of finance and business — as well as affairs of the heart — in fact, it's just about the only thing they can ever be relied upon to do! And whilst many Geminis let money just slip through their fingers, they're also capable of coming up with literally dozens of ways to remedy the shortfall and get their bank balance back in the black.

"Two of everything" is a standard Gemini catchphrase, and just as you might expect, there are two myths linked with this sign. First, there's Mercury, the messenger god, who, just like a Gemini, was always on the move, relaying messages from heaven to earth and back again. He also had a gift for talking his way out of trouble: and since he was *frequently* in trouble, it came in mighty useful!

Mercury loved to play practical jokes, to laugh and entertain, but there's also a rather shadier side to the sign. Thanks to his trickery and sleight-of-hand, Mercury was also christened "the Prince of Thieves", and it's a label that has stuck to Gemini ever since. Not every boy and girl born at this time is prone to errant ways, but a tendency to buck the system and live life the way *they* want to is certainly highly typical. Geminis have a distinct tendency to cram as much as possible into every 24-hour day, and the average Gemini behaves just like quicksilver — acting quickly, changeably and, above all, unpredictably. Geminis tend to "live on their nerves", and brittle, nervous energy is the hallmark of this sign.

The other Gemini myth is that of the heavenly twins, Castor and Pollux. Legend has it that the twins were doomed to live forever apart, one in heaven and one on earth. This story aptly reflects the restless, ever-changing nature of Geminis, who often seem as though they're constantly searching for something — perhaps their other half? The dual aspect of Geminians can make them behave like Jekyll and Hyde, switching suddenly and abruptly from one mood to another; cheery one minute and deeply depressed the next. Geminis are so changeable they can be strangers to themselves, let alone their family and friends. It's Geminis' perpetual dilemma to be forever torn between the different sides of their personality — head and heart, reason and will, freedom and intimacy, or even just right and wrong — and they are always seeking a way to blend their separate selves into a balanced whole. Little wonder, then, that they are always on the move — perhaps it's the only way they can cope with all those so many different ways of being!

Physically, Gemini men and women are among the best-looking people in the zodiac. They usually have pale complexions, expressive eyes and high foreheads, and they retain their youthful appearance and lithe figures until well into their forties — and often way beyond. Think of the stunningly attractive movie actress Joan Collins, who's still an international sex symbol at an age when most people are drawing their retirement pension. Just like Joan, many Geminis look a lot younger than they really are, which is pretty fortunate really, since they also have a horror of ageing! You can easily spot a Gemini in a crowd — or even better, at a party or gallery opening. Just look out for the people who are "talking with their hands". Wild gestures and sign language are the order of the day here, and the elaborate hand codes so beloved of the Italians were surely invented by a Gemini, too!

It's worth noting that some of the most charismatic people in history have been born under this sign. The screen goddess and sex symbol of a generation, Marilyn Monroe, and the US president JF Kennedy were both Geminis, and both were renowned for their wit and humour, as well as their physical charms. Another mutual character trait was their ceaselessly questing spirit: fame and fortune beyond her wildest dreams could not satisfy Monroe's deep inner dissatisfaction with life, and neither could her varied roll-call of husbands — and JFK, too, was a deeply restless soul.

The next thing you'll notice about Geminis is their incredible wit and their way with words. Communication is what these people are all about, and they've generally got it taped. Whatever their faults may be, Geminis are the most charming companions you could ever possibly wish for, and they're the staple and backbone of every hostess's dinner-party list. Their conversation sparkles and glitters with anecdotes and stories, and they've invariably read the latest books and seen all the latest plays. Putting it simply, they've got style.

It's often said that Geminis are "born sophisticated", and they seem to possess a deep inner élan, even when homelier signs like Cancer are also strong in their horoscope. Mercury, their ruler, keeps them constantly on the move; the city, not the countryside, is their natural home and habitat; and culture, in all its aspects, is in their very blood. Geminis are sociable to a fault, and when it comes to going out for the evening, few are content to attend a single paltry event. Not for them the sedate pleasures of a piano recital and perhaps a quiet drink afterwards. No, the ideal Gemini evening would be to begin with a star-studded cocktail party (they love to hobnob with the rich and famous), before heading on to the latest restaurant — or perhaps to a buffet party, where they can move around and won't risk getting stuck with a boring companion. Then it might be fun to take in a play or cabaret before heading on down to the new piano bar for a nightcap. Or perhaps everyone would like to come back to Gemini's house for a drink? Little wonder then that most Geminis are incapable of being punctual. They're always trying to cram so much into their day, as well as burning the candle at both ends at night, that they're constantly running to keep up with themselves. Exhausting, *n'est-ce pas?* Geminis have many virtues, but restfulness is rarely among them...

Happily, most Geminis tend to mellow out a little as they get older and their Sun progresses well into the quieter sign of Cancer. That's when they settle down a little, establish their career, and maybe even have children — though as the eternal child of the zodiac themselves, parenting isn't always something they relish — but having said that, they're truly *great* with other people's kids! Mercury's influence keeps Gemini looking and feeling young, with an open-minded approach to life that never really leaves them — and they never, ever lose touch with their own precious "inner child".

The eager questing mind and boundless curiosity of Gemini children keep parents on their toes, and making sure the playroom's well-stocked with new jigsaw puzzles, crosswords and other mentally challenging games is the best way of keeping them well-occupied and happy. Parents of Gemini children should also be well aware of the need to set limits and discipline their offspring, for Mercury-ruled children all have an urge to "push against boundaries". If this tendency is unchecked, Geminis will happily spend the rest of their lives trying to bend the rules — which will undoubtedly land them in hot water with authority later in life — whether it's the boss, the bank manager, or even the Inland Revenue!

Geminis love to feel free and unencumbered, and they keep their lives flexible so that they can change their minds at a moment's notice. That constant Gemini need for change and variety leads more serious signs, like Scorpio and Capricorn, to call them "flighty" and "superficial", and to avoid them like the plague. To a Gemini, the "grass is always greener", and they sometimes lack the staying power to see things through, whether it's a job, an investment or a marriage. Geminis have often been called the "butterflies" of the zodiac and it's easy to see why. But they do need to learn that commitment is a virtue+ too, and can often be really pleasurable, in its quiet, understated way...

Every sign has its shortcomings, though, and it must also be said that Geminis more than compensate for their "flightiness" by the sheer, utter charm of their nature. If you know a Gemini, chances are that they're such witty, charming companions, you're more than willing to forgive them their occasional lapses of memory when it comes to repaying loans, or the fact that they borrowed your lawnmower and clean forgot to return it. Or that it was their turn to pay for drinks last time you met... The bottom line is, many Geminis have a real problem handling mundane reality, and when life gets too dreary, they'll embroider it a little. But, on the plus side, your Geminis are the most delightful friends you could wish for — their jokes will make you fold up with laughter, and they'll amuse your kids for hours — as well as keeping you in touch with all the latest fashions and all the new shows in town. And all at the same time, of course! Since they're so young at heart themselves, they'll keep you young, too. The only trick to remember with Geminis is, treat them like a butterfly. Let them come and go as they please, admire their beauty, and, whatever you do, don't take them too seriously ...remember, they're probably just passing through...

II Gemini and Money

In keeping with their airy nature, when it comes to money and the task of juggling their finances, most Geminis you'll meet usually take a rational view. Money isn't something to get all hot and bothered about, as Taurus does — or to cling to tenaciously like a Cancer. You see, to Gemini, money has little intrinsic value in itself, and financial security is rarely high on their list of priorities. Rather like Aries, the typical Gemini sees money as a means to an end, rather than an end in itself. Or, as a long-standing Gemini friend of mine once remarked, "I see money as a passport to other things — like travel, culture and adventure. It's simply a currency that allows me to do what I want to in life. I don't see it as something that represents security. Money isn't something that should be squirrelled away for a rainy day. When I have money, it's there to be used — for me, of course, and also for my friends!"

Experience shows that what Geminis value most in life is seldom what you put in the bank. They love fine paintings, that's true, and they're always impressed by the good things of life — like dining at the trendiest restaurants and sporting the latest fashions. But the typical Gemini won't sell their soul in return for an income. They'd far rather be free to travel where the spirit leads them, for they value freedom and mobility above almost everything else in life. So if you run into a Gemini who's working really hard towards building some financial muscle, you can be pretty sure they're doing it chiefly to avoid doing jobs they hate — and well as to give them the freedom to travel the world at will.

Gemini's deep-rooted love of freedom and the ability to move at a moment's notice has rarely been better exemplified than by the late Robert Maxwell, the Gemini media tycoon who died mysteriously in 1991. "Money gives me the freedom to travel where and when I want, and that's why I appreciate it", he was once heard to remark. And Maxwell was as good as his word, for not only did he have a fleet of Rolls-Royces permanently at his disposal, but also a private jet and several helicopters, as well as his famous yacht. Maxwell's boat was naturally fully equipped with the very latest satellite communications and faxes, so that he could fire off orders to anyone in his global empire at a moment's notice! Despite the fact that Maxwell was a multimillionaire, he always said that money was not his driving force. It was the game itself that drove him, he claimed, rather than the result; like many Geminis before him, he found it better to travel than to arrive...

When it comes to making money, Geminis' chief asset is their incredible resourcefulness. If Geminis can think of one way of making a living, they can think of half a dozen, and their prodigious energy and enthusiasm also give them the drive to carry it off — despite their definite tendency to take on too much and generally overdo it. The average Gemini is more than capable of holding down an office job during the day — working as a copywriter, journalist or reporter would probably be ideal — then dashing off to work waiting on table in a trendy nightspot. Doing two, three or even half a dozen things at once suits them far, far better than just pegging away at one. For Geminis don't just thrive on variety — they positively crave it. More to the point, they're unlikely to prosper or do well financially if things get too fixed and predictable — and their lifestyle doesn't involve contact with lots of different people. For one thing's certain with a Gemini — communicate they must!

Gemini's ruling planet, Mercury, is also linked to commerce and trading, which surely explains their skill at selling. Geminis are the master salesmen of the zodiac, and the challenge of getting out on the street and hustling their wares doesn't faze them in the slightest: in fact, they just adore it. Most Geminis are blessed with prodigiously persuasive tongues and can sell coals to Newcastle or sacks of wheat to a Prairie farmer, and even have their customers coming back for more! They're also past masters at the art of selling themselves in the job market, and a Gemini will be undaunted by the prospect of redundancy or the abrupt termination of a freelance contract. Just pass them the telephone, Yellow Pages, and a notebook and pencil, and they'll have fixed up another job before the afternoon is out. Because security matters so little at them, Geminis are admirably suited to the precarious life of a freelance and the financial instability it generally tends to imply. Having an unpredictable cash flow holds no fears for Geminis, for they know they can always hustle. Self-confidence is rarely a quality they lack — in fact, they possess it in abundance, and most Geminis sleep easily at night, secure in the knowledge that they can talk themselves into a better financial position just as and when they need to.

Another great tool in Geminis' financial armoury is their mental agility, for this not only enables them to think their way out of financial problems a great deal faster than most, but also to understand and benefit from complex moneymaking schemes. Many Geminis have carved out a brilliant career in the world of financial services, as accountants, insurance brokers or financial advisers, thanks not least to their gift for grasping complex money matters in an instant. Knowing this, perhaps it's easy to speculate why there aren't more Gemini millionaires around, but remember the basic things that make Gemini tick — freedom and movement — and that gives you a valuable clue. Geminis have a notoriously low threshold of boredom, and they're far more likely to amass a fortune by accident rather than by careful design. Having built up a business that's producing a healthy income, they're more than likely to lose interest and be seized by an urge to start something new. For Geminis always long to be moving ever onwards — and moneymaking schemes that require a really long-term commitment are generally not to their taste. When it comes to money, Geminis invariably have a short-term financial focus. Or putting it more simply, they hate to feel trapped...

When it comes to handling their day-to-day finances, most Geminis prefer, whenever possible, to delegate this to their partners. It's not that they *can't* do it — far from it. When there's simply no alternative in sight, most Geminis can create a budget and manage to pay their bills on time. But the fact remains that the motivation to balance their chequebook may, more often than not, be lacking. Quite simply, they get *bored* when dealing with money and would far prefer to be doing something else. In point of fact, though, this typical Gemini attitude is actually very short-sighted . For were they to apply their excellent minds to the task of improving their finances — by reading the financial press, for instance, or keeping a lookout for good financial deals and products — they'd soon find themselves with more real independence than they knew what to do with! But Geminis' fatal financial flaw is often their "hidden twin" — who often causes trouble at the most unwelcome moments.

Many Geminis find themselves perennially torn by an inner conflict between what they know they *should* do with their money and what they'd really *like* to do with it. The typical Gemini is more than capable of blowing the rent money on a night at the opera and telling a few white lies about where the money went into the bargain! The twin aspect of Gemini sometimes rears its head in the financial arena, more often than not with unfortunate results. The scenario goes something like this: the "good" Gemini twin, the inner voice of reason and prudence, works out a budget and cash-flow that gets everything working smoothly. And then the "bad" twin — the manic, irrational side of Gemini that likes to indulge in spending sprees, gets hold of the chequebook and the cash flow goes to blazes. Angry letters from the bank manager result, and Gemini's financial situation degenerates into the kind of reality that they'd really rather not face. So the letters from the bank, and the credit card companies, too, get stuffed at the back of the drawer until Gemini feels like dealing with them. Or maybe then again, until their partner sorts out the mess. The main problem here is that many Geminis have trouble being *honest* with themselves about money, and will bury their heads in the sand until the situation becomes truly critical. When really pushed, they may even find themselves tempted to make money by somewhat illicit means. *Most* Geminis are thoroughly high-minded, though, and wouldn't dream of breaking the law. Being irresponsible with money, however, is a far more common vice. The time-honoured excuses of "The cheque's in the post", "It's my treat next time" or even, "I paid last time, didn't I?" are standard Gemini lines, but after a while, they begin to look distinctly threadbare...

Financial crises of the kind described above tend to bring out the "Peter Pan" side of Gemini, who then starts behaving like a child that won't grow up... The "Peter Pan" personality can also manifest when Geminis announce they're going to give up their job and write The Great Novel, or at the very least, a wonderful book that's bound to stay in the best-seller lists for at least a year. And while they're engaged in producing this mighty work, they'll naturally assume that their nearest and dearest won't mind plodding along at the boring old day job to pay the bills and keep them supplied with all life's little necessities. "Take care of me", coos Gemini, fluttering his or her eyelashes — and if you're a fool, you will. Thinking that the world owes them a living is a trait that many Geminis are prone to and, at best, it's pretty disagreeable. But the greatest favour you can do for Geminis who've temporarily lost contact with reality is to leave them well alone to clear up their *own* financial muddles. For it's only by taking responsibility for looking after their own money that Geminis begin to get grounded — and to develop the kind of staying power that's needed to achieve anything worthwhile in life.

II The Spending Style of Gemini

Geminis can be incredibly skilful at making a living, and although they'll often claim to be broke, that's rarely the case in reality. But most Geminis are just as good, if not better, at thinking up dozens of ways to spend their money, too! For although Geminis are rarely spendthrifts, their spending style can often be quite erratic. Geminis will stick faithfully to a budget for months, and then they'll break out and go on a spending spree that they'll soon regret. For when it comes to spending money, Geminis are perpetually subject to the varying wishes of those inner twins. One twin wants to save, the other wants to spend — one day the sensible twin gets its way, the next, it's the spendthrift who wins out!

Alternatively, they can live out the generous side of their personality one day and behave like Scrooge the next... So poor Geminis are forever torn between the two conflicting sides of their nature, and it's anybody's guess which will win. To get some clues as to how an individual Gemini is likely to behave, you need to look at the horoscope as a whole rather than just the Sun in isolation. Geminis with a heavy Saturn or earthy influence will probably be more sensible, but if fire and air are stronger, the spendthrift is likely to prevail.

Whatever their disposition, though, and however limited their budget, most Geminis love to spend. Rather like the famous T-shirt slogan, "When the going gets tough, the tough go shopping!", Geminis will often shop to cheer themselves up, especially if Gemini rules their Ascendant as well as their Sun. Although Geminis like to get value for money and will always be pleased when they get a good deal, bargain-hunting is rarely a crusade. But since spending money on culture is such a major part of their budget, they're always really delighted if they can cut a few corners elsewhere. In Gemini's book, culture isn't a luxury, it's an absolute must — and given half a chance, they'd far rather buy theatre tickets than groceries — and what about that new French film!

Since Geminis love to communicate, they're more than happy to spend money on anything that helps them connect with people quicker — mobile phones, computers, the very latest faxes — the speedier the better, and the latest model please! Mercury is also the god of transport, so a speedy little vehicle to get around in is naturally a must. Geminis adore sports cars and convertibles, with lots of little gadgets to play with, but if their funds won't stretch, then a motorcycle will do. Anything is better than public transport. They loathe it — it's so *slow!*

Geminis love to learn and so they'll happily spend money on evening classes and spare-time degrees. They'll study anything that catches their eye, from origami to picture-framing, or even ancient Japanese — all are grist to the Gemini mill. Trendsetters at heart, Geminis also love to follow fashion, and even if they're on a strict budget, they'll comb the sale rails for eye-catching bargains. Good haircuts and innovative accessories are also a must for Gemini, and they enjoy scouring craft fairs for unusual-looking jewellery.

Geminis often have problems stretching their budget to accommodate all the things they want to do, and that's where their ability to hustle can often come in handy. Journalist Geminis can talk themselves into free trips — but if that's not always possible, then they'll track down the cheapest tickets. Soaking up the sun on a fashionable beach is Gemini's idea of heaven, and frequent trips and weekends away are also *de rigeur*. Since home is the place where Gemini entertains, you can be sure the Gemini living-room will be designed to be truly impressive. Geminis have a keen eye for style and decor; Mercury's approach to interior design is to spend as much money as possible, make it look good, and then forget all about it. Geminis are great art collectors and also adore giving parties, so both these pastimes also feature on their budget. Buffet soirees rather than sit-down dinners are their passion, and they'll always get outside caterers in if their budget will stretch that far.

As a final pointer on Geminis and their spending, it should be noted that people born with Gemini strong in the chart should be especially wary of the temptation to "impulse buy" when Mercury, the ruler of Gemini, goes retrograde. These are the times when Mercury appears to stop and move backwards in the heavens, and many Geminis don't know whether they're coming or going! Interestingly, many shops and stores seem to hold their sales when Mercury is retrograde. Who knows why — perhaps it's just another of Mercury's little jokes! Mercury goes retrograde three times a year, so if you're an impulsive Gemini, leave your wallet at home! The Mercury Retrograde tables in the Appendix at the back of this book will show you the exact dates to beware of any impulse spending...

II Gemini: Saving and Investing

The Gemini approach to savings and investment is generally governed by their three main character traits: their short attention span, love of constant change and fear of being trapped! When it comes to saving money, Geminians aren't usually the zodiac's star performers, but they'll store their cash surplus if they have a pet project in mind. Ideally, they like short-call, highly flexible savings accounts that allow them easy access to their money, and are highly adept at scanning a spread of complex schemes to find the one savings plan that suits them best. Geminis have a tendency to build up reserves of money and then cash them in at a moment's notice. It sounds like a butterfly approach to finance, and that's exactly what it is. So if you live or work with a Gemini, be aware that this is how they are.

Leaping from scheme to scheme is not the best way to accumulate financial reserves, but that's of little interest to most Geminis. What they really want are freedom and excitement! Most Geminis learn, sooner or later, however, that saving up their money gives them greater freedom in the end. For having some reserves of money allows them to choose, and also to travel...

Perhaps the best way to persuade reluctant Geminis to save is to persuade them to set up not just one, but several accounts, called "Travel", "Art Fund", "Holidays", etc. — so that the prospect of pleasure in the future facilitates their saving in the present. Freelance Geminis in particular should always remember to put money aside for those inevitable tax bills — and if they can save a little extra for their projects, well, that's all to the good as well.

Most Geminis also have a short-term approach to investment. Their low threshold of boredom, coupled with their longing to "get rich quick", means they always prefer investments that can be cashed in without too much fuss. The concept of making money quickly appeals more to Geminis than to many other signs, and they rarely have the patience for 10- or 20-year investments. Things like property don't hold much appeal either. Land is a bit too fixed, and you can't put houses in your suitcase! Since Geminis like to move around a lot, and often end up living abroad for a spell, they rarely invest in property until the second half of life. With their agile minds and love of deal-making, Geminis are naturally drawn to the stock-market — but, unless they're doing their own deals, it's not the best milieu for growing their money — unless, of course, they've employed a Gemini broker.

Another problem that often snares Gemini investors, is their tendency to spread their energies too widely. It's all very tempting to dash off after half a dozen rainbows, but they'll find it far more profitable to stick with two or three ...and wait, if they can, for these to come to fruition before moving on quickly to the next round of possibilities.

One of the best investments for Gemini is art — and that means art in all its diverse forms, including paintings, sculpture and prints. With their keen instinct for spotting the top-selling artists of tomorrow and their knack of clinching a deal, Geminis investing in art can generally make a profit.

Geminis who are seeking to invest in business could consider any kind of company in the transportation field — from delivery services, to trains, to taxis. Mail-order is another potentially lucrative sector, along with giftware manufacturing, "magic" products, conjuring and art- and auction- houses. Other good investment opportunities may lie in communications — so look at advertising, marketing publishing, newspapers and radio, TV and travel. Telecommunications and high-technology companies are another likely field — as are companies producing computers, computer games and all kinds of audio equipment. Geminis may also be drawn to investing in companies producing games, puzzles and magic tricks. Think of "Trivial Pursuit" and you have the perfect Gemini way to make a fortune.

II The Earning Power of Gemini

Mercurial, volatile and ever-changing, Gemini's restless nature is a bag of mixed blessings when it comes to earning a living. For in their work, as in everything else, Geminis *demand* change, spontaneity and a massive amount of variety. They abhor routine, so if their workaday life becomes too fixed and predictable, they'll soon become listless, bored and depressed.

Although Gemini, frequently reach great heights in their chosen field — think of Joan Collins, Boy George and JFK — few Geminis ever really consider themselves to be ambitious. Keeping their mind buzzing with new ideas is generally far more important to a Gemini than reaching the top of the corporate ladder, and they're always more interested in today than in what they'll be doing in five years time. So if they do, perchance, end up in the president's office, it's usually by accident rather than design. And although Gemini generally knows *exactly* what's going on in the company — who said what to whom, who did what to whom, etc., etc. — they're rarely seen as key players in office politics.

Few colleagues and superiors see them as a threat, for the simple reason that once Geminis have mastered a job, unless they're getting lots of mental stimulation, they'll very quickly grow bored and soon start thinking of moving on...

In their early working years, most Geminis tend to flit from job to job rather like the proverbial butterfly, and when they're well into their thirties, many still indulge in "career-hopping". My friend Sue, a delightfully archetypal Gemini, was a schoolteacher when we first became friends, over twenty years ago. Geminis love jobs where they can "play", so teaching can often suit a Gemini quite well. But, after three or four years of teaching, the job began to pall. Then Sue met a businessman who honed in on her native wordpower — *all* Geminis have a brilliant way with words — and offered to train her as a journalist. Before long, she had carved out a niche for herself as a freelance writer — no mean feat in today's competitive media world. Then she decided to dabble in a little PR, and, being a true-blue Gemini lady, she was pretty good at that, too. *Nobody* can sell like a Gemini, and their quicksilver tongues and intellects are truly in their element when it comes to selling and marketing. And although Sue soon discovered that she didn't like PR as much as writing, her phone was constantly buzzing with clients who wanted her to promote their wares. The life of a freelance journalist, with its endless telephone calls, parties and press launches seems to have provided her with just about enough variety for her to stay with it for the last fifteen years, but she still takes plenty of time out to travel and to live out the freedom loving side of her sign. She once spent a year at art school, so she could learn to sculpt — like many Geminis, she's a gifted craftswoman, too! She's also a passionate hot-air balloonist, and clocks flying hours whenever she can. From time to time, she wistfully murmurs that she'd like to write a book — or maybe even a novel — but I sometimes wonder if she could sit still long enough to finish it!

All Geminis perform at their best when the working environment is as stimulating and varied as possible, and it's this alone that spurs them on to great achievements. They love to work with ideas, rather than things, but the social aspect of their work is also very important. Geminis don't just like people — they absolutely *need* them! No doubt it's the heritage of those mythic twins, of course, but whether they're working as copywriters, screenwriters, or running an import business, Geminis are always far happier with someone to bounce ideas around with. They always produce the best results when they work with a partner, rather than alone. Queen Victoria, for instance, (a triple Gemini) flourished alongside Prince Albert. And think of Gemini Paul McCartney and the classics he penned with John Lennon... This dual, twinning aspect of Gemini also applies to their native skills and abilities, for it can never be disputed that Geminis are amazingly versatile — and many reach very high standards in more than one career in a lifetime.

Given that Geminis work better in pairs, Gemini businesses probably stand a better chance if there's someone a bit more earthy around — a Virgo, perhaps, or a Capricorn — to take care of the practical details. Since Geminis can live quite happily with a fairly high level of uncertainty, they cope pretty well with the risks of building a business. But they do need to be careful not to delude themselves about details — for that's when the problems can begin. So if you're doing business with a Gemini, be sure to schedule regular financial meetings and keep a tab on the accounts. And bear in mind that Gemini's best role in business, by far, is as an "ideas" person and creative genius, and very rarely as an administrator or an accountant!

Although they relish a working environment that crackles and buzzes with activity, Geminis have a marked dislike of working under too much pressure. This may sound paradoxical, but just think of the way that Gemini's ruling metal, mercury, behaves when you squeeze it. Left to find its own form, mercury will nestle happily in the hollow of your hand, but if you try and force it into shape, it disintegrates and runs away completely — Geminis are a little like that, too. For though they like excitement, they don't like too much stress. They need to monitor themselves carefully when deadlines loom, and the pace of work hots up, or else they'll fall by the wayside — and just when they're needed most!

Since Geminis like nothing better than to feel free and unconstrained, they'll always baulk at rules and regulations and frequently run foul of the bureaucracy of big business. They may well fare better when they work in smaller, more individual companies, such as advertising agencies — where their idiosyncratic and irregular working style can be better appreciated for what they have to offer in return.

Geminis like to keep their career options fluid and open, so they're often accused of lack of commitment to their work — and even, sometimes, of being downright irresponsible! But whilst all Geminis love to explore the working world to its fullest extent when they're young, most of them settle down when they've discovered their true vocation. And once Geminis find the right arena for their multitudinous gifts, where they can show off their talents to their very best advantage, then they'll sprinkle all around them with a glittering trail of stardust. And who knows? If you're lucky, some of that Gemini brilliance may rub off on you too !

II The Gemini Boss

Geminis, it must be said, are not the born business managers of the zodiac. They may well end up in the president's chair by default, as a result of their dazzling abilities — but, by and large, the mantle of leadership sits somewhat uneasily on their highly-strung shoulders. So when Geminis find themselves cast in the role of taking responsibility for everything, they need to ask themselves honestly if it's a role that they really want. Geminis are unpredictable at the best of times, but the higher up the corporate ladder they climb, the more volatile they become. Media tycoon Robert Maxwell was notorious for his dark moods, which would descend like lightning out of the sky, and would hire and fire his staff on the most fleeting of whims. And when Geminis become overly constrained by the mundane realities of business, they become moody, depressed and extremely difficult to deal with...

Gemini is an air sign, and all air signs are happiest when dealing in the currency of ideas. Dreaming up new campaigns, new projects and new ways of doing things is far more to Gemini's taste — and that's why

Gemini bosses do best in top creative roles in businesses like management consultancy and advertising. The plus side of having a Gemini boss is, owing to their changeable nature, they're often very flexible — but you should also be aware that they can change their minds at a moment's notice.

II The Gemini Employee

Gemini employees look younger, think quicker and talk faster than just about any other sign of the zodiac, and what's more, they're amazingly versatile. They also have a dizzying ability to carry out a multitude of tasks at the same time. The prospect of writing a report or filing copy, fielding phone calls and totting up accounts, all at the same time, won't faze a Gemini at all. In fact, they'll love it. And if they can meet the public simultaneously, why that would be even better. Which is undoubtedly the reason why Geminis make such excellent receptionists, salesmen and secretaries.

The thing is, Gemini employees simply *must* have people to talk to, and if their work doesn't involve enough scope for legitimate communication, then they'll quickly become the office gossip! Put Geminis in a job where they can talk or write their heads off, though, and they'll be as happy as the day is long.

That's the good news. The bad news is that unless Geminis are totally fascinated by what they are doing, they all too easily get bored. When Geminis cease to be stimulated by the task at hand, their minds dash off elsewhere, and the resultant lack of concentration inevitably manifests in shoddy work or even in their total absence from the office! But, by and large, if there's sufficient variety in their workaday agenda, most Geminis have a lot to offer.

II Gemini and Career

With their agile minds and wide-ranging interests, finding a career isn't usually a problem for Geminis. Their problem is usually deciding exactly which career to choose! Many Geminis chop and change jobs a good deal before they find a career that provides enough variety and excitement to keep them interested long-term. But since Mercury is *the* planet of communication, most Geminis eventually find themselves drawn to a career that unites people and ideas in some form.

Geminis have a natural way with words, and many, many people born under this sign eventually become writers — having first of all sampled a few other jobs along the way. Geminis relish the ability to create their own routine, and a writer's life provides plenty of flexibility, along with a smattering of deadlines just to keep them on their toes! W.B. Yeats, Pushkin and Walt Whitman are just three of the literary giants born under this sign, and more recently there's Allen Ginsberg and William Styron. For Gemini, the pen will always be mightier than the sword: think of gossip columnist Hedda Hopper, who turned tittle-tattle into an art form, and U.S. comedienne Joan Rivers, whose classic opening line — "Can we talk?" — belies her highly caustic wit.

Geminis also flock to journalism, where the rapid turnover of stories and personalities suits them to a T. The world of newspapers and magazines is Gemini heaven, for they love dealing in information as well as up-to-the-minute trends. Geminis also adore radio and

TV, and many great film directors have been born under this sign: there's Jacques Cousteau and James Ivory, both renowned in their widely differing fields. And, according to statistics, you're more than likely to find a Gemini reading the news on TV each night. Geminis frequently have a great aptitude for languages, and many become successful interpreters, linguists and translators.

With their persuasive patter and native wit, Geminis are also the most gifted salespeople of the zodiac, and they enjoy few things as much as closing a deal. Gemini Donald Trump was an arch deal-maker of the 80s, and media tycoon Robert Maxwell claimed he only worked for "the thrill of the deal". Lesser-known Geminis are always in their element when selling: like Libra and Aquarius, the two other air signs, they thoroughly excel at negotiating — they don't get emotionally involved and always manage to keep a cool head. Telesales and mail-order distribution are two more natural outlets for their talents, whether they work for others or choose to go it alone. Geminis are also the great promoters of the zodiac, and no-one, not even an Aries, can outperform them when it comes to PR! And needless to say, they love all the partys that go with the job...

Since Geminis also like to keep their fingers firmly on the pulse of the moment, many are drawn to the glitzy world of advertising, where they revel in producing pithy slogans for every occasion. You'll also find many Geminis working in art galleries and auction houses, where the fashionable ambience and ever-changing merchandise are endlessly pleasing to their chic, sophisticated souls.

The Gemini love of travel leads many to become couriers and messengers, while others carve out a successful niche as travel agents and brokers. This is a job where more administration-oriented Geminis can truly shine, for it brings them into contact with the public, as well as allowing them to move around!

The worlds of acting and entertainment also abound with Geminis, and many great actors and singers have been born under this sign. Sir Lawrence Olivier and Cole Porter were both Geminis, along with Bob Dylan and Joan Collins. Gemini also has a long-standing association with magic, and many conjurors and stage hypnotists are born under its influence. Perhaps it's got something to do with the classic Mercury love of practical jokes!

There's can be plenty of laughter in the classroom, too, which is yet another place where Geminis can excel. Most Geminis possess a gift for understanding young children — giving them an ability to teach them in a highly accessible way. Last but not least, Geminis often make excellent therapists and counsellors — despite their preference for steering clear of the darker side of life. In ancient mythology, Mercury was the only god who was allowed to travel at will into the underworld — and many latter-day Geminis possess a similar gift for plumbing the depths of the unconscious and coming up with crystal-clear insights to help their clients move forward in a new, more positive way. Colour therapist Marie-Louise Lacy is a leading light in the therapy field, and combines her writing, public speaking and counselling roles in a unique Geminian way, bringing help and solace to many people.

II Gemini: Keys to Financial Success

- DO let your sterling asset of versatility work *for* you, and not against, and never scatter your energies too widely. Make "two of everything" your rule, if you like — but please don't make it a dozen.

- DO try and focus on the long-term financial future, as well as simply the present — it's the only way you'll ever achieve any lasting financial freedom. If you're in need of inspiration, read some biographies of famous writers, and find out how they did it!

- DO try and team up with the right kind of people to spark your creativity, and make your talents grow — and when you've found them, please do *listen* to what they say!

- DO use your excellent mental abilities to create a financial structure that really works. You'll be amazed to find it won't take up nearly as much time as you think — and will also give you far more freedom in the end...

- DO be honest with yourself — and others. You'll never get very far financially by creating a false reality for yourself, even if it seems more comforting at the time.

II Rich & Famous Geminis

Queen Victoria
Sir Arthur Conan Doyle
WB Yeats
Jean-Paul Sartre
Wallis Simpson (Duchess of Windsor)
Douglas Fairbanks
Frank Lloyd Wright
Judy Garland
Duke of Edinburgh
Sir Laurence Olivier
Bob Hope
Catherine Cookson
Salman Rushdie
Cole Porter
Bob Dylan
Boy George
Janet Jackson
Suzi Quatro
Gladys Knight
Laurie Anderson
Tony Curtis
Edward Woodward
Olympia Dukakis
Helena Bonham-Carter
Steffi Graf
Bjorn Borg

Richard Wagner
Paul Gauguin
Thomas Hardy
Walt Whitman
Vincent Price
Marilyn Monroe
J F Kennedy
George Bush
Errol Flynn
Joan Rivers
Saul Bellow
Colleen McCullough
Miles Davis
Paul McCartney
Prince
Priscilla Presley
Kylie Minogue
Nancy Sinatra
Gene Wilder
Clint Eastwood
Joan Collins
Brooke Shields
Pat Cash
Jackie Stewart

CANCER
June 22nd to July 23rd

Getting to know Cancer the crab is rather like setting off on a sea-voyage in uncharted waters. The day starts out fine and the water is smooth. Then all of a sudden, the skies grow dark, a squall blows up and the sea becomes exceedingly choppy. And then, before you know it, the sun is shining again ...and all that remains of the passing storm are just a few gentle ripples on the surface of the water. For just like the sea, Cancerians are thoroughly inscrutable and mysterious ...this is a sign that marches solely to the drumbeat of the emotions. With Cancer, the emphasis is firmly on intuition rather than logic — using their own special "sixth sense", Cancerians feel, rather than think their way through life. They also place a high priority on feeling safe and secure, and this is the reason why Cancer has such a well-deserved reputation for financial brilliance — rivalled only by Taurus or perhaps by Capricorn. Having money in the bank is one of the few things in life which makes Cancers feel at ease, the others being their home — the proverbial crab's shell — and a well-stocked larder...

Astrologically, Cancer is ruled by the Moon, and there's little doubt that all Cancerians are profoundly affected by its shifting, sea-change rhythms. The silvery moonbeams which light up the skies at full moon were once thought to drive men crazy (the word "lunatic" is derived from the Latin word for moon — 'luna'), and studying the Moon's cycle can provide invaluable insights into the mood-swings of the crab. At full moon, the typical Cancer is more extrovert than usual, or maybe slightly manic. Their sense of humour can be wackier too, and they'll often prefer to go partying, rather than stay at home and read a book. When the moon is new, on the other hand, and the night skies are at their darkest, Cancerians tend to be prone to irrational fears and worries. They'll often withdraw into their shell and retreat from the outside world, to quietly brood and plan their next move. For Cancerians are strategists par excellence, and can rarely be goaded into spontaneous, impulsive action, whether the issues at stake relate to finance or to their feelings. In between the two extremes of full- and new-moon falls the whole gamut of Cancerian feelings, ranging from serenity to sulking and every imaginable variation on these emotional themes! So if you want to understand a Cancer, just take some time to study the Moon. Cancer's moods unfold strictly according to its silvery cycles — and if you get to know the lunar phases well enough, you can even learn to predict those crabby moods in advance...

Many Cancerians find an outlet for their creativity through cooking and entertaining. Others, like Dame Iris Murdoch, for instance, express their creative gifts through writing and storytelling. The Moon endows Cancer with tremendous powers of memory and imagination, and also gives them unparalleled access to inner fantasy worlds. Cancer is strongly attuned to the inspirational energies of the unconscious mind, and it's no coincidence that a higher than average number of writers are born under this sign. Many a crab writes poetry, paints pictures, or has a few chapters of an unfinished novel tucked away in their bottom drawer, waiting for the day when they can give up their day-job and pursue their art full-time... Some Cancerians find their sensitivity makes them highly attuned to atmospheres and vibrations, sometimes to such an extent that they experience psychic manifestations or strange, supernatural events. Cancerian writer Colin Wilson has made a lifetime's study of such phenomena, including reincarnation, hauntings and ESP, and achieved world renown with his landmark book, *The Occult.*

Just like their animal counterparts, most crabs go about life in a distinctly defensive mode, and never, ever go directly for what they really want. The typical Cancerian tends to hang back quite a bit, and may even pretend to go in the opposite direction entirely — just to throw their rivals off the scent. Everyone is then completely taken by surprise when the Cancerian finally pounces! And once a crab has seized hold of something they want, don't ever think they'll let go, unless their life itself is in danger. For crabs, both human and animal, are tenacious to a fault!

The sign of Cancer embodies something of a subtle paradox, though, for Cancerians can be both caring and steely — and all at the very same time. You may think you are dealing with a great soft pussycat, but one day, all of a sudden, they'll surprise you with their bold and determined manner. And when they feel threatened, as they frequently do, they'll retreat into their shell until they think it's safe to come out. For when the chips are down, their shell is their armour, and their best defence against a world that's almost as unpredictable as they are. You can telephone them, or write them letters until you're blue in the face — they won't come out until they're good and ready!

Since Cancerians' feelings are what really make them "tick", it's vitally important for both male and female crabs to keep themselves balanced emotionally, or else their health is bound to suffer. Cancerians all have sensitive stomachs and, if they worry too much, as they sometimes do, it's a sure-fire recipe for an ulcer. Practising relaxation techniques such as meditation or autogenic training, or relaxing in a herbal bath each night, are great ways to defuse the stresses and strains of everyday living and help the poor old crab to take things a little more smoothly.

As children, Cancerians are like little crabs who haven't yet acquired a shell, for they're exceedingly sensitive and vulnerable to any criticism or rejection. All children need ample amounts of encouragement, love and affection, but baby Cancerians need it rather more than most. Cancer's ruler, the moon, is strongly linked with motherhood, and if these little ones are disciplined too harshly, or deprived of affection at an early age, they can grow up into emotionally damaged adults who never emerge from their shell at all. It's true that all children need discipline, but in Cancer's case, it should always be sugar-coated! Unhappy Cancerians are particularly prone to eating disorders like anorexia nervosa or bulaemia — Lady Diana, the Princess of Wales, has the sun in Cancer and has openly revealed her own problems in this area. And sometimes, a Cancer who hasn't received enough love in childhood may project their unsatisfied longings onto money and social status. Such a child may grow up to become an archetypal ruthless millionaire or industrialist, still looking for the love that they never received in childhood. Even as adults, all Cancerians need liberal amounts of encouragement and affection in order to flourish — a fact which their partners should never overlook. Little compliments and social niceties mean a great deal to Cancerians. They're extremely gifted at giving them, too, always knowing just how to "say the right thing at the right time."

Just like their animal counterpart, the human crab is a creature of constantly changing moods, who lives in two worlds. Cancerians need the real world of terra firma — the world of facts, money, bills and commitments — for the simple reason that it grounds them and makes them feel secure. But they also need to spend time exploring the bottomless depths of their fantasy world, the secret hiding-place of their dreams and imaginings. For this is the thing that illumines their life with moonlight and magic, and existence is a dull round without it.

It isn't all magic and moonbeams down on the seashore though. Cancerians have oodles of drive and an iron will, along with a highly developed desire nature, and when their ambitions are thwarted, all that gentleness quickly turns to ice. Crabs hate to let go and concede that they have lost, and they'll resort to all kinds of tactics to hang on to what they feel is theirs. Spying, smear campaigns, even emotional blackmail — all are grist to the Cancerian mill. In the long term, however, all that bitterness takes a toll of the body. Cancerians hate to let go of anything — even their negative emotions. But they must learn to let go before all that stored-up resentment makes them physically ill. Far better to take a trip to the seashore and let the billowing waves and fresh salt air just wash it all away. Spending time by the sea never fails to heal a Cancerian's wounds, and it's also the perfect place to sit and plan their next money-move — as only a Cancer can....

♋ Cancer and Money

In keeping with their deep-seated need for comfort and security, you'd have to travel a long way indeed to find a Cancer who didn't like money! The fact is, Cancerians appreciate money almost as much as Taureans and Capricorns do, and it's a constant source of speculation amongst astrologers as to which sign tops the league financially. Taureans might have the edge when it comes to accumulating money and stashing it away, and few can equal the goat for sheer Capricornian persistence. But fewer still can hold a candle to Cancer's flair for moneymaking: Cancer's "way with money" is often envied, but rarely surpassed.

All Cancerians, both men and women, are born with a profoundly businesslike head on their shoulders, though many prefer not to broadcast this fact. The truth is, Cancer's keen interest in money can sometimes sharply conflict with their caring public image. But back in the privacy of their home domain, that old caddy in the kitchen is always well stacked with crinkly banknotes, and there's sure to be plenty tucked away in their bank account too. As a rule, Cancerians put a great deal of energy into making money, and life has a habit of rewarding their efforts. The ranks of top business people, bankers and financiers swarm with men and women born under this sign, such as airline tycoon Richard Branson, and John and Nelson Rockefeller — but it's the men, rather than the females, who tend to become household names...

To a greater extent than with most other signs, Cancer's basic sense of personal security is tied up with money. But this longing for security is more complex in its nature than the plain and simple desire for more. That's the Taurean version of "safe and secure", and it's relatively uncomplicated. With Cancer, however, the issue of financial security has more to do with bolstering their own sense of self-worth and self-esteem — which can sometimes be distinctly fragile.

Shy and diffident as they are, on the surface at least, self-confidence isn't necessarily one of Cancer's strongest qualities, and making money can go a long way towards helping them "walk tall". Cancerians like money, not least because it makes them feel more confident — and there's a strong relationship between the crab's bankbalance and how good they feel about themselves. When the sign of Cancer is strong in a birthchart, the individual's whole energy, vitality and sense of self worth is directly related to their financial standing. When their earning power diminishes, their general sense of wellbeing tends to plummet too. Should a Cancerian's livelihood be threatened, a shadow falls across their whole being, and it's not unusual for a crab to get depressed, fall ill or even suffer some kind of accident. Indeed, the intimate connection between money and self-esteem is an area which every Cancer would do well to spend some time exploring. It's never a wise move to have one's sense of security and wellbeing totally invested in money, for if you lose your money, what happens then? For Cancer, at this point, the whole world can fall apart — and surely it's unwise to build your entire universe around something that's so capable of collapsing?

All Cancerians have a keen awareness of money from an early age. Even when they're barely into their teens, most crabs will have a weekend job, or some other way of earning extra pocket money. For all Cancerians, young and old, earning and having money is a sure-fire way of proving themselves and stemming those dark lunar fears that they're somehow not quite "good enough"... On a basic, more primitive level, having money is also the best way Cancerians know of taking care of their family, and this is a major factor which often underpins their striving. When I asked health guru and novelist Leslie Kenton how she'd managed to scale such heights of literary achievement at the same time as raising four children, she gave the answer that every Cancer mother would: "I did it for my family. All the things I've ever achieved in my career, I did for the plain and simple reason that I had to feed my children!"

Another reason why Cancerians love making money is because it's the most splendid "cosmic buffer." To Cancer, the world can be a difficult, worrying, unpredictable place, and acquiring plenty of money is a sure-fire way of keeping it at bay. Money allows Cancer to buy a house they can retreat to, to provide for their family, and to make the future more predictable. Money allows them to hide from the world when they feel like it, to scuttle about the seashore just as they please, and also, to plan for their old age — another thing that's very important to the crab. On so many levels, money allows Cancer to worry a lot less, to sleep better at night, and to feel in control — and in the mind of a crab, that's worth a great deal...

People who have fallen foul of the crab's great skill with money can often come to view it in a harsh, uncharitable way. Cancer's talent for self-preservation can sometimes make them quite a few enemies — or as an astrologer friend of mine once said, "When it comes to money, all Cancerians have a mind like a steel trap". And although this view is extreme, it nevertheless contains a tiny grain of truth... It's a character trait that holds true across the sexes too, for despite their fragile, fluffy appearance and air of ingenuous helplessness, Cancerian women often have brilliant heads for money — although many Cancerian ladies have a breathless, romantic air which totally belies their real-life toughness and resilience. Don't forget, Cancer is a water sign, and given enough time, water simply washes away all resistance. When a Cancerian female is unable to get what she wants straight away, she'll simply sits tight until everyone else gives up! And although Cancerian women may not enter the world of finance and banking as frequently as the men, their keen business sense should never be underestimated. So when you're discussing money with a Cancer — male or female, young or old — do remember that though they may look and sound disinterested, their awareness is more than likely to be keenly focused on that crucial bottom line!

A publisher friend of mine once told me of a Cancerian author he'd had dealings with, who murmured naively that she really didn't understand those "complicated contracts". Like most crabs, she was frustratingly evasive to deal with, particularly when it came to finalizing financial arrangements that might benefit her more if they were left open-ended. "Can't we sort it out later?", was her constant refrain. But when the discussion turned to those parts of the contract which would have benefited my publisher friend, had these been left till later, she firmly insisted that all be sorted out there and then. This tactic of quietly turning matters to their advantage whilst hiding their motives behind a smokescreen of ignorance is typical of the way many Cancerians behave when it comes to money — the reason being that crabs rarely feel safe enough to come out into the open and ask for what they really want.

When it comes to the practical, everyday task of balancing the household budget, if there's a Cancer in the relationship, be they male or female, you'll usually find them controlling the purse-strings. A wise partner will just let them get on with it, for the crab is an eminently practical soul and is genuinely gifted at financial matters. Householder crabs will keep daily tabs on all outgoings, make the family pennies stretch as though they were made of elastic, and perform some dazzling feats of recycling. In traditional astrology, Cancer rules Scotland, and it's no coincidence that the Scots are so widely famed for their frugal ways. But beware the Cancerian whose passion for recycling gets out of control, for they never ever want to throw anything away, "just in case it comes in useful". You can protest in vain that there's really no use for that ten-year old box of used Christmas cards, or that fading packet of birthday stickers, or that suitcase full of worn-out clothes. Your pleas will fall on deaf ears, and you may have to resort to a surreptitious clear-out when you're sure that your crab isn't looking! The kind of compulsive hoarding that some Cancerians indulge in is yet another symptom of their deep-seated insecurity, their perennial fear that there "won't be enough". Hoarding food, money and objects is an excellent hedge against the future and it's a habit they are loath to let go of!

On the plus side, though, most Cancerians are thoughtful, conscientious and reliable in their financial habits. They like to pay their bills on time, and they avoid consumer debt like the plague. And when it comes to lending and borrowing, their approach is equally cautious. Even when their funds are well in surplus, they'll rarely rush to lend them out, unless, of course, a family member is involved. Then, and only then, their generosity knows no limits. But generally speaking, they'll never lend money unless their inner "sixth sense" says they'll be sure to get it back. There's one important exception to their general financial caution, however. Many Cancerians who have used their excellent money skills to build sizeable personal fortunes may then turn around in middle- or old-age and become thoroughgoing philanthropists. Some of the world's greatest foundations and charities have been founded by sun sign Cancerians — just think of the name Rockefeller for a moment. So the upside of all that financial shrewdness is that it often ends up being put to the very best possible use. Rich, altruistic Cancerians prefer donating their money to charities, rather than individuals, and once they've built their own security, helping other people often becomes the primary focus of their lives. Businessman and banker Peter Rae, who has pioneered the concept of the "not-for-profit" business, is a top-level financier who's thoroughly typical of his sign. Rae now uses his considerable financial acumen to help raise money for holistic education and, like many sun sign Cancerians, he's made children's charities a major focus.

Most Cancerians spend a major part of their time and energy worrying about what could go wrong financially, and their prosperity will usually improve by leaps and bounds when they begin to face their fears and cultivate a more relaxed attitude about money. Happily, their sense of self-esteem grows stronger as they get older, and they begin to feel more secure within themselves. Nevertheless, Cancerians of all age-groups would do well to value themselves more for their creative gifts and strengths — as well as for their ability to make and hang on to their money!

℃ The Spending Style of Cancer

The Cancerian approach to spending money is quite simple. Broadly speaking, they'd rather not! Since money in the bank spells security, they'd far rather leave it there, to accumulate and grow, like the tomatoes in their greenhouse. Spending money is never Cancer's favourite occupation, and in this respect, they're not dissimilar to their opposite sign of Capricorn, which is also renowned for its frugal ways. But unlike Capricorns, who tend to discipline their expenditure with the utmost rigour, Cancerians are subject to the ever-changing influence of the Moon — which means that even the thriftiest crabs are prone to occasional spending binges, when their lunar emotions get the better of them and their strict financial discipline goes totally out of the window!

When crabs do finally get around to doing some spending, though, you'll tend to find that they plump for quality every time. Whether it's a sweater, a pair of shoes or a motorcar, they'll always buy the very best that they can afford: "Those handmade loafers may be expensive, but they'll last at least three summers" — or so the crablike logic goes. Cancerians are great bargain-hunters too, and they'll patiently wait until the sales come round before buying those top-of-the-range items that they've been coveting all year.

There are two major areas, however, that crabs will quite happily and freely spend on — their home, not surprisingly, and also their family, too. Since home is their "shell", and their first line of defence against an uncertain world, they spend a great deal of time there, and the typical Cancer home is always cosy and inviting. Cancerian houses and apartments are comfortable, rather than chic, and they're unlikely to have modelled the decor on the latest interior designs. They'd far rather choose all the furnishings themselves — or better still, recycle those treasured velvet curtains and mahogany armoires they inherited from their dear old mother. Cancerians are deeply sentimental people, and the most prized piece of furniture a crab possesses may well be a rather battered chest which once belonged to their Grandmama. They won't mind at all that it's a bit tatty — to them, the memory is what matters most.

Crabs are great collectors, too, so their homes are often quite cluttered. Whether their passion is for ducks, old teacups or military medals, once the collecting bug has bitten them, they'll indulge it whenever they can, spurred on by their urge to accumulate. Crabs love anything which has a past or a history, and have a real talent for spotting the one good piece in a roomful of junk. Many Cancerians turn their passion for antiques into a lucrative spare-time hobby. The only problem here is that they sometimes find it difficult to let go of things, even when they're offered a temptingly high price! Cancerians also don't mind paying out for help around the home. For although they're supremely domesticated, most Cancerians loathe housework and always prefer to pay someone else to do it — finances permitting, of course. And Cancerians never, ever scrimp on their children. A Cancer mother will go without new clothes, or even a much-needed holiday, in order to ensure that her children get the best education money can buy. And you can be sure that Cancer's offspring will be the best-dressed kids in the street...

Cancer being a water sign, Cancerians have a real affinity for the sea, and most crabs like to head for the coast whenever the fancy takes them. It's as though they need to touch base with the shifting tides of the ocean every now and then, in order to regain their inner equilibrium. Many crabs have a second home by the seashore, even if it's just a humble caravan or chalet. Even if they don't have a seaside base, they may own a yacht or a dinghy, or have a stake in one at least. And when their busy lifestyle keeps them city-bound for months at a time, many crabs will recreate a sense of the seashore in their home. Some content themselves with a humble goldfish bowl; others, like ex-fashion designer Cynthia Morgan, who has Cancer on the ascendant, have even built their very own grotto — which is a source of fascination to all her visitors, young and old.

There's a self-indulgent side to Cancer too, and both male and female crabs alike are fond of giving themselves little treats. Both sexes enjoy dressing well, and the women, in particular, always like to feel well-groomed. Romantic, lace-trimmed outfits in gentle pastel shades and soft feminine tones are the stock-in-trade of the female Cancer's wardrobe. Cancerian ladies also love antique jewellery, old-fashioned cameos and mother-of-pearl necklaces that glow by the light of the moon. The men like to look good, too, and they're also likely to spend considerable sums of money on photography and amateur movie-making — both favourite Cancer hobbies.

With their love of good food and wine, Cancerians love to eat out from time to time. The typical Cancer eaterie won't be a flashy, expensive place though. They tend to plump for jolly Italian trattorias, where the decor may be a bit shabby, but the food is tasty and comforting, the portions are large, and the prices are — well, old-fashioned! Crabs also love to entertain at home and will never pass up the opportunity for a celebration or family get-together.

A final area where Cancer will quite happily spend large sums of money is on travel. Holidays are sacred to the crab; they're a wonderful reward for all that hard work throughout the year, and the more exotic the location, the better. Since they like to travel in comfort, they always avoid low-cost options, such as camping. The only problem is, sooner or later the crab will need to build an extension for all those souvenirs and mementoes they keep bringing home year after year — each one holds a memory, so naturally, there's never any question of letting it go. A garage sale? — perish the thought!

♋ Cancer: Saving and Investing

Saving money is an area where Cancerians really come into their own. The crab is one of the thriftiest signs of the zodiac, and the habit of putting something aside for the future comes as naturally to a crab as blowing it all on the latest "toy" would seem to an Aries or Leo. Cancerians usually acquire the habit of saving quite early in life, and rarely need to be encouraged. Salting their pennies away in the piggy-bank is something that little Cancers seem to be born knowing how to do, and wise parents will take steps to ensure that their baby bankers also know that it's OK to spend their pocket-money too...

Crabs of all ages take a special delight in watching their money grow. They enjoy saving for specific items and projects, especially when these are related to home and family. For example: renovating their house; building an extension or a conservatory for their plants; summer courses for the children; or perhaps a trip to Disneyland.

The Cancerian's skill at saving is second to none, but choosing the right investments can frequently cause them headaches. When crabs are faced with the job of deciding exactly where to place their funds, all their deep-seated fears and insecurities come flooding to the surface, and niggling doubts and irrational worries can cloud their clarity of judgement.

Since Cancerians loathe risk-taking in any shape or form, their prime investment criterion is security, first and foremost; above all else, they want their money to be safe . The high-risk, high-yield speculation of the stock exchange or money markets doesn't appeal to the crab one whit, despite the allure of high profits. Cancerians are all too aware that "what goes up must come down", and they like to feel they can go on holiday and come back knowing their money will be just where they left it — growing nicely of course, but still there, nevertheless. Astrological investment consultant Dan Pallant reports that he's never once been approached by a single Cancerian who wished to invest in the volatile futures market. But when he worked as a property developer back in the early '70s, it was a different matter entirely...

Since they love their homes above almost all else, perhaps it's hardly surprising that Cancers love to invest in property. Owning their own home is an absolute necessity for most crabs, and they'll usually make sure that the mortgage is paid off in record time, too. Cancers view paying rent as "money down the drain", and if at all possible, they'll buy their business premises, as well. Many Cancerians have built up fortunes, large and small, by the shrewd buying and selling of both residential and commercial property. Despite the reverses suffered in the world property markets over the last few years, most Cancerians still persist in the view that property is one of the best investments around.

With their long-term outlook and cautious temperament, most crabs also place a high priority on investing in pension funds and insurance policies. To a Cancer, the idea of putting money aside for use in twenty or thirty years' time seems eminently practical, for little matters more to them than ensuring a comfortable old age. Cancerians also like to travel in retirement, and that takes money, too. For the most part, they'll be too busy working to spare much time for globe-trotting before they retire — apart from their holidays of course...

Another investment pitfall that many Cancerians encounter stems from their all-too-frequent tendency to let good opportunities pass them by — for the very simple reason that they hesitate too long. Learning to trust their finely-tuned intuition is the best, if not the only way of dealing with this problem. Cancerians would do well to remember that deep-down, they always do know whether it's right to go ahead or not. They need to remind themselves that it's OK to trust — and that it's perfectly all right to get involved in exciting new investments, provided of course, that they pass that important 'feel right' test.

As well as bricks and mortar, items for the home also make good Cancerian investments. With their love of history and all things of the past, many crabs enjoy investing in antiques. Buying beautiful, rare collectibles, such as china, porcelain, glassware and paintings allows Cancerians to both decorate their home and make money at the same time — a double-edged prospect that's truly hard to resist. In traditional astrology, the Moon is linked with the metal silver, and investing in fine silverware can also prove to be profitable.

Entrepreneurial crabs, who are looking to invest in business, should seek out enterprises with a sharing, caring face. Cancer's favourite and most profitable ventures are always companies which benefit and nurture others, whether it's a luxury hotel (Peter de Savary), an airline (Richard Branson), or a fashion house (Pierre Cardin). Retirement homes and clinics can also prove to be good investments, along with schools, kindergartens and nurseries. Some Cancerians put their money into pioneering "alternative" schools and holistic education. Others get involved in hotels, cafes, health resorts and restaurants. Holiday companies, catering ventures or even cookery-book publishing could prove lucrative too. But any kind of business where the primary emphasis is taking care of people will be a likely avenue for the crab to explore. Home-related businesses such as interior design, hand-crafted items, property renovation, dressmaking, soft furnishings and ladies' and childrens' clothing, could also prove rewarding, in many more senses than one.

ॐ The Earning Power of Cancer

With their cautious, sideways, "two steps forward, one step back" approach to life, it's easy to make the mistake of thinking that Cancer is one of the less ambitious signs in the zodiac. In reality, however, nothing could be further from the truth. Don't forget, Cancer the crab is a cardinal sign, which means crabs have the strongest possible drive to drive to achieve and make their mark in life. This may be well disguised, but it's still there, all the same. Crabs are always waiting — waiting patiently for just the right moment to make their next move...

To the Cancerian way of thinking, work and money are intimately related to a far greater degree than they are for most other signs. Just like their opposite sign of

Capricorn, people born under the sign of the crab are extremely hard-working. But with Cancer, it's the desire to boost their earnings ever skyward which generally drives them on, rather than the need for status and approval. Cancer likes to be noticed, that's true, and they thrive on appreciation: a pat on the back won't come amiss, but, given the choice, they'll always plump for a financial bonus instead. Money spells security and a long line of safe tomorrows, and the way Cancer sees it, that's what work is all about. For although typical Cancerians hate to leave a job once they're happily settled, they won't hang around for long if the salary doesn't measure up and the pay rises don't keep coming. Promotion, they can wait for, yes — but money? That's another matter entirely.

For Cancer, a peaceful working environment is a necessity rather than a luxury. Noisy, open-plan offices are ill-suited to their sensitive, reflective natures, and they'll go to considerable lengths to avoid them. The crab's office can often become a sort of home-from-home, pleasantly cluttered with family photos and memorabilia. Knock before entering, though, for Cancerians value their privacy, and they often need to withdraw into their shell before making important business decisions.

Above all else, Cancerians love to work near water. High-flying Cancer tycoon Richard Branson of Virgin Atlantic fame is a perfect example. His own personal office and "empire HQ" has for many years been located on a houseboat moored on a quiet backwater of a London canal. Branson has always prided himself on his empire's "family" feel: any company that grows beyond a comfortable fifty employees is automatically broken up into smaller, more family-sized units — and he also conducts a lot of business from the comfort of his London family home.

When Branson decided to branch out from his tried and tested music business into the risky, cutthroat world of aviation, his company accountants asked him, "Why an airline?" "Because it feels right", was Branson's reply. The success of Virgin Airlines speaks for itself, furnishing abundant proof, if proof were needed, that Branson's Cancerian "feelings" are usually thoroughly correct. Earlier on, he built a music empire by selling cut-price records, a strategy also based firmly on intuition. In business astrology, the Moon rules mass markets, and Moon-ruled Cancerians are particularly adept at tuning in to what the general public wants to buy. Branson's glittering career once again perfectly proves this point...

Many lesser-known Cancerians share Branson's talent for gauging the mass-market, and crabs' intuitive gift for knowing just what people want is one of their greatest working assets. Coupled with their innately practical nature and unwavering attention to the balance-sheet, most crabs are natural businesspeople. It's a curious thing, though, that with a few noteworthy exceptions, Cancerian women often do better in business than men. Perhaps that's because the male crab finds his sensitivity and intuition harder to handle than does his female counterpart. And he's often browbeaten into going against his feelings simply because he cannot really explain them in a logical, rational way.

Crabs of both sexes tend to be highly secretive about their work, and most Cancerians will never tell anyone their business plans, unless that person's support is indispensable. Whether it's a merger, a takeover or simply the last piece of gateau at the office party, the typical Cancerian wouldn't dream of showing their hand until the deal is firmly in the bag. Cancerians often dither and demur until the very last minute, and then they'll suddenly pounce and make an unstoppable move towards their goal!

Crabs are excellent salespeople, too, but their way of selling is not the gift-of-the-gab style of Gemini. A Cancerian salesperson is far more likely to close the deal by looking almost tearful and getting the unsuspecting customer to feel quite sorry for them. And although Cancerians may sometimes lack the boundless energy of the fire signs, their steady persistence often yields greater dividends long-term. Patience is Cancer's great virtue, and it's this that allows them to take a longer-term view and create a thriving enterprise across a time-frame that would make an Aries, say, chafe with frustration. Thanks to their lunar nature, Cancerians also have a keen awareness that business and finance operate in cycles, and never lose sight of the fact that when winter comes, as it surely must, then spring is bound to follow!

The main problem which holds Cancerians back in business is their tendency to be overly cautious. Every business must sometimes "speculate to accumulate", but Cancerians can become so obsessed with conserving resources that they fail to take advantage of even the best opportunities to expand. Their intention is always to protect the business, but by holding it back, they can sometimes damage it instead. Cancerians generally dislike taking risks, and often do best when they team up with a fiery partner — preferably an Aries or a Leo — who will move the business forward while Cancer watches the budget.

Cancerians can also do extremely well when working in partnership with a husband, wife or family member. This arrangement helps them to create a close-knit working environment in which they can safely express their creative gifts and practicality to the full. Incidentally, since Cancer also adores food and socializing, all crabs will be in the seventh heaven when their work-schedule requires them to socialize and entertain business guests and clients.

♋ The Cancer Boss

Generally speaking, most Cancerians prefer giving orders to taking them. They like to be the boss, and for the most part, they make a good job of it. Cancer likes to take care of others, but they also need space to express their drive and native ambition. Self-starters at heart, they're eminently suited to the competitive world of freelance employment — provided, of course, that they have a base of regular clients.

Cancerians can and do prosper as executives within large organizations, but they usually prefer smaller, more intimate companies with a friendly, personal feel. The nurturing qualities of Cancer bosses are always firmly to the fore, no matter how exalted their corporate role. Cancerian bosses expect their underlings to work as long and hard as they do, but they're hugely understanding when any personal problems arise, particularly if these are family-related. Cancerians take great care of their employees, but they can become possessive and difficult when their staff wish to leave or branch out in new directions. Crabs hate letting go of people, as well as things, and Cancer bosses can behave distinctly like the archetypal "Jewish Mother" when one of their "children" wishes to fly the nest.

☙ The Cancer Employee

Diligent and hard-working by nature, Cancerians usually make excellent employees — the only problem being, they're so very, very emotional! For there's no getting round it, the feeling nature of crabs sometimes overrules their customary clear-headedness. Cancerians always make moody workmates, and a crab who's going through a major emotional upheaval — like divorce, or some other "disaster" — can disrupt the office for weeks with tempests of tears and tantrums. Your best strategy is to be gently supportive and caring, for your patience will usually be richly rewarded once the crab is more balanced again. Often, the most sensible course of action is to give them a few weeks leave to sort themselves out — or, better still, go home to Mother!

It's also advisable to talk regularly with Cancer employees, for crabs who feel they're not getting a fair deal will resort to sulking, silence or even sabotage, rather than confront the issues directly. Finally, never pay too much attention to any outlandish things that a Cancerian employee says or does when the moon is full — it's bound to be just a case of temporary insanity!

☙ Cancer and Career

Cancerians care. Yes, they really do care, despite their well-developed instinct for self-preservation! The statistical research into astrology and career carried out by Professor Alan Smithers of Manchester University in 1984 clearly showed that Cancerians typically opt for careers where they can serve the needs of others, and it's their ability to nurture just about anything you can think of, from pensioners to piranhas, that is really the key to Cancer's greatest career success. For when crabs choose a working role where they can minister to the needs of others as well as their own, then they're well and truly on the right track.

Not surprisingly, the caring professions, such as nursing, teaching and social work, are natural magnets for Cancer. You'll find many, many crabs working happily in the health service: Cancer women often choose nursing or nutrition, and many Cancerian doctors specialise in obstetrics and gynaecology — the Cancer link with motherhood is, it would seem, inescapable.

Patience is another Cancerian virtue, and Cancerians make great agony aunts. They're happy to sit and listen while a client or colleague blows off steam, and then they'll offer a few, well-chosen words of advice to help remedy the problem at hand. The customer care and personnel divisions of companies, large and small, are also places where crabs are likely to excel: they thrive in any job which involves a counselling or mentoring role.

Many crabs become youth workers, teachers and nursery nurses, too. It's no coincidence that Diana, Princess of Wales, one of the world's most famous Cancerians, was a nursery teacher before her marriage, for looking after small children is a natural Cancer calling. The crab's nurturing skills also extend to animals and plants, and crabs often have green fingers, as well as helping hands. Many Cancerians find their true vocation as veterinary surgeons or farmers, or through working with plants in nursery gardens.

Another way of nurturing others is by working with food and wine. Many, many Cancerians can be found either running or working in restaurants, wine bars or hotels, and their culinary skills, together with their innate ability to create a welcoming and soothing ambience, usually guarantee their commercial success.

But let's not allow all this talk of caring and nurturing to obscure the fact that Cancerians are ambitious. Every crab, however altruistic at heart, wants to make his or her mark on the world, and Cancer the crab is also the sign of the entrepreneur. You'll find many, many crabs running their own business — be it a small corner store, a boutique, or a huge, multi-million dollar corporation. Cancerians' native commonsense and shrewdness stand them in good stead when it comes to buying, selling and retailing, and, even more than "watching the store", they love to watch those profits grow. Cancers excel in businesses which allow them to combine their special interests — money, property, antiques or travel — with their innate ability to relate directly to the buying public. They make great travel agents, estate agents and property developers, and you'll also find many crabs working as bank or building society managers: with their finely-tuned intuition, assessing loan prospects is second nature!

Cancer is also a highly artistic sign, and many crabs make a living as interior designers, photographers or painters. Think of artist David Hockney, or the late great photographer Henri Cartier-Bresson. Other Cancerians have channelled their natural artistry towards the field of haute couture — Pierre Cardin, Hardy Amies and Elizabeth Emanuel were all born under Cancer.

Cancer's sea-change moods and finely-tuned sensitivity mean that many crabs are endowed with a real genius for film acting. Meryl Streep, Kelly McGillis, Leslie Caron, Genevieve Bujold and Isabelle Adjani, all have the Sun in Cancer. Male Cancerian superstars include Sylvester Stallone, Tom Cruise and Harrison Ford. These actors are among the highest-paid stars in Hollywood, with Tom Cruise commanding more than $20 million per film. For when it comes to the portrayal of big-screen emotions, Cancer has few rivals and even fewer peers.

Many Cancerians also have a natural gift for writing, a moon-given ability to weave magic with words. Marcel Proust — widely considered to be one of the greatest writers of all time, was born under Cancer, as was Dame Barbara Cartland. Her prose, if not "great", is certainly prolific, and has exerted a tremendous appeal to successive generations of female readers.

☏ Cancer: Keys to Financial Success

- DO trust your intuition: when something 'feels right' to you, it generally is, and your innermost feelings will always point the way to success.

- DO make a point of identifying and dealing with your fears about money. Put aside some time each week to see where these fears originate from, and create some positive statements for dealing with them.

- DON'T hesitate too much when choosing your investments. Although a little caution is probably prudent, if you hang back too long, precious opportunities may be lost.

- DO take some risks: ring a new acquaintance up and ask them over for dinner; try a new way of dressing or a new hairstyle. If you overcome your fear of looking foolish, you'll begin to look and feel more confident, which will, in turn, draw new financial opportunities to you, too.

- DO work on your self-esteem. Listen to your 'inner tapes', and try to identify those times and situations when you find that you're doing yourself down. Use positive statements daily to strengthen your inner belief that you really *do* deserve to be successful and wealthy — otherwise you may find that your progress towards your financial goals is slower than you had hoped...

෨ Rich & Famous Cancerians

Julius Caesar
John D. Rockefeller
Edgar Degas
Marc Chagall
Jean Cocteau
Nathaniel Hawthorne
George Orwell
Jean-Paul Sartre
Ernest Hemingway
Natalie Wood
Stavros Niarchos
H J Heinz II
Donald Sutherland
David Hockney
Iris Murdoch
Ken Russell
Pierre Cardin
Norma Kamali
Diana Rigg
Peter de Savary
Carmen Callil
Barbara Cartland
Jean Marsh
Leslie Kenton
Jennifer Saunders

Thomas Jefferson
George Eastman
Camille Corot
Gustav Klimt
Camille Pissarro
Joseph Wedgewood
Mervyn Peake
Gertrude Lawrence
Nelson Rockefeller
Tom Cruise
Sylvester Stallone
Princess Diana
Nelson Mandela
Ringo Starr
Ingmar Bergman
Meryl Streep
Kelly McGillis
Elizabeth Emmanuel
Geraldine James
Richard Branson
Anita Brookner
Colin Wilson
Bill Cosby
Alice Munro
The Dalai Lama

♌

LEO
July 24th to August 23rd

As the days lengthen into high summer, and Big Sol climbs ever skywards, our thoughts invariably turn to leisure and pleasure. Suddenly, it seems far more tempting to take a snooze after lunch, or head for the beach, instead of going back to work. But cast your guilt aside, good people, and seize the sun-block. The Sun God's in his heaven and all's just as it should be — for we're now in the realm of Leo, the most fun-loving sign of them all!

Leo has always been regarded as the "royal" sign, because it's ruled by the Sun, the biggest and brightest star in the heavens. Although astrologers call the Sun a planet for the sake of convenience, it's actually a very bright star — and that's precisely how most Leos tend to see themselves, too. Just as the Sun shines, dazzling all in its orbit with its radiance and brilliance, so, too, do Leos shine — especially when they have an audience! Which is most of the time, since Leos are so sociable — and no lion likes to languish unseen with no-one around to talk to. Leos love to hold court, and what good is a court with no courtiers? Even the quieter Leos, the strong, silent types, who don't seem as flamboyant and outgoing as their noisier brothers and sisters, still know how to gather an attentive retinue around them — even if it's just their workmates in the bar after work.

Leo loves to be the king or queen of the moment, and by a curious coincidence, the sign of Leo is also prominent in the charts of the British royal family. Queen Elizabeth's sister, Princess Margaret, her mother, the Queen Mother, and her daughter, Princess Anne, all have the Sun in Leo: Prince Charles, the heir to the throne, although a Sun Scorpio, also has Leo rising — which helps to explain his whimsical acts of extravagance, like sending his chauffeur on a 300-mile round trip just to fetch a bunch of carrots from his garden! For it must be said at the outset that Leo is one of the most extravagant signs of the zodiac — and although many lions are blessed with lives of wealth and prosperity, it's generally a result of luck, hard work, or their boundless faith in life, rather than any innate financial wisdom.

The fact that Leo is ruled by the Sun tells us a great deal about the lion's character. Just about every culture of the ancient world had its own Sun-God — the Egyptians had Ra, who drove his fiery chariot across the heavens day after day, the Persians had Mithra, who inspired a whole religion, and so on and so on. These ancient Sun-Gods were widely revered — and just as all the planets in our own solar system orbit the Sun, so, too, do most Leos expect "life, the universe and everything" to revolve round their own sweet selves. Every Sun-God myth tells of a hero and his "journey" — and most Leos also feel they have a great "life mission" to fulfil. It's usually a mission that's got a lot to do with "finding themselves" — and, more importantly, discovering that field in life where they can shine, and stand out, and be "king" — or, naturally, "queen"!

The regal bearing of Leo, means they generally stand out from the crowd, and lions and lionesses are usually pretty easy to recognise. Look out for well-built people with an impressive mane of thick, healthy hair and a rosy, almost florid complexion. Leos usually carry themselves well, with their shoulders drawn back and their noble heads held high! Their eyes, whether blue or brown — more frequently the latter — are often flecked with hazel; they have loud, booming voices and a firm and vigorous handshake — unless they're the quieter kind of lion — which does exist, you know. Their solid frames, which sometimes stray the wrong side of "well-rounded", are generally clothed in classically tailored garments — usually in strong, bright colours and quality fabrics. Leos love to be well-dressed, and nothing depresses them more than feeling shabby in any way. Designer labels are generally the order of the day in Leo's wardrobe, and even the hard-up lions will find the classiest-looking clothes in the thrift shop or "sale rail". Aside from their physical characteristics, however, Leos are eminently noticeable because they're so powerfully charismatic. No-one, with the possible exception of Scorpio, exudes such an aura of magnetism as Leos do, especially when they're feeling good about themselves. And one way to make them feel good is to notice them a lot — which is pretty easy, really, given their bearing and superior air. Above all else, all Leos love attention, and they regard not being noticed is a fate worse than death to them. The Leo who doesn't get enough recognition in childhood is generally scarred for life. Since they're such larger-than-life characters, though, that's unlikely ever to happen — for, love them or loathe them, they're pretty hard to ignore!

Even as children, Leo's urge to be "the leader of the pack" is often plainly apparent. Young Leos often automatically assume the lead, and insist on choosing all the games and pastimes that their local gang should play. But parents should be extremely careful how and, more importantly, when they discipline their budding leaders. Leo's sense of dignity is well-developed, even at a tender age, and there's nothing they hate more than being reprimanded in public. So if you need to lecture a renegade lion cub who's guilty of bossiness or showing-off, please be sure to do it in private. Ridicule the lion cub in front of their friends and you'll damage their self-esteem. Even at this early age, the lion's ego is vulnerable: they hate to look small, and need as much love as you can muster!

The dread of looking foolish is a fear that follows Leos long into adult life, despite the fact that they're often the zodiac's biggest risk-takers. Although sun-sign columns wax lyrical about Leo's self-confidence, that air of Leonine bravado is something many lions find they need to spend their whole lives cultivating — for, sadly, it rarely comes naturally. Behind their buoyant facade lies a fragile ego, which needs to be constantly fed and bolstered. Leos' Achilles' heel, however, is often their pride, which motivates a surprisingly high percentage of their actions and decisions. Lions plump for activities, careers and projects that will make them look good in the public eye, and they tend to run a mile from anything that might possibly have the opposite effect. Leos' overwhelming pride makes them highly susceptible to flattery, and their otherwise excellent judgement can sometimes be clouded by the promptings of their ego — leading them into business ventures that sound wonderful, but later turn out to be duds.

Leos' innate sense of drama and theatre means that whatever they do, they do it in style. When they decorate their house, it's usually in a grand manner that wouldn't look out of place in "Homes and Gardens", with masses of royal crimson and gold. When they give a party, only the finest food and drink will do. Forget the paltry wine and cheese affairs that lesser mortals throw — funds permitting, Leo's guests will dine on lobster and caviar, liberally washed down with champagne! Incidentally, Leos' taste for the good life can sometimes incline them to eat and drink to excess, but since the heart is also their weak spot, that's a habit they should firmly avoid. Moderation in food and drink and regular, gentle exercise are essential requirements for lions who desire longevity — but alas, it's a regime that not every lion manages to stick to.

Although Leos' famous pride can lead them to do and say great things, it also has a downside, as those who have seen it know only too well. When the Sun is badly aspected in their horoscope, some Leos can have a truly compulsive desire to prove themselves, and their proud, haughty ambitions can sometimes lead them badly astray. Their arrogance sometimes makes them "bite off more than they can chew", often with disastrous results. Not only that, they can sometimes turn into Mr or Ms Know-It-All, and there's a sudden rush for the door as their friends all clear the room!

To even the score, however, one of their greatest assets is their wonderful loyalty, and when a Leo befriends you, you've made a friend for life. Lions and lionesses are invariably kind-natured, and if you do them a favour, they'll never forget it: in fact, they'll always do their best to reciprocate. Warm-hearted and sentimental to a fault, Leos never forget old friends or lovers − which may be a little hard to bear if you're married to one! On the plus side though, they're among the zodiac's greatest givers. And whether it's a party, a present, or a bear-hug, Leos like to do it BIG. And although their spontaneous behaviour can sometimes verge on being plain childish, their wacky, loud manners conceal a heart of purest gold. Remember, Mother Nature created Leos to cheer the rest of us up ...and when the going gets tough, there's always a Leo around to remind us how to relax, how to party, or simply how to recover our joie de vivre − for, however far you travel, you'll rarely discover a sign with more zest!

♌ Leo and Money

To the typical Leo, money exists for one thing and for one thing only: to help them express their deep-seated belief that they deserve the best that life has to offer. And express it they do, as often as possible — or at least every bit as often as their credit-card will permit! To a Leo, money stands for pleasure, pure and simple, and they rarely waste time in worrying about it, even when it's in short supply. Which can be quite often, since most Leos aspire to a lifestyle that's bold and dashing, and a source of inspiration to everyone they meet. They simply must have a nice home, or even two, to entertain in, and maybe even a boat, perhaps — or at the very least, an extremely comfortable car. And all that takes cash — quite a bit of cash, in fact. But although most lions have quite a high regard for money, viewing it as indispensable for fuelling their taste for good living, they very rarely see it as a worthwhile goal in itself. Unlike Cancer, say, or Taurus, very few Leos will overtly devote their life's energies to the simple accumulation of wealth.

Fame, fun and pleasure are the things that Leos really prize above all else, and money is simply a means to those ends: it's the green-coloured passport to the life of luxury that most lions firmly believe is their god-given birthright — except maybe those with a more conservative Virgo ascendant. Leos want a lot out of life — they want to earn a lot of money, and hopefully spend a great deal too! Many Leos often live well beyond their means, and they're pretty extravagant people — just watch out for the Leos in action down at your local mall — they're the ones who'll be flexing the plastic to its limits, and quite probably way beyond.

Unless there are mitigating factors in their birthchart — such as a strongly placed Saturn or lots of earth, most Leos handle their finances in a carefree, cavalier style that frequently lands them in hot water, especially during their younger adult years. Few lions are cautious with money, and they can rarely be bothered with financial planning — that's for old fogies and pessimists: "To a Leo, money is just part of their crown jewels", says investment astrologer Dan Pallant. "Leos don't tend to discuss money too much — they simply assume it will always be there." Some might call Leos lavish. Less charitable souls say they're profligate. But the love of life and good living is what you'll find writ large across the columns of Leo's profit and loss account — and to give them their due, they'll usually try and make sure that everyone they mix with has a Leo-style good time, too!

Leos' greatest financial assets are their boundless creativity and gift of seeing the positive in every situation. The key to their prosperity invariably goes hand in hand with their great Leo mission or "quest" — for once they've discovered where their true life's calling lies, financial abundance is bound to surely follow. In addition, most lions also have a deep-seated faith in providence — or good old Lady Luck. Some rely on faith to see them through even the direst difficulties, and Leos often believe that money will always just somehow "turn up". They persist in this mode of thinking until something — usually a harsh financial crunch — comes along to convince them otherwise. That's when Leo learns that along with providence and luck, hard work is also needed to make their dreams come true. But when Leos really follow those dreams, more often than not the money they need to keep themselves going will turn up without too much trouble. I know one Leo who inherited a substantial sum of money at just the right moment to finance a film project that was the culmination of his whole life's work! And that's just the sort of thing that happens to a Leo when they *really* follow their dreams!

When it comes to handling the household finances though, Leo is rarely the best person to be left exclusively in charge. It's not that they're not a dab hand with the calculator when they want to be. Nor will they ever keep a tradesman waiting to be paid for a moment longer than necessary. The problem lies rather in their over-reliance on providence, along with their deep dislike of budgeting — which they see as a petty restriction of their freedom to live as lavishly as they choose. In extreme cases, I've known Leos who can't even be bothered to work out their bank balance, and just carry on spending until the bank starts bouncing their cheques!

Leos all too often have a problem with looking after details, and that can play havoc with their money management. They'll sign their cheques with a bold flourish, for instance, but forget to fill in the counterfoils to record just where the money's been spent! So it's all too easy for them to lose track of how much money they have... In an ideal world, of course, they'd have someone to take care of all that menial stuff, preferably a Virgo, say, or a Taurus. But if they're forced to deal with it themselves, they can sometimes come badly unstuck — and wind up with a bad credit rating into the bargain.

Many Leos also have an irrepressible urge to flaunt their money and "show off" financially, and this is another habit that can pave the way to disaster. But although Leos' forgetfulness and extravagance can often lead them into "cash crises", they're very seldom daunted. And since they're so very resourceful, they usually succeed in finding a way out.

Then there's Leo's "gambling streak", which can also sometimes cause problems. Leo rules the fifth house of speculation in the natural zodiac, and many lions like nothing better than a flutter on the tote — or the cards, or even the roulette table. Their natural optimism and sense that "they know best" sometimes pays off and leads them to "win big" — but they frequently "lose big", too. Some Leos will gamble with the holiday fund in their efforts to take the family off to the Bahamas — but if things don't go according to plan, they could end up vacationing in the backyard instead!

If you live with a Leo who appears to be irredeemably careless, it's best to seize the financial reins and take over the housekeeping yourself. Take your lion by the hand and guide him or her gently back to their Great Novel, screenplay — or whatever this year's project is: that way, at least, you'll be sure that the bills are likely to be paid. Male readers who live with lionesses shouldn't have too much trouble persuading their ladies that they should be handling the finances, but male Leos you'll find can be slightly harder to coerce. Along with Ariens and Taureans, Leo men can be just a touch chauvinistic, with a pretty unshakable conviction that they should always be in charge. Probably your best line of argument is to tell him that really, his time is far too precious to be taken up with silly little things like remembering to pay the electricity bill — and since he has such a high opinion of himself, he's bound to agree. Oh, and by the way, if you happen to start earning more than your Leo spouse, you might well be advised to keep it to yourself — that kind of information can be fairly damning to his ego, and can even cause a permanent rift. It's that pride again, you see.

In keeping with that Leo pride, lions are very, very unlikely to ever borrow from their friends. Lions hardly ever borrow money from people they know and care about if they run aground financially. They're just too proud to admit that they haven't risen fully to the challenge of generating their own crock of gold. One of the most important things in a Leo's life is "keeping up appearances", and, even if they're practically starving or almost bankrupt, they'll never, ever admit it. They're far more likely to run up a huge overdraft instead, or take out a personal loan. Lions' pride allows them to borrow from big, faceless institutions to finance their dreams, but from their loved ones — never!

Should a friend or relative approach Leo for a loan and they're temporarily unable to oblige, they're more than likely to rush round to the bank and borrow the money, so that they can say "Yes" to the request for help. Sounds strange, doesn't it, but it's a kind of royal thing — how could the king possibly let down his subjects? It's that pride again, you see: Leos simply love to take care of people and make them happy, even when they can't afford it. Lions are instinctively generous by nature, and it's a source of genuine pain when they're unable to give as much as they'd like. There's nothing they like more than treating all their friends, and picking up the bill is a kind of Leo reflex. But even a Leo who's fallen on hard times will still contrive to live in style...

Sebastian, a Leo friend of mine, took a considerable drop in income in order to follow his dream of training as a homoeopathy, but his innate sense of style meant that he was always well-dressed — despite the fact that his clothes and footware all came from thrift shops! He had a real talent for spotting cashmere coats and designer shoes amid the tattiest pile of junk, not to mention rare china and crystal. "I'll always buy the best I can afford within the limits of my income", said Sebastian. "And top-quality items are the only things I really like. I can always tell whether something's South Sea Island cotton, and that's the only thing I like wearing. I wouldn't dream of wearing polyester, so I either have to go to Jermyn Street and pay £70 per shirt, or scout around for the same stuff second-hand! And when I can't afford to give a dinner-party, I'll have all my friends round for tea and serve the very best cakes instead." Indeed, tea at Sebastian's was always a treat — with a log fire burning heartily, and gourmet cakes from the best store in town, washed down with finest Darjeeling, it always felt like "royal treatment": that's Leo's way, and the world is far richer for it. For no matter how little they have, Leos will always give — generosity is the secret of their true financial strength. No-one has deeper pockets than the lion, and because they're so good at giving, their large-hearted ways will always be rewarded — and very often when they happen to need it most.

So if you happen to live with a Leo, you'd better just accept that your finances may not always run smoothly. If that's your top priority, then go find yourself a Virgo or a Capricorn instead. But if your heart's set on Leo, don't brood and get resentful over their shortcomings in the financial department: after all, they've so much to offer in so many other ways. Look on the bright side, just as they always do! Leos will always be life's "big spenders" at heart, but they'll calm down a bit when their Sun progresses into Virgo, and they begin, at long last, to acquire a tad more commonsense.

More practical-minded souls should see Leo's extravagance for what it really is ...an exuberant expression of their faith in the bounty of life, and of their deep-seated belief that all their needs will be taken care of. Like everything else in life, Leos think money is just there to be enjoyed. Leos are blessed with a natural "prosperity consciousness": they'll never allow thoughts of financial lack or scarcity to get them down for too long ...and that's an attitude we'd all do well to copy, no matter what our sun sign happens to be!

♌ The Spending Style Of Leo

The spending style of Leo is, as you might imagine, truly flamboyant — what else would be appropriate at the court of the King? No other sign in the zodiac is prouder of telling you what their sun sign is than Leo, for they think they're the very best and they want everyone else to know ! And because they're the best, they deserve the very best — or so the lion's reasoning goes. Leos place a premium on quality and excellence and they'll only buy something if it's sure to impress. "Big is better" is a Leo catchphrase, and only the biggest and best will ever really do...

Money tends to burn a proverbial hole in the lion's pocket, and they'll rarely miss a chance to indulge their costly tastes. Leos never wait for the articles they covet to be marked down at sale time. Provided they have cash in the bank, or a valid piece of plastic, they'll just go ahead and buy. If a Leo wants something, they want it now, and since they nearly always live beyond their income, the average Leo is a credit card company's dream — provided, of course, that their income can keep up with their lavish tastes!

Since one of Leos' major preoccupations in life is looking their best, clothes feature high on the lion's shopping list. As well as stylish casuals and smart, tailored outfits for the office, male and female Leos alike usually have an impressive range of evening clothes. Traditional astrology texts describe Leo's taste in clothes as being "loud and garish", but this isn't necessarily so. You'll always notice Leos, that's true — but generally because they're beautifully dressed, not because they're gaudy or flashy. Strident, shrieking colours are far more typical of Gemini than Leo, who favours classic, well cut clothes in rich and jewel-like shades. Leos' taste can sometimes be almost conventional, for they like well-made, top-quality clothes that announce that the wearer has class! Leo's hair is usually immaculately styled, too, for lions are proud of their manes, and will always frequent the best coiffeur in town. And there's not a lioness I know who won't treat herself to a lengthy facial and beauty treatment at her local salon whenever she has time and money to spare.

Head for the best restaurants in any city, and you'll find Leos aplenty living it up in style. Even the quiet Leos go out a lot, though they usually favour more serious pursuits, such as concerts, recitals and plays. The opera, ballet and theatre are happy hunting-grounds for Leo, too, along with trendy tearooms and brasseries. But every once in a while, even the liveliest Leos need to stay home and recharge their batteries...

Since a lion's home is their castle, interior design is another favourite Leo pastime. Lions loathe shabbiness in any shape or form, and even when they're reduced to operating on a shoestring, they'll still manage to live in style. Leos are instinctive decorators and can make even the humblest home look like a palace. They favour bold, bright colours, such as red and gold, fuchsia, amethyst and electric blue. You'll find large, well-padded armchairs and sofas for lazing around in ranged alongside their china and glass, as well as the prize pieces of French furniture they've bought to look at, rather than sit on. Once a Leo has decorated their home the way they like it, however, it rarely gets changed, for they're creatures of habit and get very attached to their surroundings. For this reason, few Leos will "trade down" to smaller houses once their children have left home.

Entertaining is another favourite Leo extravagance, for very few signs are more hospitable than they. Leos will always give their guests the very best wine and food they can afford, and if they're sufficiently affluent, they'll send a driver to collect their guests and also deliver them home again! High-class cars, such as Rolls-Royces or Bentleys, are their favourites — and even for less affluent Leos, a comfortable, speedy car, preferably with leather seats and a CD player is pretty well a must. All Leos loathe even the mere idea of 'roughing it', so they won't travel at all unless they're sure they can do so in style. Of course, not all Leos can afford to go first class, but if they possibly can, they will.

Generous to a fault, Leos love buying gifts for their friends and family, and if you're being courted by a Leo, the sky really is the limit! Lions like to shower their loved ones with flowers, chocolates and champagne, as well as the odd plane ticket to a romantic destination. Or you might be the happy recipient of a beautiful marble Cupid they just happened to pick up at an auction. But since Leos usually suffer from an irresistible urge to outbid everyone else in the saleroom, they really should avoid auctions if it's humanly possible! Remember, though, it's useless to try and curb Leos' excesses until *they* choose to set some limits — for there's little they hate more than anyone telling them what to do. Besides, typical Leos regard writing cheques and spending on their credit cards as a form of self-expression — and one that comes as naturally as breathing!

♌ Leo: Saving and Investing

If you happen to be the parent of a lion cub who's reached 'pocket-money' age, you've probably noticed that your offspring has a pronounced dislike of saving. Try not to worry about it too much, for your baby Leo is totally typical of their sign. The simple truth is, Leos hate saving. There isn't a Leo born who can see any point in delaying gratification for a second longer than necessary, and since they regard the occurrence of 'rainy days' as unlikely in the extreme, it follows that they generally view saving as a total waste of time. So, in order to encourage lions of all ages to save, the secret is to make it fun. If you're dealing with a young Leo, buy them a really spectacular money-box that lights up and makes noises when you put coins in it, and tell them it's their "Fun Fund". Better still, get them to save up their money for a new mountain bike, or for their holidays. And the sooner you do this the better, since Leo is a fixed sign and any habits a young Leo acquires, for good or for ill, will have a tendency to stick.

Adult Leos, too, will rarely see the point of saving unless they've a concrete goal in mind. And pleasure is usually the key that helps them relate to their financial future. They'll save for a lovely new home, most certainly, for a pet creative project, or even a new tuxedo. But ask a Leo to save just for the sake of it? Not a chance...

Leos' attitude towards investment is similarly governed by their tendency to seek short-term gratification. The Leo who receives a surprise windfall or inheritance will rarely put the money on deposit and live off the income. At best they may invest some of it, but a sizeable chunk of the money will almost certainly be spent on good living. I know many Leos who managed to squander their entire inheritance within a startlingly short space of time: one lion gave lavish parties, went on a trip to India and totally revamped his home. Another spent the better part of £250,000 on holidays, gifts for friends and staying in the best hotels on the West Coast of America. My Leo friend protested that this last extravagance was absolutely essential for his work as a budding Hollywood scriptwriter. "People wouldn't take me seriously unless I was staying somewhere grand ...and I'd never be invited to any of the really important parties!"

The urge for quick returns means that most lions are irresistibly drawn to 'get-rich-quick' schemes that often fail to pay off. In order to achieve lasting prosperity, however, Leos need to quell their urge for rapid returns and invest in areas like property instead. This is usually a popular choice for Leo, since a house is the kind of asset that you can show off to your friends. Indeed, many Leos revel in the process of buying and selling both commercial and residential property.

With their love of speculation, many lions are also drawn to the stock market, but this is also an investment area where they need to tread with care. Leos are strongly intuitive investors, and can sometimes be masters of the 'long shot' that pays off, but they also need to learn to seek the right kind of advice. Advisers and brokers are essential to Leo, since most people born under this sign have neither the patience nor the inclination to sift through the minutiae of market indicators and keep abreast of new business developments. Their extreme optimism can also sometimes lead them into trouble, for they can carry on investing in a stock that seems set to rise forever, and indeed, invest their all without stopping to consider its potential. All Leos find it hard to take advice — but they do need it more than most. Every year, a higher than average percentage of Leos go bankrupt — and many a Leo has been led down the primrose path to financial disaster by an unscrupulous or slapdash advisor who flattered their ego, but neglected their portfolio — as they later discovered to their cost. Lions will always do well to remember that "all that glitters is not gold".

Fine art, antiques and china make excellent investments for Leo, for with their cultured eye for quality and their salesmanlike gift of the gab, most lions can not only pick out the best pieces in the room, but also turn them around to the tune of a handsome profit. Gold and jewellery are also good Leo investments, for the combination of looking good and making money at the same time is one they find hard to resist. Interestingly, gold is also Leo's ruling metal!

Leos can also profit by investing in any kind of business which exists to give pleasure to others — such as theatres, sports complexes, hotels and health spas. Property which is related to these forms of business — such as sports arenas, bowling alleys, golf courses, theatres and cinemas, can also sometimes prove lucrative. Musicals and stage shows are also worth exploring. Film production companies, advertising agencies, PR agencies, goldsmithing and jewellery manufacturing are also be good areas to consider.

♌ The Earning Power Of Leo

For Leo, "all the world's a stage", and what better place to act out their many roles and indulge their natural sense of drama than the workplace? With their love of the limelight, Leos are the zodiac's star performers: just think of Madonna, Mae West and Mick Jagger, all born with the Sun in Leo, or Marilyn Monroe, who had Leo on the ascendant. Lions who are just starting out can find themselves running into problems, though, because the only role they ever really want to play is the lead! Sadly, precious few jobs ever allow them to start right at the top — apart from the ones they create themselves, that is — and for Leo, there's the rub. For in common with the other fire signs, Leos make little effort to disguise their ambitions, which are often pretty substantial. As king of the zodiac, they feel their natural place is at the top — and the sooner they get there, the better!

It must be said in their defence, though, that Leos are natural leaders, and most people born under this sign are brimming with executive ability and zeal. The typical lion is enthusiastic, lively, full of energy and ideas, a great organizer and totally brilliant at getting things done. It's no coincidence that quite a few great generals — Napoleon Bonaparte and, more recently, Norman Schwarzkopf, to name but two — were born under Leo, for this is the sign of the master strategist — he who sees the Grand Plan and "goes for it", without hesitation. Leos excel at grasping the essentials of a project — the broad brush-strokes, in other words — and assembling a team to see the job through. They don't like dealing with details, either, so they rarely have trouble in delegating. And since they make such cheerful and generous team leaders, they rarely have problems recruiting staff.

Creativity and self-expression are the key to Leo's happiness at work and, more so than for many other signs, it's vital for Leos to have work that they really enjoy. Young Leos on the threshold of their working lives should take time out to explore their creative potentials and native talents. For life lived without creativity means little to Leos, and they become genuinely miserable and depressed if forced to dance to another person's tune for too long. That's when they succumb to gluttony, heart disease and even an early grave. The creativity we're talking about here doesn't necessarily mean painting pictures or becoming a concert pianist, although many Leos do, in fact, express themselves through the arts. Countless other lions are equally happy running a restaurant, managing a sales team or leading a mountaineering expedition — it's not the form the work takes that's important, it's the fact that Leo's in charge — and ideally, it should be *their* restaurant, *their* sales team or *their* mountain assault party. They love to be in charge, for they know that it's the role they were born to, the job they do best. The only area where Leos tend not to make good managers is — you guessed it — the financial department! Leos love spending money — especially other people's —

and if they're put in charge of the company coffers, that budget may go out of the window.

The wise Leos who've worked on developing their skills and talents are a joy to work with, for they excel at bringing out the creative spark within others and encouraging their gifts to flower. But if their self-esteem and confidence have been damaged in childhood, because they didn't receive enough praise, they may fall into the fatal Leo trap of passing others' work off as their own. Think of the role Sigourney Weaver played as the opportunistic boss in the film "Working Girl", plundering Melanie Griffith's ideas and pretending she'd dreamed them up herself. That kind of situation is a classic Leo temptation and one they should aim to steer clear of...

Leos love a touch of drama, too, and should always choose work that's sufficiently exciting and original to satisfy their deep-seated need for a colourful, interesting life. That's the reason so many Leos opt for a theatrical vocation — for whether they tread the boards, or run the show backstage, life in show business is rarely dull. But whatever career they choose, Leos should never allow themselves to get backed into a boring, mundane position through family pressure or financial necessity — for if they do, the sparks are bound to fly... Leos must have stimulation in their life, and if they can't get it from their work, then they'll get it by throwing tantrums and losing their temper. Far better for them to take a more constructive route, by picking the right career.

Many Leos have a curiously spasmodic work pattern that sometimes perplexes their workmates. They will work tirelessly to get an important report out, say, or complete a presentation to a very tight deadline, with no thought of rest until the goal has been accomplished. Then they'll head straight for the sofa or, better still, their bed, for a long and well-earned rest. It's not unusual for Leos to work manically for a stretch and then take several days out to completely recoup their energy. Perhaps that's why they're often accused of being lazy, but the expression "lazy Leo" doesn't really take account of their capacity for hard work! Granted, Leos do know how to relax and take it easy — they're experts at it — but when the lion's heart is engaged in a task, no-one, but no-one, works harder.

Leos bring a great deal to any job they undertake, but they also ask a lot in return. Approval and appreciation are the fuel that drives their engine, and their abilities and energy expand in direct proportion to the amount of attention they receive. When Leos are in charge, they are happy — but even if they're the boss, they vitally need those verbal "strokes". Leos who are deprived of praise and appreciation soon start behaving like spoiled, self-seeking children, constantly drawing attention to their efforts and achievements ...and the classic phrase "Do you know what I did today?" will pepper their conversation with mind-numbing regularity. Leos hate to be ignored, and the more you ignore them, the louder their "trumpet-blowing" becomes!

Leos can also sometimes be extremely vain and self-centred — just like the sun, all must revolve around Leo, and their ideas alone are what count. Since this attitude usually produces exactly the reverse of what they intended (most people just ignore them), that's when the lion begins to roar, and a lion whose pride's been wounded can roar extremely loudly indeed. But when their errant behaviour is pointed out, they are often deeply abashed and make a concerted effort to see things from other peoples' point of view. For even the most determinedly headstrong lion has a childlike, almost naive desire to please, and sooner or later they'll be tackling the next challenge — or even more likely, getting an existing project to take off. For Leo is a fixed sign, and one of its greatest strengths is its persistence. Whether it's a job, a project or a relationship, Leos rarely give up, and they're great believers in that time-honoured dictum, "If at first you don't succeed, try, try again"... This ability to see things through stands Leos in good stead in all their creative endeavours. For Leo rules the fifth house of creativity in the natural zodiac — and whether the Leos you happen to know are creating a painting, a play, a book or a business, or raising a child, their approach is bound to be one of the most creative you'll find anywhere on the planet. Everything that Leo touches is brushed with magic and gold-dust, and their ideas are always interesting and dazzlingly original!

♌ The Leo Boss

A Leo at the top is a happy Leo and, not surprisingly, a high percentage of top executives, managers and company directors are born under this sign. In many ways, Leos are wonderful people to work for: their skill at morale-boosting is second to none, and they're usually the most sunny and generous people you could ever hope to work for. As long as you agree with them, that is...

The fact is, Leos are mightily keen that everyone around them think the same way that they do, and they get highly offended indeed if their opinions are ever questioned. Since this is a fixed sign, Leos are unlikely to change course or modify their thinking — they'll just find themselves some other employees who reflect their own views more closely or are simply willing to bend. For this reason, Leos frequently clash when they work with the other fixed signs — Taurus, Scorpio and Aquarius; workaday harmony is more likely to prevail if lions work with people who have a more flexible approach — like Libra, say, or Gemini or Pisces. But the lions' working environment only becomes really fraught when they've been ridiculed, snubbed or upstaged — the three big Leo No-Nos. That's the time you'll really hear them roar and see their claws, for Leos who feel they've been slighted can become quite vicious in their thirst for revenge. Leos' determination to have things go their way may bring out their "dictator shadow", and it's not a pretty sight. There's just a touch of Napoleon or Mussolini buried deep within every Leo's psyche, and if you tread hard enough on their paws, you may just get to see it — and also live to wish that you hadn't. Incidentally, if you work with or for a Leo executive, be sure to look the part, too, for lions like their satellites to reflect a good image, too — which means dressing well at all times and also behaving with decorum.

♌ The Leo Employee

Leos' pride makes it hard for them to work in a subordinate position, and though they may work for others while they're on their way to the top, taking orders is never something that a Leo really enjoys. So if you *do* have a Leo working for you in a junior capacity, there are a few rules that you'd be wise to observe. First and foremost, never, never reprimand or ridicule them in public. Be aware that you're dealing with a highly competitive, ambitious individual, and if you do them an injury, they'll never forget it. What's more, they'll pay you back as soon as they're able, for, just like elephants, Leos never forget...

As employees, Leos do best in positions where they're given the chance to express themselves, and even to show off a little. Put them in a mundane, boring job tucked away in a back-office somewhere, and they'll very soon get up and leave. Be sure to pay them well, too, for Leos need a generous income to finance that lavish lifestyle and they'll grow restless pretty quickly if the pay rises don't keep coming just as thick and fast as the compliments. Giving Leo a fancy job-title also helps tremendously — as does a generous expense account and a sufficiently long lunch-hour to enjoy it. It may sound as though working Leos demand special treatment, and indeed they do, but keep them happy and they'll be a sterling asset to the business till the day they take over as Chairman!

♌ Leo and Career

Leos love to lead, and their natural executive ability means they excel at running and managing businesses of all kinds. In particular, lions are drawn to film and television, travel, PR and the law. Just think of the legal eagle Leos, all dressed up in wig and gown, defending their clients with flowery, rhetorical prose — they're truly in their element. So, too, are the many

Leos who are drawn to the helping professions and become doctors and counsellors — for not only do most lions have a genuine desire to help others, they're equally fond, if not fonder, of telling them what to do!

Leos also love to be centre stage in the literal sense, and a great many lions gravitate to the performing arts, where their exhibitionism and self-confidence tend to stand them in very good stead. Although Leos aren't necessarily the showiest sign in the zodiac — Sagittarians vie closely with them for that role — it's hard to imagine three performers more larger-than-life than Mick Jagger, Mae West and Madonna — all born with the Sun in Leo. Many of the most charismatic movie stars of our time are also Leos — think of Dustin Hoffman, Robert de Niro and Robert Redford, as well as "golden oldies" like Robert Mitchum and Ava Gardner. Interestingly, Marilyn Monroe, arguably the most charismatic screen goddess of the century, had Leo rising. Leos love to call the shots behind the camera, and there's a curious paradox whereby many Leo film directors — such as Alfred Hitchcock, Roman Polanski and the epic movie-maker Cecil B. de Mille — have become almost more famous than the stars they have directed! Many other Leos find contentment working backstage in the theatre. With their superb organizational skills, they make great house managers, and when a crisis arises, lions *always* manage to keep their heads.

Some Leos express their creative gifts by becoming writers, painters and poets. Think of Emily Bronte, Percy Shelley and George Bernard Shaw and the sabre-tongued wit, Dorothy Parker. Then there's sculptor Henry Moore, and the tirelessly flamboyant Andy

Warhol, who had the Leonine gift of turning everyone around him into a star, even if only for a day! With their superb sense of style, many Leos are drawn to the world of high fashion: think of Coco Chanel and, more recently, Yves St. Laurent. Many lions carve out a comfortable niche for themselves in the gold and jewellery trade. More technically-minded lions find their talents lie in innovation and invention, like John Logie Baird, Clive Sinclair and Henry Ford, whose Leonine shrewdness also helped him build his business empire.

Many Leos opt for politics, since it provides ample opportunity to speechify, perform and pose for the cameras! The former UK Premier Margaret Thatcher had the Moon in Leo, so tellingly revealed by her untiring love of publicity. Many great political wives and hostesses have had the Sun in Leo, too, including Rosalynn Carter and the most famous First Lady of all, Jacqueline Kennedy Onassis, whose elegance, grace and composure made her the heroine of a whole generation.

Many Leos are drawn to teaching, for it's a career where they can do two of their favourite things at the same time: namely, hold centre stage and also work with youngsters! Finally, there's that time-honoured link between Leos and the metal gold, which provides many career-seeking lions with their working inspiration. Leos who like playing with money tend to head for the Stock Exchange, while more altruistic lions opt for fund-raising and charity work. With their oratorical skills and gift of the gab, they're simply superb at persuading people to give, especially to a good cause. At the other end of the charity industry, you may well find kind-hearted Leos with time and energy to spare helping out at your local Volunteer Bureau, where they're amply appreciated for being "worth their weight in gold!"

♌ Leo: Keys to Financial Success

- DO remember that one of the most important things in life is finding pleasure in your work. In order to really prosper, you must always really love what you do.

- DO make a point of listening to others sometimes — or at least, make the effort to. It's easy to believe that you always know best, but human beings are all interdependent and, believe it or not, others are sometimes better informed than you are!

- DO look for projects, investments and, most importantly, a career that allows you to take centre stage and perform in some way. You're far more likely to prosper if you do.

- DO try to create a workable budget — but make sure it's one that allows you some scope for spending on pleasure. That's the only kind of budget you'll ever stick to!

- DON'T let your excellent powers of judgement be clouded by over-optimism. You're a natural devotee of the gamble or long-shot, but for best results you should always balance speculation with persistence and effort.

♌ Rich & Famous Leos

Napoleon Bonaparte
T E Lawrence
Cecil B de Mille
Neil Armstrong
Eddie Fisher
Emily Bronte
George Bernard Shaw
Sir Clive Sinclair
Debussy
Percy Shelley
Princess Anne
Bernice Rubens
Whitney Houston
Yves St Laurent
Stanley Kubrick
Robert de Niro
Shelley Winters
Peter O'Toole
Dustin Hoffman
Mick Jagger
Helen Mirren
Melanie Griffith
Katharine Hamnett

Mussolini
Alfred Lord Tennyson
Jacqueline Kennedy
Norman Schwarzkopf
Mae West
Beatrix Potter
Henry Ford
Carl Jung
Jacqueline Susann
HRH The Queen Mother
Princess Margaret
Madonna
Coco Chanel
Roman Polanski
Robert Redford
Robert Mitchum
Rosanna Arquette
Martin Sheen
Arnold Schwarzenegger
Sarah Brightman
Marie Helvin
Madhur Jaffrey
Sherry Lansing

♍

VIRGO
August 24th to September 23rd

As the heat of high summer reaches its peak and then
gives way to harvest time, we enter the sign of Virgo.
Traditionally depicted as the goddess of the wheat-
fields, Virgo the virgin has received a pretty poor press
over the centuries, owing to her much-maligned love
of domestic order. But although most Virgos like to
run a "tight ship", there's far more to this complex,
discriminating sign than its fondness for cleanliness
and tidiness. But since Virgos tend to be quite modest,
retiring people, you'll never find them bragging about
their virtues — which are often quite extensive. Virgos
love to be needed and to feel that they're useful — and
since they're such talented, resourceful, subtle creatures,

they usually prove themselves to be more than useful. They're also pretty good at managing their money and, following on the heels of luxury-loving Leo, their prudence and commonsense are like a refreshing breath of fresh air.

It's probably a good idea to put the record straight on the sexual front right at the outset, for, contrary to popular opinion, the sign of Virgo has nothing whatsoever to do with sexual experience, or with the lack of it, either. Virgo is an earth sign, and *all* earth signs have a taste for the pleasures of the flesh, even if they *do* come across as a little shy at first. No, Virgo's so-called "virginity" describes the sign's air of self-sufficiency rather than its sexuality, for the Latin expression, "Virgo intacta" means simply "a woman complete unto herself". That is, one who lives life according to her own terms and values. The temple maidens or "virgins" of ancient Greece and Rome freely engaged in sexual practices as and when the temple rituals demanded, but most of the time, they lived alone ...and it's this idea of independence and self-containment that is the key to the Virgo personality.

Think about it for a moment — doesn't just about every Virgo you've ever met have a curious air of detachment, which sometimes verges on aloofness? Virgos are deeply cautious people and, wherever they find themselves, they always prefer to stand back, size up a situation and ponder a little before taking any action. Greta Garbo, perhaps the greatest screen goddess of all time, had the Sun in Virgo, and she doubtless spoke for millions of her fellows when she uttered the immortal phrase, "I want to be alone". For the need to withdraw from time to time and reflect on the process of life is totally essential to Virgo's nature.

Although many astrologers believe that the yet-to-be discovered planet Vulcan is the true planetary ruler of Virgo, this sign has long been linked with Mercury, the selfsame planet of communication that rules the sign of Gemini. In Gemini, Mercury is a chatty, pranksterish fellow, but in Virgo he reappears in a far more serious guise. There's a strong connection between the planet Mercury and the written word and, in ancient mythology, Virgo is linked with the Egyptian-style Mercury, the ibis-headed Thoth. Thoth was the scribe of the gods — which is interesting really, when you consider how many first-rate writers have been born under Virgo. There's Goethe, D.H. Lawrence and H.G. Wells and, in our own time, A.S. Byatt, Stephen King and Shirley Conran. Incidentally, although Conran's racy "bonkbuster" novels are the books that have made her fortune, she originally came to fame with "Superwoman", which is essentially all about housework — a classic Virgo theme! Mercury also gives Virgo a talent for mimicry and, perhaps more surprisingly, acting. Think of the late, great Peter Sellers and Sophia Loren, with their brilliant comic timing. Even the shyest Virgos can regale you with a side-splitting imitation of their boss or bank manager — provided they're feeling relaxed enough, that is. So if you offer them a glass of wine to chase away their inhibitions, you can sit back and enjoy the show...

Most of the time, it's quite easy to overlook Virgos in a crowd, because their native reserve and modesty disincline them to seek attention. Virgos are usually slender and spare of frame, and it's only when you get up close that you'll notice their most attractive feature — their lovely, crystal-clear eyes. Think of top Virgo model Twiggy, pin-up and role model for an entire generation of women. Although females everywhere strove to copy her pin-thin figure, it was her extraordinary kohl-rimmed eyes, staring out from a million magazine covers that captured the world's imagination, and made her the heroine of the Sixties. Virgo's eyes are light and lustrous, usually cornflower-blue or blue-grey and, rather like their owners, they're positively brimming with integrity. Indeed, you'd have to go a long way to find a Virgo who wasn't as honest as the day is long, and eminently trustworthy too.

The simplicity and straightforwardness of the Virgo nature is usually mirrored by their dress sense, which is — well, simple and straightforward. Colour therapists say that people who want to be respected and taken seriously wear navy blue and, funnily enough, it's often Virgo's favourite colour ...not that they don't spice it up occasionally with a little white, cream, brown or beige, of course, and maybe even emerald green, when they're feeling really festive. Virgos *never* go for loud Hawaiian prints or gaudy checks, even when they're on vacation. Neat plaids and weaves, polka-dots and paisleys, or small, intricate prints are what you'll find in Virgo's wardrobe — unless of course, they've a fire sign on the ascendant, when they might just break out into red or even black! Occasionally, you'll find odd Virgos living out their opposite Piscean polarity, and then they'll dress in floaty, hippie garb like a real Sloppy Joe — but this *is* the exception rather than the rule.

The other thing that you'll usually find Virgo wearing along with that customary navy blue is a faintly furrowed brow, for Virgos are the great worriers of the zodiac ...and even Virgo children are known to fret and fuss more than average! Life never runs quite smoothly enough for Virgos, and they frequently misuse their excellent minds by conjuring up horrific fantasies of "what will happen *if*"... For the sake of their health and sanity, that little expression is one that every Virgo should aim to use as seldom as possible! The Virgoan propensity for worry and anxiety can actually be a threat to their health, for, taken to extremes, it leads to insomnia and ulcers and makes it hard to relax and unwind. Every Virgo should learn some kind of stress management technique, such as autogenics, or Transcendental Meditation, or simply make a habit of taking a long, relaxing bath each night, scented with herbal oils.

Even in childhood, Virgo's native modesty, retiring nature and propensity to worry are plainly apparent, and they rarely have to be reminded to tidy away their toys. Their shy, watchful natures conceal a delicately sensitive spirit, and it's important to give all Virgo children lots of encouragement, as well as the best education possible — along with the space to develop their mental abilities and interests, which will no doubt be considerable. Don't miss out on the hugs and kisses either — for despite the fact that Virgos aren't the most demonstrative of children, they crave warmth and closeness every bit as much as other signs.

Virgo rules the 6th house of health and healing in the natural zodiac, and since most Virgos eat fussily, pop vitamins, and diligently remember to take exercise, by and large, this is a pretty healthy sign. You'll occasionally find a Virgo who's really gone to town on the health kick one way or another, and in the general run of things, there are two kinds of Virgo "health nut". There's the health-food freak who wouldn't dream of eating a piece of toast unless it's stone-ground, organically-grown wholewheat and liberally studded with sunflower seeds ...or there's the arch hypochondriac, who fairly rattles with conventional drugs. *These* Virgos never leave home without a caseful of their favourite patent medicines, plus an ample supply of bottled water, as they claim the slightest change of water has a deep effect on their bowels!

The striving for optimum health is all part and parcel of Virgo's great longing for perfection, which is another of their major traits. Since all Virgos are perfectionists at heart, and have a burning desire that the universe should run as smoothly and punctually as the Italian railways did in Mussolini's time, they tend to find day-to-day living a highly stressful process in itself. For it's sad, but true, that real life is rarely perfectly ordered. Virgos want life to be perfect, and they want the people around them to be perfect, too. But since we live in an imperfect world, they're being constantly disappointed.

The way that most Virgos I've encountered deal with this problem is to take every step possible to ensure that their own little corner of the world — their work, their home, their spouse, their children, etc. — is as perfect as possible — and this is what lies at the root of their tendency to be rather critical. If you live with a Virgo, you'll doubtless be only too familiar with the early-morning scenario wherein your nearest and dearest delivers a lengthy discourse on what's wrong with the house, the kids, and your dress sense, before you've even had your first cup of coffee. It can be infuriating — but take heart please — because if Virgos are tough on the people they live with, remember that they're always even tougher on themselves. One of Virgo's pet hates is being criticised by others, and in fact it's rarely necessary to do so, since they're always so quick and eager to do the job for themselves! But tempting though it is to strike back, stop for a moment and reflect on the fact that your Virgo's only saying these things because they want you — and everyone else, for that matter — to be just that little bit better. No-one has higher standards than Virgo, and their love of excellence shines out from everything they do, whether it's building a house, writing a book or embroidering a cushion. So, although Virgo's behaviour can seem petty at times, never forget that their intentions are every bit as snowy as their shirt-cuffs!

Virgo's obsession with order can be rather irritating, too, till you take the time and trouble to examine it more closely. Although the stereotype of the "neat and tidy", ashtray-emptying Virgo lingers on and on, I've known at least two Virgo writers who, though clean and tidy about their person, lived in total domestic squalor whilst they pursued their passion for ideas. The piles of dirty washing and washing-up grew ever higher day by day, but Bruce and Elizabeth didn't even notice. They were far too preoccupied with their composing, thinking and writing! Virgo loves order, that's true — but it doesn't have to be order in the literal sense. Many Virgos spend a lifetime ordering information and ideas, and have scrupulously tidy minds, rather than tidy desks and homes. But if one thing's certain, it's that in order to find any happiness and fulfilment in life, all Virgos need to push back the boundaries of chaos in at least one major area of their lives.

So, although it's the easiest thing in the world to get irritated with Virgo, don't forget that Mother Nature put these people here for a reason, and a jolly good one at that. Namely, to teach all the rest of us how to do things properly, and not to slack on the job! So why don't you all just take your medicine and get on with it? You know Mr or Ms Virgo is right — they always are ...well, nearly always.

♍ Virgo and Money

Money is something you can see, feel and touch, so when it comes to handling it, most Virgos are in their element. With their flair for analysis, and skill at looking after details, most Virgos also have a well-deserved reputation for financial expertise. No-one can balance a chequebook with such speed and adroitness, and it's a total mystery to Virgo's astrological neighbours, Leo and Libra (both noted for their extravagance), how on earth they manage to make their money stretch so far. Virgos are past masters of the art of living well on little, because they naturally incline towards both prudence and economy. But the Virgo habit of watching the pennies can be a source of profound irritation to many a less financially gifted sign — which is another way of saying, more spendthrift souls often call them mean.

"Mean?" squeals Virgo in self-defence. "Me? Never! I'm just careful, that's all. Of course I'm not going to rush out and buy brand-new birthday presents for my friends when I've got some perfectly good make-up in the cupboard at home that isn't quite the right colour for me. I've only used it once, after all. And I'm sure my mother won't even notice that the jacket I got her at Christmas came from the thrift shop. It's still in perfectly good condition. Why should I waste money when I don't need to?" Why indeed? Deep in the heart of every Virgo lies a profound loathing of waste which is every bit as instinctive as their longing to be useful. But to uncover the hidden motives behind Virgo's money attitudes, it will now be necessary to dig a little deeper...

People born under the sign of Virgo tend to worry a great deal about money, and they see having cash in the bank as a passport to greater peace of mind. They're rarely inspired to acquire money for its own sake, like Taurus, nor do they tend to flaunt it, like Leo. Virgo is an idealistic sign at heart, and generally places a higher premium on the things that can't be stored in the bank. They value knowledge, Nature and beauty, to begin with, far more than simply having money per se. But all Virgos need a steady stream of money, because they *need* to feel secure. Once they've made it, they can relax — but up until then, they generally find it hard to.

Many Virgos suffer from a less than trusting attitude to life, and their attitudes to money are often tinged with fear, most notably a fear of the future. They're frequently haunted by a vague, nameless feeling that "anything could happen, so I'd better be prepared." The roots of this fear are hard to unravel, but they usually lie in Virgo's childhood, which may not have been a particularly happy time. Whether the stresses their parents faced were financial or emotional ones, Virgos usually grow up with the distinct impression that it's really not such a great idea to have to depend on people. Hence that famous Virgo independence. Virgo's classic fearfulness also determines their financial priorities, for they usually begin working to establish their security as soon as they possibly can. Most Virgos starting out in their first job, for instance, will set up a pension fund straight away, despite the fact that they've barely turned twenty! So, what with their mortgage payments, and pension payments, there's precious little left over once the bills have been paid — but Virgos don't usually mind. To tell the truth, they're really not that bothered, since they're nearly always working! And that pension fund is an absolute necessity, for it will save them from the old folks' home and obviate the need to rely on handouts, which, to Virgo, would be a fate worse than death.

But let's look on the bright side first, for just as Virgos can be frugal, careful souls, they're also among the best money-managers on the planet. If you live with a Virgo, male or female, you can rest assured that the financial wheels of your existence will always run smoothly. So please don't even think about doing the accounts yourself. Most Virgos have a real genius for budgeting, and it would be truly senseless to deny them the opportunity to exercise their very real gifts. When Virgo's in charge, it means that the bills are always paid on time, and there's never a shortage of cash at the really important times of the year, like Christmas and anniversaries. A Virgo can teach you the art of living well on less, and make it enjoyable, too. A Virgo dad may seem like a bit of a kill-joy at times, because he'll always insist on taking sandwiches to the football match (why waste money on hot-dogs?), but his moneysaving ways can also be fun in other ways. He'll take you rowing up the river to gather wood for the fire, or tramping through the forest in search of mushrooms and berries "baksheesh". Virgos delight in all the natural bounty of the earth, and they know in their hearts that many of the best things in life really *are* free. The others they work hard for.

Since their needs are usually quite modest, most Virgos tend to live well within their means. But by a curious twist of irony, they often end up with a spendthrift partner. It's as though they need someone in their life to live out all those extravagant urges that lie buried deep in their subconscious — so deep they didn't even know they were there! And although *all* couples row about money sometimes, more tiffs than average in the Virgo household tend to centre around this issue. For if Virgos don't approve of their partner's purchases, or feel they've spent too much, they'll never suffer in silence. Paradoxically, though, they'll often maintain silence about their own finances. And if they don't want their partner to know how much money is in the bank, well, they simply won't say anything. For though Virgos rarely lie about money, they can be as economical with the truth as they are with the housekeeping!

Alternatively, a Virgo may choose a partner who works freelance, and whose earnings are therefore subject to considerable ups and downs. Virgos themselves usually prefer regular work at regular pay, and the more regular the better. A salaried Virgo will always prefer to be paid weekly if possible, and freelance Virgos often like to be paid in cash. "Sooner, rather than later", is Virgo's golden maxim on payment, and they take the view that cash in the hand is worth more than a "cheque in the post"...

But just as Virgos' insistence on rapid returns underlines their lack of trust in life, it can also actually curtail their longer-term prosperity. That's because Virgos will always play safe financially, never taking risks unless they absolutely have to. They'll *never* trade a secure job with an average salary for a not-so-secure job with far greater financial potential. Not that they'll stay anywhere that they're underpaid — it's just that their attention is always firmly focused on what they're earning *now*, rather than their future financial prospects. Of course they *care* about the future — they worry about it every night, after all. But they'll never gamble on it, if they feel there's the slightest risk they'll lose out. I have seen Virgo clients forego a once-in-a-lifetime opportunity of starting their own business, despite the fact that their prospects looked great, because going it alone felt just too risky. One Virgo client stayed for years in a job that she hated before taking the leap into becoming self-employed. With a thoroughness that was admirable to observe, she refused to take the plunge until she had paid off her mortgage and done everything humanly possible to make her new job as a therapist almost as secure as the old.

Most Virgos also have a keen sense of "financial self-preservation", that's why they hang on to their money the way they do. So if Virgo seems tightfisted, it's just because they're scared of not having enough to pay their way. That's a prospect they find just too horrible to contemplate, and it constantly plays on their mind. That's why Virgos never, ever throw money around, rarely spend money on pleasure, and will *never* lend out a penny unless they're sure that they'll get it back. Virgos reluctance to lend out their money is closely matched by their fear of debt, and they're always loath to borrow. Even the rare Virgos with an overdraft will go to strenuous steps to pay it off, and sleep far better once they have!

But take heart, for every Virgo has flashes of generosity, too, and you may get to see one of these rare financial events if you're really, really lucky. In order to qualify, though, you'll either have to work for a Virgo, or else be related, and they'll only loosen their purse-strings if you get sick or fall on hard times. Then, and only then, will Virgo give freely — but it's a mighty rare occurrence, so please don't hold your breath.

Virgo's insistence on tangible financial security sounds like a praiseworthy virtue, and in lots of ways it is, but it also has its drawbacks. Virgos can get so hung on "watching the pennies" that they overlook the need for proper financial planning. Rather like the man who spends a fortune driving to the garage where he can buy cheap petrol, Virgos need to "see the forest as well as the trees", and set some longer-term goals and priorities.

On the plus side, one of Virgo's greatest assets is patience, and Virgos are amply endowed with the ability to *wait* for what they want in life. And once they've achieved their money goals — be they financial independence, paying off the mortgage, or simply getting the kids through college, then they begin to lighten up a little, and that's a refreshing sight to behold. It's as though Virgos suddenly discover where their "spending muscles" are and, since it's quite a change of pace, their partners can often be taken by surprise.

Astrologically, this corresponds to the Virgo Sun's progression into Libra, traditionally a far more pleasure-loving sign: that's the time many Virgos finally get to indulge their love of the arts, or take up that hobby they've always dreamed of. It can be a bit of a shock watching a prim and dutiful Virgo mother suddenly kick over the traces and shell out hundreds of pounds on learning how to dance the tango! Or seeing a middle-aged Virgo father finally indulge his long-standing longing for the very best stereo system that money can buy. When Virgos finally relax their financial stranglehold, partners who are used to relying on their financial savoir-faire may not always care for the change. But since Virgos usually discover where their "giving muscles" are, too, and will always give to their family first and last, the sea-change in outlook is generally good news, rather than bad.

♍ The Spending Style of Virgo

In keeping with their general approach to life, Virgo's attitude to spending is marked by prudence, caution, and above all, careful planning. It's a rare Virgo indeed who'll step out to buy a hi-fi or TV set without having studied all the audio magazines and discount catalogues for months with as much zeal as the priests of old studied the Ten Commandments. Otherwise, Virgos might find they've been spending money needlessly, and that's a prospect that's just far too upsetting to even contemplate!

Not that there's anything wrong with being careful with money, of course. If there's one thing that the economic downturn of recent years has taught us all, it's that wise husbanding of resources is a virtue to be cultivated. It's just that when you've worked as hard for your money as Virgos generally do, it's good to have some fun spending it too — but sadly, that's a luxury few Virgos allow themselves to indulge in.

Rather like their fellow earth sign Capricorn, Virgos generally get far more pleasure out of saving money than spending it, and their needs and requirements usually tend to be modest. Virgos seldom opt for big, flashy houses like Leos — they'll be just as happy in a small house on an estate. If it's easy to maintain and keep clean, so much the better, since they also have an aptitude for DIY and carpentry. They're more than happy to spend money on a good set of tools, since they know they'll save a great deal more than they cost, in the long run. Virgos love to mend and renovate household items, and may even grow their own vegetables, too ...home-grown greens are both economical *and* healthy, which is a double bonus that's hard to resist. Having pointed out Virgo's penchant for domestic economy, however, it's only fair to mention that they'll always buy good-quality gifts when birthdays and anniversaries come round. They're always surprised and delighted to receive presents themselves — though they may start to worry if they fear the giver has spent more than they could afford.

Extravagance, even in others, will always upset a Virgo! Since frugality is their middle name, Virgos are among the zodiac's great bargain-hunters, and they're fond of ransacking garage and car-boot sales for goods at a knockdown price. My Virgo friend David is a car-boot sale devotee, and also has a great eye for antiques. But true to sign, his very best pieces are all safely stored away well out of sight — "just in case a burglar should ever call". Like oh-so many Virgos, he finds it hard to simply *enjoy* his wealth...

When Virgos do finally get round to spending money, though, their first priority is always quality: then come usefulness and reliability. Functionality is the key that never fails to unlock Virgo's wallet, and they'll invariably go for goods that are useful and safe (even if they don't look very exciting) over eye-catching items that might possibly be unpredictable. This rule applies just the same whether Virgo's buying a house, a car or a winter coat. So when you hear Virgos utter those magic words, "Hmm, that ski-jacket looks so sensible — do you have it in beige?", you know they're about to buy! The typical Virgo spending pattern is to buy seldom, but to buy the very best that they can afford. Despite the fact that they're seldom vain by nature, Virgo's lack of self-confidence makes them want to look their best, so they always opt for good-quality clothes. Besides, good clothes last longer, and that's always a plus in Virgo's book.

Mercury-ruled Virgoans have a great love of knowledge, too, and they'll rarely stint on buying books and magazines. With their love of learning and desire for self-improvement, they're particularly fond of self-help psychology books, and texts on business and management. The typical Virgo bookshelf will also contain books on increasing your learning skills — another Virgo passion — as well as lots of "How To" guides. Many Virgos have a real aptitude and feel for computers, and millions of hard-earned Virgo pennies are spent each year on top-of-the-line word-processors so that they can get round to composing "that novel I keep meaning to write" — or perhaps earning a few extra pennies writing short stories and features. Finally, no Mercury-ruled Virgo would be happy without a car of their own — though, naturally, it doesn't have to be especially flashy or luxurious. Young Virgos favour bicycles as a means of transport, since they help them to keep fit as well as to get from A to B.

Virgos' preoccupation with health is also reflected in their spending habits. Many people born with the Sun in Virgo, or Virgo placed strongly in their birthchart, find themselves drawn to explore all kinds of therapies- such as massage, rolfing, shiatsu and reflexology — along with vitamins, herbs and nutrition. Virgo's bill at the local health food store is likely to be quite substantial — unless, of course, they happen to own or run it!

♍ Virgo: Saving and Investing

When it comes to saving money, Virgo needs no lessons. In fact, most Virgos have honed and perfected the habit of salting away their pennies to the point where it becomes an art form — or an obsession — depending on just how far they take it. Virgos are the kind of students who manage to save money out of their grants — or even help pay off their parents' mortgage whilst they're still at college! But Virgos rarely, if ever, save for pleasure. These people don't set out to amass a crock of gold so that they can buy a yacht and sail it round the world. Virgos like to save money "for a rainy day", or "just in case" ...because their cautious, pessimistic nature (they call it realistic) always takes into account the possibility that financial disaster may be lurking around the next corner. To be caught without a well-padded monetary safety-net is, quite simply, unthinkable.

Virgos are often accused of being the champion hoarders of the zodiac, and just as many Virgos find it hard to throw anything away, so, too, do they hang on to their money — and do I mean that quite literally. The old joke about keeping your money under the floorboards may sound a bit ridiculous in this computerised day and age, but I personally know two Virgos who make a habit of actually doing just that. Most Virgos like to squirrel away some money somewhere in the home so that they can get their hands on it easily, but few will run to the expense of installing a proper domestic safe. A major problem can arise, however, when they forget just where they stashed it. One ageing Virgo I know stowed a whole bag full of banknotes under the floorboards, and then forgot where he'd put it! By the time he'd finished his excavations, it cost him a considerable sum to put the floor straight again! ...not to mention the interest he lost out on by not depositing his money in a more conventional savings account. By all means keep a cache of cash,

Virgo, but it's also a good idea to check out savings accounts that combine good interest with easy access — just in case you need your money in a hurry one day.

People born under the sign of Virgo have an equally cautious approach to investment, and prefer putting their money into tangible assets like silver or antiques, or better still, into property. The expression "safe as houses" gives Virgo a nice, warm glow inside — it sounds, well, safe, and that's exactly what they like. But Virgos can sometimes let their obsession with financial security get a little out of hand. Firstly, an appropriately large proportion of their income may be allocated to pension funds and annuities. Secondly, they're so obsessed with hanging on to what they have *now* that they never stop to think of what they *could* have, if only they'd alter their approach just a little.

Most Virgos are profoundly suspicious of anything even remotely resembling speculation, which they tend to regard as gambling. The Virgo threshold of risk-taking is low, which means they often miss out on opportunities. They'll never, ever invest in a business unless and until they've analysed it in detail, and fully explored its potential. Well that's no bad thing, I hear you say. But the fact remains that Virgo's investment decisions are often based on fear and lack of confidence, rather than the facts: Virgos are reluctant to trust their judgement, and can often err too far on the side of so-called caution. Paradoxical though it may sound, Virgos can often do well on the stock exchange. This is an area they usually avoid, since it always sounds so risky, but their keen intellect and powers of analysis mean they're admirably equipped to assess and evaluate the relative merits of companies and corporations for the purposes of investment. Few signs can make as much money on the stock market as Virgos — if they only put their minds to it. The key here is to start small, with money they can afford to lose, and just take it from there.

Virgos are often happiest investing in their *own* businesses, as they certainly feel more in control. Entrepreneurial Virgos should look at all enterprises linked with health and healing in the broadest sense. These could include health clinics, therapy centres, vitamin companies, medical technology, and even the veterinary business. Any business associated with the printed word could also be profitable for Virgo, such as publishing, printing, newspaper production or news cuttings agencies and information bureaux. Other profitable areas for Virgo investors may include financial services, stockbroking, management consultancy, and film production and processing. Many Virgos are also greatly fascinated by astrology, so investing in astrological products could also turn out to be lucrative!

♍ The Earning Power Of Virgo

Work occupies an all-important role way above and beyond mere economic survival for Virgos. It's often their primary source of pleasure and enjoyment, too, and many Virgos regard it as the most important thing in their life. People born under Virgo often find it easier to commit to a career than a relationship, which helps to explain their traditional reluctance to get married. You might say that whereas other signs may work to live, Virgo lives to work! And since work is where Virgo shines, generally speaking, they tend to excel at whatever they chose to do.

To a greater degree than many of the signs we've looked at so far, Virgos are motivated by the desire to be useful and to serve humanity, rather than by money or by burning ambition. Not that Virgos don't want to be rewarded for what they do — far from it. Though they often find it hard to ask for a pay-rise, they usually insist on being paid the going rate, for their self-respect demands it. They're not averse to the odd compliment, either, provided it's not overdone — they just find that kind of thing embarrassing. It's just that for the most part, Virgos are simply far more interested in *doing* their work, rather than having an audience for their efforts. There's a kind of humility about Virgos and their work that is really quite humbling, for this is the sign that teaches us the true meaning of service to humanity in a way that's like no other. Think of Mother Teresa of Calcutta — it's hard to think of anyone who's done as much to help her fellow man as she, and there are no prizes for guessing what her sun sign happens to be! Astrologically speaking, it's as though all Virgos are trying to put the creative skills they learned in the 5th house of Leo to some useful purpose — the emphasis here being on *useful*.

It's a rare Virgo indeed who actively courts the limelight and seeks to be famous — most Virgos get thoroughly ill-at-ease if they're thrust into the public eye. So if you do happen to meet a Virgoan who wants to be famous as well as being useful, you can be certain there's a healthy dose of fire in their horoscope, as well... I know a painter with the Archer on the ascendant and the Sun in Virgo, and although he enjoys the fame his paintings have brought him, he always confesses that he's far more interested in the process of painting itself. Left to his own devices, he'll work seven days a week, long into the night, and not even notice time passing...

Virgos tend to identify with their work to a far greater extent than many other signs, and their sense of personal identity is often directly derived from their work. To quote my painter friend again: "I am what I do, it's as simple as that. Unless I'm painting, I don't really feel that I exist — it's as though there's no-one there unless I'm working." To say, "I am what I do" is all very well, but people born under this sign can be dangerously vulnerable to those sudden changes of fortune which can arise out of the blue and alter their lives at a single stroke. Take redundancy, for instance — a not uncommon occurrence in these economically troubled times. Virgos who derive their sense of identity totally from their work may be hard hit indeed if they wake up one morning to find that their job has disappeared — as indeed, so many have. Little wonder then that Virgos value job security to a greater degree than many other signs, for having a reliable job goes a very long way towards helping them relax.

It's also a good idea for Virgos to cultivate a broad spread of interests, work and hobbies. Virgos hate to be idle, and since they're often so good with their hands, most Virgos have a favourite pastime which can also produce extra income — flower arranging, for instance, or tapestry-making, boat-building, model-making, or even freelance writing. All are classic Virgo pastimes which can often be made to pay.

Most Virgos genuinely love their work, and since Virgo rules the 6th house of work in the natural zodiac, that's exactly as it should be. But since Virgo can also be a slightly obsessive sign, you'll also often find that they take things a little too far. Virgo is the sign of work, but it's also the sign of the workaholic. If you've a workmate who always looks spick and span and well turned-out, arrives at the office early and stays on long after everyone else has left, you can bet your bottom dollar they're a Virgo. Try and get them to slow down a little if you can, for the chances are they're so hardworking that the company is piling on the work. But if they're not careful, they'll wind up suffering from that classic Virgo complaint — burnout. The danger of overworking is one that all Virgos need to guard against. But since they're also so fond of routine, one of the best antidotes is simply to schedule time each week to get out in the great outdoors. For whether it's cross-country hiking, canoeing or rafting in the wilds, few things are so therapeutic as simply getting "back to Nature."

On the plus side, though, Virgos are the true craftspeople of the zodiac. All Virgos take a tremendous pride in their work, and it's not uncommon for them to spend many years training and perfecting their skills, frequently at low wages, whilst they serve their latter-day "apprenticeship". I know Virgo boat-builders, dried flower artists, painters and at least one craftsman bookbinder: without exception, their work is always beautifully executed, even if they aren't always the fastest workers you'll ever meet. And since Virgos need solitude and a peaceful working environment, a craftsman's lifestyle often suits them very well. But even if they opt for the hectic pace of corporate life instead, they'll usually create a quiet corner where they can do their thinking undisturbed.

Virgos' other great working asset is their genius for analysis, which should never be underestimated. Whether they're the company chairman or simply a lowly clerk, Virgos have the unique ability to spot the weak link in the chain that could bring a company down. That's the good news. The bad news is, Virgos are skilled at finding fault with everything and everyone, which makes them tricky to work with, since they find fault at every turn. Little wonder, then, that they often prefer to work alone. Virgos also excel at leading research teams, large and small, where their ability to analyse results and apply new technology really comes into its own. Surprisingly for a sign that's very craft-oriented at heart, many Virgos have a passion for computers that's almost on a par with that of Aquarius. Mercury-ruled Virgos are natural teachers, too, and since they're so patient, they excel at training others. Problems can arise, though, if they're forced to stick to a strict methodology, for Virgos always have their own ideas about the very best way to do things — and they equally always believe that *their* special way is best. Or, in the words of Frank Sinatra (who incidentally has Virgo on his ascendant), "I did it my way!"... For in work, as in every activity, self-reliance and self-determination are the keystones of the Virgo philosophy.

Virgos may prefer to serve rather than lead, but watch a Virgo at work and you'll be forced to conclude that there's far more to the sign than the secretary stereotype we've come to know so well. Virgos are the true administrative geniuses of the zodiac and their organizing abilities are second to none. Virgos are the team-builders, the managers, the cogs that make the big wheel turn, and, without them, most businesses would just come grinding to a halt. It's Virgo who ties all the myriad strands together, unifying them into a workable whole, making sure the business runs smoothly, whilst some other poor fellow does all the wining and dining of clients that they detest. And they do their job wonderfully, too, provided they don't fall victim to the classic Virgo trap of seeing the trees, but not the forest! Virgos thrive on details — taking care of them, sorting them, classifying them and ordering them, but they often get overwhelmed by the volume of information that lands on their desk. Although they frequently construct defences against it in the shape of endless charts, schedules and reports, it's important for them to learn to try and see the broader picture, too. Having a routine can help — but keeping to a set routine can often become yet another defence against chaos. It's essential for Virgos to learn when to stop chasing footnotes and focus on essentials! Incidentally, although this is not a fixed sign, you might sometimes believe otherwise when you see how upset most Virgos can become when their tidy routine is disrupted!

All Virgos can be pedantic at times, and their occasional outbreaks of "Know-it-all"-itis, obsessive-compulsive behaviour and plain old irritability mean they're not the easiest people to work with. But try turning to your Virgo boss or colleague when you're sick, or life has dealt you a blow, and you'll very soon see the better side of their nature — the caring, compassionate, generous person behind the navy blue suit or polka-dot dress. For niggles and nit-picks classic Virgo are a small price to pay for the privilege of working with such gifted, helpful people. And if, as the poet Kahlil Gibran said, "Work is love made visible", there's a great deal we can all learn about the art of working — and loving — from this humble, self-effacing and vastly underrated sign.

♍ The Virgo Boss

Just as Virgos shun the limelight, so they also tend to pass up many opportunities to become the MD, preferring rather to act as the "power behind the throne" — despite the fact that they're often more than qualified for the job. Virgo's reluctance to lead doesn't just spring from shyness. It's just that they know instinctively that their real talent lies in organizing the action behind the scenes, and making sure that everything runs smoothly. That's what they really love doing, and it's also what they do best. You can often see this "invisible " side of Virgo at its best in politics. Think of Joseph Kennedy, a Virgo "fixer" if ever there was one, masterminding his sons' careers and using his influence, money and connections to get them right to the top.

There are exceptions to every rule, of course, and, in some situations, Virgo thrives in the hot seat. They don't mind heading up small businesses, provided they don't grow too large! Big business just isn't their scene, unless they've a strong Saturn theme in their chart or can come and go as a consultant.

If you happen to have a Virgo boss, just accept the fact that you're working for a perfectionist. People who react badly to criticism had best stay away, for Virgo bosses will always speak their mind. But whatever you do, don't criticise them back. To suggest that there might be something wrong with Virgo is to invoke their deepest, darkest nightmares, and they're bound to get terribly upset. Don't do it more than once, or you could find yourself out on your ear. On the plus side, though, they're unfailingly loyal, and genuinely pleased when you do your job well. And be sure to dress neatly, for they hate sloppiness in any shape or form!

♍ The Virgo Employee

Virgo employees must be counted among the best in the zodiac, for they're hardworking, trustworthy and honest, and can always be relied upon to do their job well. The phrase "If a thing's worth doing, it's worth doing well" must surely have been coined by a Virgo, and it's usually almost impossible to find anything seriously wrong with their work.

Although Virgos often prefer to work alone, and without supervision, they usually prefer the security of a salaried position to the precarious life of a freelance; so self-employed Virgos are usually few and far between. Virgo employees thrive on a fairly regular schedule and excel at tasks that call upon them to handle a great many details at once. They appear to work slowly, but in truth they're just being thorough ...and remember, too, that though their desk may be cluttered, their mind most certainly isn't!

♍ Virgo & Career

Virgo is the sign of service and selflessness, and many Virgoans have a deep and compelling need to be of service to their fellow men. This "call to service" can take many forms, but it's rare to find a Virgo who isn't working to improve life for others in some way, however subtle it may be. Virgo is traditionally linked with agriculture and the land: many Virgos grow or produce food, or take care of animals, either as vets or by running a farm. Virgo has a particular connection with small animals too, and you may well find a Virgo running your local petshop or shelter for waifs and strays.

Other Virgos enter the helping professions as doctors, dentists and nurses, or as healers working with acupuncture, massage and nutrition. You'll find many Virgos with conventional day jobs helping out in voluntary organizations at evenings and weekends, and others still travelling abroad with VSO.

Virgos love to pass their knowledge on to others and they often make excellent teachers. Their innate patience means they're ideally suited to conveying ideas to people of all ages. One of the very first teachers I learned astrology from was a Virgo, and her methods were thorough, to say the least. Week after week, she'd find subtly different ways to put across the complex ideas of "the ancient wisdom" until everyone in the group understood it perfectly. Incidentally, many, many Virgos are drawn to study, teach and write about astrology: it's a treasure-trove of categories, concepts and methods and so it appeals to their tidy minds no end.

Many Virgos find a niche within business where they can make themselves thoroughly indispensable. There's more than a grain of truth in the old chestnut that Virgos make great typists — for indeed they often do! And since they're always cool, calm and collected under pressure, they also make brilliant executive PAs, medical secretaries and para-medics. A government office is a happy hunting-ground for Virgos too: with all that data to organize, it's their idea of seventh heaven.

Virgos also excel at careers requiring precision and attention to detail, two qualities they possess in abundance. Many are drawn to the law, where their nimble minds can get to grips with complex cases and briefs that would dwarf less agile intellects. Financially-minded Virgos find contentment working with figures — either as qualified accountants, or as cashiers or record-keepers. They love to count the pennies, after all, and find little so satisfying as a set of perfectly balanced accounts! More artistically-oriented Virgos can opt for calligraphy or graphics — two careers that combine precision with visual flair. Virgos also excel at the art of horology — making and mending clocks and watches.

Many Virgos enjoy working with the written word, and you'll find thousands of them employed as proofreaders, journalists and editors. When I worked in Rome as a reporter on an English-language paper, I once did an astrological headcount to see which signs predominated in the office — a staggering 70% were Virgos, and it's pretty easy to see why. The challenge of writing pithy copy to tight deadlines and fitting it exactly into neat and tidy columns was one that suited them down to the ground. Virgos also make brilliant critics and reviewers — two more natural outlets for their excellent powers of analysis.

Writing is both an art and a craft, so it's an area where Virgos excel. Virgo writers seem to have a real knack for tuning in to what people really want to read, and a great many best-selling authors happen to have been born with the sun in Virgo. There's William Golding, Dame Agatha Christie, H.G. Wells and Christoper Isherwood — not to mention Antonia Fraser, Roald Dahl and Stephen King. Booker Prizewinners A.S. Byatt and Anita Brookner are also Virgos, as is the darkly humorous Alice Thomas Ellis. With their perfectionist tendencies, rigorous self-discipline and love of routine, the typical Virgo can see even the longest of novels right through to completion. Think of "War and Peace" — yes, Tolstoy was a Virgo too!

Acting is another profession where Virgo excels ...and Virgo actresses are sometimes famous for their icy-cool, poise. Think of Greta Garbo, Lauren Bacall and Ingrid Bergman. They can also be stunningly sensual too — like Raquel Welch, for instance, or Jackie Bissett and Sophia Loren. Supercool screen hero Sean Connery is also a Virgo, as are Richard Gere, Jeremy Irons and also Larry Hagman. Many Virgo actors are brilliant mimics: think of Peter Sellers (a double-Virgo, with Virgo on his ascendant, as well) whose humour was tinged with true genius.

♍ Virgo: Keys to Financial Success

- DO try and focus your critical and analytical abilities toward *things* rather than people. Criticising your family or business colleagues will only antagonize them and make them far less likely to want to help you reach your goals.

- DO learn to have more *fun* with your money — start a savings account devoted exclusively to pleasure — or if that feels too daring, a holiday or hobby account.

- DO relax and try not to worry so much about money. To get some perspective, try this. How would it be if you had all the money in the world, but were too ill to enjoy it. See?!

- DO try and learn to take more risks. Your financial judgement is among the best in the zodiac and you can lose out a lot by hanging back too long.

- DO be sure to set some long-term financial goals and priorities. Your emphasis on having "cash in hand" may be stopping you from enjoying greater wealth in the longer term. For example: would you be better off working for yourself? Think about it!

♍ Rich & Famous Virgos

Lyndon B Johnson
Dr Samuel Johnson
Agatha Christie
Arnold Palmer
James Hunt
Herbert Lom
Sean Connery
Christoper Isherwood
Goethe
Ingrid Bergman
Fay Weldon
Shirley Conran
Frederick Forsyth
Pauline Collins
Michael Jackson
Richard Gere
Gloria Estefan
Anne Archer
Lady Antonia Fraser
Roald Dahl
William Golding
Peter Falk
Van Morrison
Freddie Mercury
Martin Amis

Deng Xiao-Ping
Dante
Mary Stuart
Jimmy Connors
Stirling Moss
Linda Gray
Jeremy Irons
Mother Theresa
J.B. Priestley
Alice Thomas Ellis
Greta Garbo
H G Wells
Stephen King
Roald Dahl
Oliver Stone
Sir Richard Attenborough
Jacqueline Bissett
Jessica Mitford
Arthur Koestler
Larry Hagman
Lauren Bacall
Anne Bancroft
Elvis Costello
Leonard Bernstein
Hugh Grant

♎

LIBRA
September 24th to October 23rd

Libra is the seventh sign, the midway point of the astrological year — the sign in the zodiac where we reach a point of perfect balance! Well, that's the theory at any rate. Perfect, you'll notice, is a word that Librans use often. And although the Libran ideal of perfect equilibrium is aptly reflected by Libra's astrological symbol — the scales — most Librans find that perfect balance is something they spend their whole lives working at — not least when it comes to finance!

The perennial Libran search for perfection explains the curious restlessness which often underlies their calm facade. Rather like ducks on a village pond, they swim along so smoothly, looking thoroughly serene — but just below the surface, their legs are frantically paddling! In just the same way, many Librans are constantly striving to meet their own high standards and even higher expectations. For in an ideal world, they aspire to nothing less than the perfect lifestyle — which means the perfect job and the perfect home, along with the perfect marriage, and, last but not least, the perfectly balanced chequebook...

Libra is ruled by Venus, the goddess of love, beauty and the arts. It's also an air sign, which means that Librans figure things out with their minds, rather than with their senses or their intuition. For although Librans "love to love", and are among the greatest romantics in the zodiac, they'll rarely allow themselves to be swept off their feet in a wild fit passion. It's the head, rather than the heart, which makes the decisions with this sign — provided they're in the mood, that is... For Librans can also be notoriously indecisive. Just as Virgo is renowned for its endless nit-picking, and Scorpio for its pent-up passion, so too have volumes been penned on the subject of Libra and its reluctance to get off the fence. But a brief sortie into the pages of mythology will reveal the roots of the problem...

The sign of Libra is usually associated with the tale of the Judgement of Paris. Paris, a handsome youth in ancient Greece, was called upon to choose which of three goddesses — Athene, Hera and Aphrodite — was the fairest. Not an easy task, as you might imagine, but Paris finally plumped for Aphrodite, who promised him the hand of Helen of Troy, the fairest woman in the world, in return. True to the myth, you'll find that many latter-day Librans place the highest premium on romantic relationships. But the other two goddesses were so angry at being slighted that they started the Trojan War — thus leaving poor Paris with the unmistakeable feeling that his decision, though made with the very best intentions, had triggered a disastrous chain of events. The thought-processes of many Librans run along strikingly similar lines, for they hate upsetting people, and usually live in mortal dread that their decisions might have unfortunate consequences. So, when Libras have an important decision to make, they like to be absolutely sure they've considered all the alternatives and weighed them up thoroughly on those inner mental "scales", to see which of all their options is likely to lead to the happiest outcome. Then, and only then, will they make their final choice.

That famous Libran indecision is something that needs to be carefully handled in childhood, too, for people born under this sign are prone to dithering over trifles, even when they're still toddlers! Parents of Libran youngsters need to encourage them to have confidence in their judgement and follow through on their reasoning. Beware of the tendency to rush a Libran child into choosing, or, worse still, to choose for them — for once learned, the habit of leaving major decisions to others is one they'll never grow out of.

Despite the troublesome furrow that clouds their handsome brow whenever they have to choose, Librans are often among the best-looking people in the zodiac. Along with the legendary Libran dimples and a good speaking voice, their physical charms are legion. The men are classically handsome, smooth and sartorial — think of Roger Moore, the classic James Bond hero —

and the women are often blessed with the kind of "peaches and cream" prettiness that's straight off the lid of a chocolate box. Their hair is smooth and wavy, they're rarely troubled by pimples, and their figures, even when plumpish, are always well-proportioned. Having said that, you'll rarely meet a skinny Libran, for even the slender ones are curved in a way that's subtly pleasing and easy on the eye. Then there's the Libran smile — which, in a word, is totally dazzling. Most Librans learn how to use it from the very earliest age in order to get them exactly what they want! They need it, too, for most Librans aim to please all the people all the time, and that's no easy task, by any stretch of the imagination. Librans are usually highly fashion-conscious, too, and have instinctive flair and dress sense. Later in life, though, they may run into problems as a result of their legendary love of sweets — a tendency that can sadly play havoc with their health, as well as with their wardrobe. As in all things Libran, balance is the keyword here.

Most Librans have an instinctive awareness of their need to balance periods of activity with periods of rest, and this is a sign that needs no lessons in relaxation! This penchant for taking things easy can be a bone of contention if they happen to live or work with one of the more industrious signs, like Virgo, say, or Capricorn. But although some Librans may well be guilty of sitting back and letting the other people in their lives make the running, it's just that mostly they know how and when to "listen to the body." A Libran will head for the hammock whenever they know it's time to rest ...and when they've recharged their batteries, they'll be back on the job, as bright as a button, and maybe even more productive than that Virgo or Capricorn who worked straight through the lunch hour!

Libras' love of ease and the good things of life is equalled only by their love of beauty and harmony, and if they're forced to live in ugly or squalid surroundings, or in an atmosphere of discord, sooner or later, it will literally make them ill. Seething atmospheres and silent agendas may be mother's milk to a Scorpio, but they're total anathema to Libra. Hence the sign's great reputation as a peacemaker and troubleshooter, for whenever Librans find themselves in troubled surroundings, they'll work ceaselessly to smooth things over. All Librans believe that cooperation is better than conflict, but sometimes their love of conciliation and pleasing others leads them to put everyone else's dreams and wishes before their own. This may be all very well as a short-term strategy, but in the long run it can make them resentful. That's when they seek refuge in alcohol or overeating — both classic Libran escape-routes. Finding the middle ground between meeting the needs of self and the needs of others is Libra's challenge here, and it's often the work of a lifetime.

Getting the balance right in relationships is a peculiarly Libran dilemma, however, for this is also *the* sign of one-to-one relationships. Libra rules the seventh house of "significant others" in the natural zodiac, and life means little to a Libran without someone to share it with. Many Librans marry early, but being such perfectionists, they often marry more than once. And once the "honeymoon" phase is over, they sometimes find the nitty-gritty of everyday coupledom a little hard to cope with. But more often than not, it's only when Librans have found their mate that they really do come into their own.

Curiously, both male and female Librans alike often embody the qualities of the opposite sex, whilst still retaining the strongest possible sense of their own masculinity or femininity. So you'll find that a Libran man may well be a hunky Adonis who sweeps you off your feet, but he may also be a deeply sensitive soul who's great at listening, and has a brilliant fashion sense as well as a love of the arts! I know a Libran man who's so tuned in to changing fashions, he changes his image so often that it's really hard to keep up. Every time we meet, he's sporting a new hairstyle − be it permed and dyed, long and wavy, or simply cropped − along with a totally new way of dressing. And that Libran lady you met the other day at the business seminar? She may be as beautifully dressed and groomed as a top model, but you can bet your bottom dollar she also has a mind like a razor and can out-argue every man in the boardroom. No-one knows the cause of this strange, but undeniable "switching" effect − but perhaps it's just because *all* Librans, male or female, are seeking a perfect balance within themselves, as well as in the world outside.

The Libran quest for balance can also lead to some pretty extreme behaviour. A Libran at a boring cocktail party may well start telling a few off-colour jokes just to "restore the balance" and liven things up a little! Or they'll play devil's advocate in a discussion − even if they don't believe it − just to show that there's another point of view. More often, however, you'll find them speaking up for the underdog, or a cause that's crying out to be defended, for there's little they hate more than injustice. "It isn't fair" is an expression that's never far from Libra's lips, even from the earliest age, and most Librans find it hard to accept that life quite often just *isn't* fair. So wherever they can, they'll do their utmost to help. Sometimes Librans even devote their whole lives to the struggle — like Mahatma Gandhi, who sacrificed his life to liberate India. More recently, the whole world dug deep in its pockets and gave to help the starving in Africa, thanks to the stirring words and sterling deeds of Bob Geldof, who masterminded "Band Aid". Geldof didn't mince his words either, when he called on the world to give, using righteous Libran anger to shame millions into paying up!

With their deep-seated love of the Good, the True and Beautiful, it's true that many Librans view life through rose-tinted spectacles. It's also true that their burning need to "please all the people all the time" may sometimes lead them to be slightly less than truthful, and also to come across as distinctly wishy-washy. And then there's their dithering and their indecision, as well as their monopoly of the bathroom mirror. But when all's said and done, these little faults are a small price to pay for the gentle pleasures of a Libran's friendship. For though the head rules the heart in the Libran home, a Libran's heart is usually firmly in the right place — and more often than not, they make the world a better place to be. And all things considered, that's no mean feat indeed.

Ω Libra and Money

Just as one might expect with a sign that, ruled by Venus, the zodiac's planet of pleasure, most Librans you'll ever run into have a keen appreciation of money. It's as though, even from childhood, they know that money can buy them pretty things — a lovely house, a well-stacked wardrobe and an eye-catching motor to go cruising in! But, as in all things, the Libran approach to finance is instinctively balanced, and although Librans like money, they seldom afford it undue importance. Librans rarely *worry* about money, and, in keeping with their relaxed and "laid-back" attitude, it seldom proves, to be a source of major problems in their lives.

For Librans, money is simply a bridge to beauty, a green-edged passport to the finer things in life. They value money because it allows them to enjoy the pleasures of a comfortable lifestyle and this is always their motive for making it — along with the ability it bestows to make other people happy. Most Librans have a pretty strong sense of self-worth, which means that their basic needs include a nice home, a stylish car, fashionable clothes to wear, and the wherewithal to amuse themselves as and when the fancy takes them. Money also allows Libra a sure means of escape from all that's mean, squalid or ugly — and this is a thing that they value highly, too. Yet even a Libra who's constrained by circumstances to live on the slenderest of shoestrings will somehow contrive to do so in the greatest of style indeed. A Libran can make sardines on toast taste like blinis and caviar, home-made lemonade sparkle like champagne, and can give an attic studio a penthouse feel with a splash of paint and a simple roll of calico !

Having money also allows Librans to express their love of beauty — another thing, too, that's essential to their nature. And whether those Libran tastes incline toward fine sculpture, fine wine or designer dressing, they're usually quite costly. The pressed wildflowers and fir-cone arrangements that come courtesy of Mother Nature and delight the humble Virgo nature simply don't impress them a bit. Librans like their little luxuries, and they usually like them gold-plated — or hallmarked at the very least. And although love, rather than money, is Libra's primary driving force, in practice, the two often seem to go very much hand in hand. Bouquets of red roses, weekends in Paris and candlelit dinners — the little romantic rituals that Libra loves so much — they all cost money, as all Librans soon discover.

The bottom line is, Librans like money — but they rarely seek more than they need to finance their pleasure-loving lifestyle. Wealth brings power and responsibility, and most Librans don't really want to be bothered with all that — unless, of course, they've lots of Scorpio or Capricorn planets too. Security isn't something they get overly het-up about either, and the average Libran would far rather leave the burden of financial decision-making to someone else. So even when Librans become very successful and wealthy — and since they're so talented, they very often do — they invariably delegate their financial management to a team of advisors and professionals.

Looking at moneymaking in a broader astrological context, there are two main ways that most people tend to approach it — let's call them the "Mars" way and the "Venus" way. You can go out into the marketplace and struggle and strive — that's the Mars way (the way that Aries and Scorpio do it) — or you can lie back and let it come to *you* instead — and that, pure and simple, is what I call the way of Venus. Countless canvases have been painted of the goddess Venus sprawled on a chaise-longue being showered with gifts and, since she's the ruler of this sign, that's the approach that most Librans prefer... For although Librans are often stunningly successful in their chosen careers, they also practically invented the principle of attraction. Indeed, they sometimes rely on their physical assets and looks as a way of attracting what they need. Libran women are often the very epitome of the ravishing siren, whose charms are so magnetic that men can't help but heap them with jewels. Think of Elizabeth Taylor and that huge diamond ring Richard Burton once gave her... That's pure Libran stuff, and it's no surprise to learn that La Burton has Libra rising. Sadly, Librans who haven't succeeded in finding their true niche in life sometimes decide to "marry money" instead, and people born under this sign have a higher-than-average tendency to stay trapped in loveless marriages for fear of losing their comfortable lifestyle.

By harnessing their "Venus energy", though, all Librans can attract all the money they could ever need — and the secret is actually quite simple. Libra is an air sign, so people born under this sign have a wonderful capacity for using mental images and pictures. Librans can use the subconscious power of the mind to attract whatever they need, simply by mentally imaging their goals — twice a day at least — until those goals have been attained. This imaging technique — or "creative visualization" — was first developed many centuries ago, and is based on the simple idea that "You are what you think". It has recently come to be widely practised in the west, mainly thanks to the work of Shakti Gawain, who, by a curious coincidence, just happens to be a Libra! Shakti used mental imaging to achieve what she wanted in her own life and then went on to explain how it worked in her book, *Creative Visualization*. Many Librans I know seem to use it quite unconsciously. As an impeccably-groomed lady Libran friend of mine once said, "If you think 'beer and cigarettes', that's what you'll receive — so why not think 'champagne and caviar' instead? That's what I focus on — and that's what I always get!"

As a cardinal sign, Librans are among the great go-getters of the zodiac and get enormous satisfaction from setting and achieving their goals. On a day-to-day financial level, however, they're usually far happier when someone else is in charge. Without exception, *all* the married or cohabiting Libran clients I know leave their nearest and dearest in charge of the bills. Not that they're incapable of running the household accounts — far from it. It's just that they tend to baulk a little at making those financial decisions. We're back to the Judgement of Paris again. Suppose I don't choose the right investments or pension plans and we lose all our money? reasons Libra. So first they weigh up one option, then another ...then another... The whole business can take quite a while so, generally speaking, it's probably better if some other sign takes over.

Solo Librans, (who are quite a rare breed, incidentally), can do quite a capable job of managing their finances — though they're sometimes a touch forgetful when it comes to paying the bills. Forking out money for gas, electricity and other utilities is so dreary compared to going out for dinner, and Librans often have to steel themselves to "do their financial duty." There's also a slightly whimsical side to Librans and their money, which can sometimes manifest at the most unlikely moments. Writer and traveller Lisa St. Aubin de Teran packed two suitcases full of cash when she left her unhappy first marriage to a South American revolutionary. The money lasted for two years, but the novelist then recounts that things were a "bit lean" until her first two books were published! Lisa's approach to money certainly gave whole new meaning to the expression, "living out of a suitcase"! When things get really tough, though, a Libran who's truly desperate may simply live off others. Librans excel at borrowing money and making people feel it's an honour to part with their cash. It's that charm again, you see ...but it must also be said that Librans are highly generous souls, and will always be happy to lend their money, too — provided it's fully repaid on time.

Librans also have quite a reputation for extravagance, and it's worth pausing to explore this in more detail for a moment. It's true that Librans will spend a great deal of money on a beautiful painting for their home, or a piece of jewellery for their spouse. The fact is, they're often given to spending fairly large amounts of money on just a single item, and that's why they're sometimes called spendthrifts. But a Libran will always be sure to re-balance the accounts after they've been on a spree. *He* may well treat himself to that Frink sculpture; *she* may not be able to resist that St. Laurent shawl — but any resulting financial imbalance will disturb a Libran's peace of mind. Venusians hate upsetting people, and that includes the bank manager! So a Libran who's indulged in a pretty major extravagance will economise for months rather than lingering in the red. Debt upsets them. It's — well, it's so unbalanced. So, much as they adore luxury, they'll always strive to balance their chequebook.

Some astrologers claim that Libran men are more extravagant than women, and in my experience, too, this is very often the case. I'm reminded of a Taurean friend of mine, who's married to a Libran. When I asked about her spouse's spending habits, she simply said, "Show me the man with four hands!" Her facial expression described her spouse's profligate ways with money far better than any bank statement ...and other clients I've questioned also bear this theory out. Not that I want to start any arguments here, just venture the hypothesis that the clear, cool brains of the Libran female may have a touch more financial "savvy" than the pleasure-loving Libran male!

Generosity is one of Libra's great financial virtues and, much as they enjoy spending money on themselves, they're even fonder of spending it on others. Nothing gives them greater pleasure than making their partner happy, and their generous emotional support is always firmly backed up by their chequebook. A Libran man or woman will have absolutely no hesitation in using their life savings to bail out their partner's ailing business, or to finance a risky new venture. Indeed, when the chips are down, and there's a crisis in the offing, you can often observe Librans at their very, very best. They'll help others in need, too, if they possibly can — especially those who are suffering due to the current world imbalance of resources. Librans Anita Roddick, of Body Shop fame, and rock star Bob Geldof have both used their fortunes to come to the aid of the poor, and their energetic style of philanthropy shows idealism at its very best.

Ω The Spending Style of Libra

As the honorary children of the goddess of beauty and pleasure, there's never any doubt that Librans were "born to shop"! When it comes to spending money, though, their top priority is always beauty. Style and taste must always prevail, even if the Libran is only buying a humble toaster for the kitchen. For after all, there are good-looking toasters and ugly ones, so why not have one that graces the kitchen as well as making breakfast? No matter if it costs a couple of pounds extra. Librans will always spend freely on beauty, especially when it involves their partner. Big white weddings, romantic holidays in faraway places — this kind of spending is total Libra Heaven. But they'll *never* ever buy anything that doesn't look good, if they've the slightest choice in the matter... Ah, yes, choice — there's that word again, the one that gives them so much trouble! For the other great thing about Libras and their spending is the great length of time it takes them! The problem is that Librans can't help but compare things on those famous mental scales — and that means just about everything, in every single shop. Should they buy the maroon brogues or the tan? Or perhaps high boots would be more suitable for winter? But then again, those patents look so sensible.... You know, it can take a whole day to buy a single pair of shoes when you go shopping with a Libran, and it's a pretty exhausting activity. So please don't even think about it if you're not feeling up to the task. I speak from personal experience here, because I have a healthy dose of Libra in my own chart. Over the years my long-suffering husband has devised the perfect strategy for dealing with the problem. When he can no longer stand the sight of me dithering and hesitating over the blue sweater, or the green, he finally steps in and cries, "Buy them both! And choose the one you like best at home." It works every time, provided the store will cooperate and let you return the unwanted item! All Librans love to spend on beauty, and love to cultivate the body beautiful. Libran women will always be among the biggest spenders at the hairdresser and the beauty salon and they'll buy the best cosmetics they can possibly afford. The Libran bathroom will invariably be a pleasant place to linger, with lots of pretty jars and boxes, and sweet-smelling unguents and lotions.

Libran men and women generally spend lavishly on their wardrobes, and keep up with the latest fashions for as long as they continue to be flattering. If they can't afford an Armani original, say, they'll choose the best high street copy they can find and dress it up with costly, accessories. Libran taste is generally impeccable:

older Librans plump for well-cut, timeless classics in top-quality fabrics. Libran women love pastels, cream and beige, and these seem to suit them all, regardless of hair and skin tone.

Home is an important place to Libras, for they love to give parties and spend time with their friends and loved ones. Creating a pleasant environment figures high on their list of expenditures, and Libran homes are generally an absolute treat to visit. Librans like to decorate their houses in pale, airy tones, and usually in a contemporary, rather than traditional style. The furniture will be low and comfy, and perfectly arranged for conversation — another favourite Libran pastime. Tea — or real coffee, never instant — will be served in fine bone china cups, along with delicious cakes and pastries that will frequently be home-made.

Sociable Librans also like to do the rounds of the latest restaurants, art galleries and parties, so the right kind of car is also very important. A stylish, two-seater sports car would probably be their natural first choice, but any light-coloured, speedy saloon would do — as long as it looks good, of course! On their rare nights in, Librans are also fond of reading, and they're usually regular customers of all the local bookstores. Hardbacks are their special love, and you'll probably find a stock of Libra's secret vice — a pile of the most wonderfully escapist novels — that even the most level-headed Libran dives into from time to time...

Ω Libra: Saving and Investing

Given their natural tendency to surround themselves with objects of beauty, most Librans prefer spending to saving. But although Librans are not necessarily the zodiac's star performers in the saving stakes, their innate shrewdness impels them to put small amounts aside for the future — especially when that future involves a partner. For when there's a pleasurable joint goal in sight at the end of the day, such as a pretty house or elegant apartment, a romantic holiday or a big, splashy wedding, then Librans have no problem saving. It's just that, for the most part, they find it easier to save their pennies in a pot marked 'Pleasure,' rather than 'Rainy Day' or 'Contingency'...

Libras' innate talent for goal-setting and forward planning means that when Librans have accumulated sufficient money for investment to become an issue, they generally take a long-term approach. For although Librans aren't nearly as security-oriented as some of the other signs of the zodiac, they do still like to know what they're going to get at the end of the day. This is why assurance policies are among their favourite investments: the final pay-out is specified right from the beginning, spelled out in black and white. A major problem for Libra, though, can be finding just the right policy, for they can get thoroughly sidetracked by small print and legal niceties. Using a broker can save vast amounts of time, energy and money that could be far better spent elsewhere. Down at the shopping mall, for instance...

Libras' love of beauty and excellent aesthetic judgement mean that fine art, sculpture and textiles are among their very best investments. Here is where Libras' moneymaking instincts really come into their own: they excel at spotting tomorrow's successful artists today, so they're very well-placed to take financial risks in this sector — and more often than not, these can yield up handsome returns. Some Librans also buy and sell antiques — but generally speaking, they prefer contemporary art to old.

Property is another favourite Libran investment and, despite the slump in property values, some Librans have still made money buy buying low at auction, renovating, and then selling on. But no Libran will buy an ugly-looking building, no matter how much of a bargain it is. Concrete apartment buildings or office blocks leave them cold, but an elegant Georgian town house — why, that's quite another matter! Investing in stylish property also suits the Libran fondness for impressing others with their wealth. Libra's sense of security comes from people, not from things, and they like their friends and associates to appreciate their investments, too.

Librans' gifts of analysis and intelligence mean they're good at assessing and evaluating the relative merits of different investments, but unless they've mastered the art of decision-making, they're unlikely to get very far. Librans are fairly enterprising by nature, but in order to maximise their return on speculative investments, they must learn how to take more risks, and above all, how to choose. Windows of financial opportunity are sometimes short-lived, so Librans who find the decision-making process a problem should appoint an investment manager. Getting a personal recommendation from a friend is probably better than choosing one from Yellow Pages — where, after all, there are so many to choose from!

The worst thing in the world a Libran man or woman can do is to entrust their investments to their partner, though usually their instincts incline them to do just that. That way, if things go awry in Libras' personal life, at least their finances will still run smoothly. Hardhearted though this may sound, Librans can suffer quite badly as a result of their habit of sinking all their resources into their primary relationship, so it's not always a good idea. Better to keep 'head' and 'heart' arrangements separate to at least a certain degree, so that Librans can retain a modicum of financial independence.

As well as fine art, sculpture and property, good investments for Libra include gold, precious stones and fine furniture. Business-minded Librans may profit by investing in all businesses connected with beauty and the arts. These may include fine art, art publishing, auction-houses, ceramics, perfumery, beauty therapy, hairdressing, floristry, millinery and fashion — as well as art galleries, music studios, photographic studios, interior decorating and design, Feng Shui consultancy and landscape gardening. Accountancy, insurance and the legal profession may also make profitable investments.

Ω The Earning Power Of Libra

Just as most Librans spend a great deal of time and energy searching for the perfect relationship, so, too, do they focus on finding the "ideal" career. The ceaseless quest for career perfection can cause many Librans to chop and change jobs never-endingly — particularly in the first few years of their adult working life, until the happy day when they finally come to see that no job is ever perfect after all! It's also true that many Librans don't really "find themselves" workwise until they've settled down into a stable relationship, or until their natal Sun has progressed into the more serious sign of Scorpio. That's the time many Librans acquire a more serious approach to life, and may well take up a proper professional training, as a lawyer, for instance, or even as an accountant — much to the surprise of their family and friends.

Libra is a cardinal sign, and as with the other members of this astrological grouping — Aries, Cancer and Capricorn — the drive, ambition and initiative that exist beneath its tasteful facade should never be underestimated. Librans want to go places in life, even if external appearances might suggest that their ultimate goal is simply to find the perfect hairstyle. Thanks to the paradoxical "switching" effect of Libra, these qualities of driving ambition and go-getting are often more developed in the female than the male. For, whilst the men may well hold down good jobs, complete with impressive pay-cheques, lady Librans often climb right to the very, very top. Think of Margaret Thatcher, the former British Prime Minister, and you'll begin to see how determined a really focused lady Libran can be...

It's true that the average Libran woman may look as though she has nothing more serious on her mind than choosing what colour to decorate her office, but beneath that pretty hairdo, there usually lies a formidable intellect. Female Librans often have a string of academic degrees to their name — Mrs Thatcher studied chemistry before turning to politics — and whilst many apply their knowledge and learning in commerce and industry, still others build excellent careers as scientists, engineers or academics. Libra's intellectual ability may seem slightly at odds with the beauty-loving nature of Venus, but the airy side of the sign means that Librans like using their minds just as much as looking good. Librans of both sexes, who have spent time developing their innate executive abilities, will invariably get exactly where they want to go. You'll rarely find them taking work home in the evenings, though — a Libran's evenings and weekends are sacrosanct, for they know they need to rest and recoup their energies if they're to work at their best the next day. Librans may be many things, but workaholics they're not, and they usually succeed in striking the right balance between work, rest and play.

With their well-publicised love of leisure and taking life easy, you might be forgiven for thinking that Librans view work as a necessary evil — and in a few rare cases, unhappily, I've found this to be true. I once had a hardworking Taurean girlfriend, for instance, who took a perverse pride in telling all and sundry that her Libran lover was "strictly for decoration". Indeed, young Michael liked nothing better than to lie in bed all day reading the newspaper, with occasional trips to the off-license or betting-shop for entertainment! But such dyed-in-the-wool "lazy Librans" are definitely the exception rather than the rule. For I also know another Libran, called Sue, who supports her entire family of four daughters, a husband and two cats, by working as an artist. In the summer months, you can find her at work by 5.30 a.m., only pausing briefly to get her family off to school. Lunch and dinner parties chez Sue are a real delight, for she's a superb cook, too − another Libran trademark − and her home is decorated with such originality, taste and flair that it's a total delight to visit. My lady friend is more typical of her sign than young Michael, I believe, for the vast majority of Librans take great pride and pleasure in their work. Building a career offers Libra an opportunity to help make the world more beautiful and just and, sooner or later, they usually find just the right niche for their talents.

As you might expect with an air sign, Librans often gravitate towards work that allows them to flex their mental muscles. They love to weigh, evaluate and compare ideas and, generally speaking, they're happier working in the abstract realm of thoughts and concepts than with the world of things. Composing reports and creating public relations campaigns might well be the Libran idea of paradise: supervising the production line in a dreary, dusty factory most definitely isn't! "Mind over matter" is Libra's ruling, and they'd far rather supervise the advertising campaign for a new brand of soap powder than oversee its production! They like to dress well, explore ideas and mingle with interesting people. And these aren't just the things they like, they're what Librans absolutely *need*.

Librans become thoroughly depressed if they're forced to work with uncongenial people in a dirty, unattractive setting. But if they're forced to work alone — horror of horrors! — the depression becomes almost terminal. For just as much as they love to use their minds, Librans love to relate, and the social dimension of work is one of the reasons they value it most. The open-plan office, with its daily diet of powder-room gossip, leisurely chats by the water-cooler and constant social intercourse, is a home-from-home to Libra, and even when they're promoted to an office of their own, you can be sure that their diary will feature plenty of lunches and meetings to vary the hours of working solo.

Although many Librans have a genuine talent for working with groups, and make great team-builders and troubleshooters, it's when they're working one-to-one that they really come into their own. If there's one thing Librans need above all else, it's a partner. And once they've found the right person, they're very often unstoppable. The beauty tycoon Anita Roddick, the founder of Body Shop and self-appointed creator of "beauty with a conscience", is a Libra who totally exemplifies the sign's very great emphasis on partnership. For although La Roddick founded Body Shop when her husband was travelling around South America, he has played a vital role in the business since its very earliest days. Whilst Roddick is very much the "ideas person" of the company, coming up with brainwave after brainwave, Gordon is her constant mentor and sounding-board, and keeps a keen eye on factory production. I was fortunate enough to spend some time with Anita a while back, and I couldn't help but notice how many aspects of her sign she embodied. Working in the beauty business is a very Libran calling, and despite her fairly casual public image, Anita dresses in the very best clothes that money can buy. She also has several beautiful homes in town and country and is frequently featured in the Sunday colour supplements — her style may be low-key, but it's also totally Venusian. Her Libran idealism also shines through in the way she fights for what "is just and true" — like championing the cause of the Third World and drawing attention to environmental problems, as well as to threatened animal species.

Anita Roddick takes a long-term, strategic view of business development and in this, she's also thoroughly typical of her sign. For Librans are among the master planners and strategists of the zodiac, and some of the greatest military minds in history were born with the sun in Libra — Alexander the Great, for instance, and Eisenhower and Churchill. The Libran aptitude for strategy and statesmanship goes hand in hand with their diplomacy, which is also, as it happens, a considerable asset in business. Librans are past masters at keeping business secrets, and will always regard a confidence as inviolable. They won't let their colleagues in on a secret until *they* choose the time. And naturally, there's always a master-plan behind it...

You might think that classic Libran indecisiveness might create a lot of problems at work, but provided they're in the right job, and have time to think things over, it's actually rarely a major drawback. Although Librans may dither and prevaricate over trifles, they can be surprisingly decisive once they've really made up their minds — or, indeed, if a crisis blows up. Then they can take command of a situation in a most impressive manner. Remember the way Mrs Thatcher masterminded the Falklands War back in the 1980s? No shillyshallying there that one might notice! Most Librans, though, are happiest in roles where they don't have to take a hard-and-fast line or make lots of decisions at short notice.

The Libran habit of cultivating anyone who can help them "get on" leads some to call them opportunists. And there's no denying that Librans at all levels of the corporate ladder have an irritating habit of saying one thing to one person and precisely the opposite to another. At times, this springs from their wish to keep everyone happy: at others, it's just a necessary move in the executive chess-game, executed with unblinking sang-froid. When confronted with their "double-talk", a Libran can be thoroughly inscrutable. It's worth noting that both China and Japan are ruled by this sign, and there will be times when it's almost impossible to tell what your Libran friend is thinking!

As a cardinal sign, Librans love to lead, and there's little doubt that they always prefer to give orders rather than take them. The key to the executive washroom, however, lies in whether or not individual Libras manage to master their own decision-making. If they're happy to take a stand on things, fine. In that case, you'll find them happily running their own business, or surviving in the ever-changing world of the freelance professional. If they prefer to sit on the fence, however, they're probably best advised to stay there, for the pressures of executive life would surely prove too taxing. But even a Libra who's climbed almost to the top of the greasy pole may opt for the job of MD rather than Chairman, preferring to let the final responsibility for decisions land at someone else's expensively-shod feet. The buck has to stop somewhere, after all — and most Librans vastly prefer that the buck should stop somewhere else!

Ω The Libran Boss

You'll find more lady bosses than male ones born under this sign, for the simply reason that the female of the species is often a good deal tougher than the male. Libran bosses of both sexes demand good presentation and high standards from their underlings — in return, though, in keeping with their love of justice, they usually treat their staff fairly and are thoroughly pleasant to work for. You can expect frequent office parties, ample Christmas bonuses and regular pay-rises, provided, that is, you're doing your job well. If not, you can expect a caustic rebuke that will set your ears ringing, for Libras who feel they have cause for complaint can be judgemental and sardonic indeed! One thing a Libran employer most definitely *won't* put up with, though, is an office feud, for Librans find it impossible to work in an atmosphere of discord.

Ω The Libra Employee

Although their sights are usually firmly set on executive roles, all Librans concede that they have to start somewhere, and they can and do make excellent employees. Work is something they take seriously, for they like praise and appreciation just as much as money and, in true Libran style, they'll always do their best to please. Since they always look smart and speak so pleasingly, they make excellent front-of-house people or public liaison staff, and they don't really ask so very much in return — just the occasional long lunch hour to try out that stylish new brasserie, or go shopping for their cousin's wedding present... Oh, and don't forget to ask them what colour they'd like the office painted, or skimp on flowers on their desk. It takes surprisingly little to tip a Libra's scales in the wrong direction and send them into a fit of the sulks. But happily, it takes little to tip those scales back to normal and make them smile again. And they do have such a lovely smile after all — isn't that what got them the job in the first place?

♎ Libra and Career

Librans are the master aesthetes of the zodiac and, with their flawless taste and unerring eye for beauty, it's no surprise to learn that some of the greatest interior designers of our day — like Sir Terence Conran, for instance — have been born under this sign. Another thoroughly Libran career is the current passion for Feng Shui, the ancient Chinese art of room placement. For what could be more Libran than re-balancing your life by rearranging the furniture in your home?

Librans love to weigh things up, to talk, to compare and to see the other person's point of view, so they're drawn to all careers that allow them to do just that. So, many Librans find that law offers a perfect home for their talents. Librans love the law because it lets them resolve others' conflicts. But the law is also concerned with disagreements and disputes, and there's also a hidden side to Libra that secretly enjoys a good fight! And what could be more socially acceptable than fighting courtroom battles for a living, elegantly attired in legal blacks and greys?

Union activity is another field where many Librans exercise their talent for debate, arbitration and rhetoric: think of Lech Walesa, the Polish Solidarity leader and premier. Librans with an intellectual bent find career satisfaction in academia or publishing, or maybe in science or in computers — for, like all the air signs, they're fascinated by new technology.

Librans also revel in politics, and many rise to become premiers and statesmen. Think of Jimmy Carter, a Sun Libra, and JFK, who had Libra rising. Other Librans exercise their mental faculties in the military. Napoleon and Hitler both had Libra rising, and then there's Horatio Nelson, Eisenhower and Churchill. Much as Librans loathe conflict, it seems to follow them around: remember poor Paris and the Trojan War! But it's often said that Librans make good generals because they seek to minimise suffering. Librans are also drawn to careers in the diplomatic service, which, with its agenda of travel and parties, often proves to be a perfect choice.

The world of beauty therapy also offers a chance for many Librans to find their vocation, for their Venusian nature endows them with many gifts in this field. Some take up careers as beauticians, hairdressers or beauty therapists: many aromatherapists and massage therapists are also born under this sign. The art of shiatsu — re-balancing the body's vital energies — is yet another therapy that can appeal. More business-minded Librans can take a leaf from Anita Roddick's book and turn their attention to creating cosmetics. For many Librans have a real skill for working with plants, herbs and rare herbal extracts. Others Librans work with plants by choosing careers in gardening. Others still create beauty indoors, by working as florists and painters.

Capitalizing on their good looks is another Libran option, and many Librans succeed in the fields of modelling, acting and the movies. Think of Elizabeth Taylor, with Libra on the Ascendant, and also Brigitte Bardot. Then there's Sigourney Weaver, Charlton Heston and Catherine Deneuve. Interestingly, Bardot has now channelled her energies into fighting for animal rights — another very Libran activity! Some Librans find a happy home in TV — like chat show host Johnny Carson and the UK's Anneka Rice. Some Librans express their artistry through literature or music: think of John Lennon or the late George Gershwin; Oscar Wilde and Truman Capote; Eugene O'Neill and Katherine Mansfield — Librans, one and all.

Super-sociable Librans are abundantly endowed with "people skills", too, and developing these gifts can help many to find their vocation. Careers with lots of built-in socializing, dressing-up and hand-shaking, like hotel work or public relations, are perfect for Libra and guarantee that they'll never be lonely!

Librans love to advise, but they also love to listen, and they excel as consultants and counsellors. The feisty Scots psychologist R.D. Laing was a Libran, and many others have become psychotherapists. Many Librans come to therapy as a second career in midlife, when their Sun has progressed well into the following sign of Scorpio. Prior to this time, they often shy away from the darker side of life — but in the Scorpio progression, they start to see things in a different way...

Finally, Librans who are logical rather than psychological in their leanings often do well as financial advisers, using their ultra-keen minds to help clients to balance their money, in a work environment where they're working mostly one-to-one.

♎ Libra: Keys to Financial Success

- DO practise the art of choosing — start with little things — develop confidence in your ability to choose the right option, then you'll find it much easier to make large-scale financial decisions.

- DO remember that all that glitters is not gold — your love of beauty and fine appearances means that you can sometimes get taken in by something that looks good. Don't be — always look a little deeper before you say Yes.

- DO set goals: create a game-plan for your work and finances and stick to it. Make it the plan that *you* want for yourself, not one that other people want for you.

- DO use your excellent judgement to help you track down the best investments — like insurance products, for instance — or spotting bargains in your local auction house.

- DO practise creative visualization on a regular basis — daily, if possible. The benefits in your bank account and in your life in general will soon repay the effort!

Ω Rich & Famous Librans

Antonio Canaletto	Christopher Wren
Mary Coleridge	Oscar Wilde
George Gershwin	F Scott Fitzgerald
Jimmy Carter	Mahatma Gandhi
Dwight Eisenhower	Lech Walesa
Mark Rothko	Buster Keaton
Lee Iacocca	Margaret Thatcher
Arthur Miller	Katharine Mansfield
Graham Greene	Jackie Collins
Truman Capote	Gore Vidal
George C.Scott	John Lennon
Paul Simon	Linda McCartney
Cliff Richard	Bryan Ferry
Julio Iglesias	Deborah Kerr
Chevy Chase	Michael Douglas
Luciano Pavarotti	Carrie Fisher
Catherine Deneuve	Johnny Carson
Julie Andrews	Susan Sarandon
George Peppard	Walter Matthau
Charles Dance	Charlton Heston
Brigitte Bardot	Dame Anna Neagle
Lisa St Aubin de Teran	Anneka Rice
Clive James	Sir Terence Conran
Martina Navaratilova	Roger Moore
Anita Roddick	Bob Geldof
Patric Walker	Dawn French

♏

SCORPIO
October 24th to November 22nd

The late October and November days when Scorpio birthdays fall are a strange and ghostly time ...for this is the time of Hallowe'en, or the great ancient Feast of the Dead. The time when the gates between the worlds stood open, it was said, and ghosts and spirits roamed abroad freely, and anything might happen, or so it seemed... And since it's also the season of Scorpio, an aura of mystery has lingered round this sign ever since. Think of the Scorpios you know, for a moment. Beyond that calm, capable facade, isn't there something just a little, well, mysterious? Something veiled and hidden, that you can't quite put your finger on? Few people on earth would claim to understand Scorpio fully, even their lifelong marriage partners. For Scorpio is the sign of sex, death and money, and it's a highly complex one, both to live with, and also to fathom....

Notwithstanding Scorpio's air of mystery, few signs, with the possible exception of Virgo and Capricorn, have received a worse press down the centuries. Scorpio is *the* sign that people love to hate, and Scorpios soon learn to shrug off the way people flinch when they bravely reveal their birth-sign. Or else there's that other stock response, the lascivious, knowing grin — because of course, we *all* know how great those Scorpios are in bed! Those are the tabloid titbits we're used to reading — and though they may contain a grain or two of truth, the real story is rather less straightforward.

Astrologically, Scorpio is ruled by two planets — Mars, the planet of war, and Pluto, the planet of rebirth. In ancient mythology, Pluto was the God of the Underworld, the Lord of Hades, and since he possessed the power of life and death, he was universally respected and dreaded. In a similar way, all Scorpios possess tremendous latent strength and inner reserves that they can call upon in times of crisis. Astrologers often consider Scorpio to be the most powerful, potent sign of all, and there's certainly no doubt that Scorpios have huge potential — for either good or evil. This is the sign of saints or sinners — though most Scorpios, it must be said — usually fall somewhere in between. But it's also a sign of extremes, and *all* Scorpios can sometimes be — well, pretty extreme. At one end of the scale, you'll find charismatic preachers and spiritual leaders, like Billy Graham or Mahatma Gandhi, who had Scorpio on the ascendant. At the other, there are low-life criminals and mass-murderers like Charles

Manson and Joseph Stalin (also with Scorpio rising). So it's hardly surprising that Scorpio inspires such caution and respect. It's as though people fear that voracious, reined-in energy that pulses just below the surface – held in like a tightly coiled spring that might just unravel at any moment.

Paradoxically, Scorpios are one of the easier signs of the zodiac to spot, for their air of intensity and quiet charisma usually make them stand out in the crowd. Since they're often quite shy, they usually try hard not to be noticed – but their hooded, "X-Ray" eyes are a sure-fire giveaway: just think of Bette Davis – she had Scorpio on the ascendant. Scorpios are mostly quite reserved and quiet. They've little taste for small talk, or social niceties, and won't even talk at all if they're really not in the mood, which can be highly disconcerting!

Scorpios are usually quite dark in colouring, with translucent complexions and noble, aquiline features. Even the blonde ones have a quality of "darkness" about them – think of the late Grace Kelly, or Billy Graham. Scorpios bodies are strong, and they're rarely overweight, for they've too much self-discipline to really let themselves go. Unless, of course, food is their demon, or their defence against the outside world.

Pluto people are masters of the art of transformation, and have the ability to act as catalysts in their own lives and in the lives of those around them. This inevitably means that the life of the average Scorpio is periodically subject to times of crisis and change. And since change is something that Scorpios aren't all that keen on, this can cause them a considerable amount of stress! Particularly if they insist on hanging on stubbornly to whatever it is that needs to go — be it a job, a relationship or even a place of residence. But the longer they resist, the worse it tends to get! Pluto-style crises can be financial, emotional, or even spiritual in nature, but whatever the cause, life is usually stripped "back to basics", as the Scorpio in question goes through the fires of purification. Then they can rise, like the phoenix from the ashes, and a whole new cycle of life can then begin anew... The late Richard Burton was a Scorpio, and his life, with its fame, fortune, multiple marriages and lifelong battle with addiction is thoroughly typical of Scorpio's fate.

Scorpios are also blessed with tremendous emotional intensity. This is a water sign and, as the saying goes, still waters run deep, and occasionally they also boil over! That's when the famous Scorpio temper is unleashed, and they're capable of saying and doing all the wrong things, all at the worst possible moments. Scorpio's strong feelings can land them in the most terrible trouble at times: at others, they're the very thing that saves them. Learning to control these emotions is often a lifelong battle, and is also at the root of that famous Scorpio reserve — which is, in essence, a great defence against getting hurt. For Scorpios may look tough on the outside, but they're really very softhearted...

Then there's the passion, ah yes, that famous Scorpio passion. Poor Scorpio has the unenviable reputation for being the sex maniac of the zodiac, which means they often come in for some pretty suggestive comments at parties. And though there's no denying that this IS a deeply sensual sign, with a keen understanding of the pleasures of the flesh, Scorpio's passion is usually grossly misunderstood. It's simply one more expression of their strong feeling nature and extends to *all* areas of life — not simply the bedroom! Scorpios are passionate about their work, about the environment, about social injustice and the starving millions, their lover, their kids — in short, about *everything*.

Scorpios also have strong feelings of an entirely different nature, for their intuition is usually developed to the point of being psychic. Scorpios have an inbuilt "sixth sense" about things, and it's their most infallible guide through life, if they can only learn to trust it. Scorpios rarely need to be told what's going on ...they just *know*. Most Scorpios are also deeply fascinated by the occult, and you're more than likely to find a pack of tarot cards tucked away in the drawer of even the most level-headed Scorpio lady — or Scorpio man, for that matter... The sign of Scorpio is strongly linked with astrology, and there's scarcely an astrologer I know that doesn't have Scorpio — or Pluto — strongly placed in their horoscope. Scorpios always have a deep feeling for the great mysteries of life, like being born or dying, and they're wonderful to have around when a soul is entering or leaving the planet. Their tremendous psychic strength and vitality are a pillar of strength to those around them, and this is when Pluto's power really does come into its own.

Astrology teaches that there are three different levels or types of Scorpio, and most people born under this sign spend their lives moving twixt all three. At the bottom rung of the ladder, there are the grey lizard or scorpion types, who are totally ruled by their baser desires. Lizards are generally ruthless, lustful, dishonest and mean and have given the sign of Scorpio a thoroughly bad name! They won't think twice before stealing your money or your spouse. They're also quick to anger, and even quicker to seek revenge. Grey lizards live in a world of fear and paranoia, always convinced that others are plotting against them. Frequently, the only way they can escape from their irrational terrors is through drugs or drink, and this is also the level where Scorpio shows its self-destructive side.

Then there's the eagle, who is a far, far nobler sort. Eagle-type Scorpios are proud, dignified and well in control of their passions — well, that's the theory, at any rate. Their ability to "rise above things" gives them great objectivity, but although they'll forgive an injury, they certainly won't forget. As the late Bobby Kennedy (Sun in Scorpio) once said, "Forgive your enemies, but don't forget their names". For although eagles can be magnanimous, they have pretty long memories, too. It works both ways, though, for if you do them a kindness, they'll never forget that either. Eagles see things clearly, and they don't take things at face value. For their great mission in life is to discover the true essence of things — and that also, quite naturally, includes themselves! Finally, there's the third type, the rare Scorpio who can be classified as a dove. One who has acquired real wisdom on their journey through life, and who understands people's motives well enough to forgive and forget. But as I said before, this kind of Scorpio is rare indeed...

For most Scorpios, life can often feel like a battlefield. Generally speaking, the unfolding of their destiny usually leaves them little choice but to fight their inner demons at some point, whether they be depression, negativity, anger, addiction or jealousy. The inner torment this "fight" can evoke often inspires many Scorpios to dig right to the depths of their being. "Know thyself" is a Scorpio dictum par excellence and, through exploring their own inner make-up, many Scorpios discover psychology. Scorpio comedian and author John Cleese became world-famous through acting out his anger and frustration in the classic comedy TV programmes, "Monty Python" and "Fawlty Towers". Subsequently, however, he went into therapy and, having explored his own inner conflicts, went on to co-write a book called *Families And How To Survive Them*. A constructive use of Scorpionic anger, if ever there was one! That Scorpio sarcasm is legendary, but when the "sting in the tail" is expressed through satire and wit, it can often be immensely entertaining — think of Scorpio comic Peter Cook — and also Oscar Wilde, whose Mercury was placed in Scorpio.

Physical exercise is an absolute must for Scorpios, since they desperately need an outlet for all that Mars and Pluto aggression! Jogging, hiking and swimming are all perfect Scorpio sports, as are the martial arts and yoga, which call on their powers of concentration, too. Exercise not only helps Scorpios to recharge their batteries, but also to release the petty resentments of their everyday life, which may otherwise fester unseen. Scorpios are quick to take offence, but slow to forgive, and this tendency to harbour grudges can take its toll of both body and mind. City-bound Scorpios who live far from the coast or seashore will benefit greatly from sessions in a float tank — a pleasurable, sure-fire route to inner peace and relaxation!

When you have the good fortune to meet Scorpios who have discovered their essential nature, fought and conquered their demons, and acquired enough insight into human nature to allow others to live and let live, you'll be bound to admit that they're really a rather special person. And if you succeed in winning their trust and friendship, do pat yourself on the back. For you've just earned yourself the priceless gift of unswerving devotion and loyalty, and a friend who will always be there when you need them. A friend who'll follow you to the grave — and who knows? Maybe even beyond...

♏ Scorpio and Money

Scorpio may mostly be known as the sign of "sex and death" , but it's also the sign of wealth and, by implication, financial power. Which sounds as though I'm saying, if you're a Scorpio, you're brilliant with money! Yes, it's a fact that software baron Bill Gates is the richest self-made man in America, and that he also happens to be a Scorpio! But unfortunately, folks, it's not *quite* as simple as that. Many Scorpios *are* financial wizards, it's true, but it's also true that money can provide Scorpios with some of their greatest lessons in life. Scorpio's ruling planet Pluto also rules the "goods of the dead" and "shared resources", and it's strange, but true, that many acquire wealth by inheritance, and also through their partners...

The urge to acquire and accumulate wealth begins in Scorpio's opposite sign of Taurus, where it's a simple matter of "I want it", and "The more, the merrier, please!". Scorpios want money, too, but for entirely different reasons, and Scorpios' motives for acquiring great wealth are seldom totally straightforward. Firstly, there's the basic, primitive urge to feel secure. Scorpio is a water sign, and like all the water signs, they have a deep-seated need for a secure foundation in life. Like Cancerians and, to a lesser degree, Pisceans, Scorpios need a place they can retreat to from the world, although in Scorpio's case, the retreat is often a veritable fortress! The act of buying a home is often Scorpios' first step on the financial ladder, and such is their need for privacy that they regard it as totally essential.

Way beyond the level of domestic security, however, what Scorpios really desire is to be totally in control of their destiny — and it's this, above all else, that really drives their financial endeavours. "I am the captain of my ship, I am the master of my fate" is a phrase that all Scorpios are instinctively in tune with. They see money as their route to total freedom — and to a Scorpio that's a state "more precious than rubies." Scorpios loathe feeling beholden to others, and they resent the restrictions of salaried employment far more keenly than many other signs. So once a Scorpio has secured a stable home base, their next priority is usually achieving financial independence. Which leads us to an interesting paradox — namely, that although Scorpio is often a far from materialistic sign, many Scorpios are truly obsessed with the goal of acquiring great wealth. But Scorpios don't seek wealth as an end in itself — but for the control it gives them over their lives — and also, sometimes, over the lives of others, too. For after security and control, Scorpios also value money for its power... For Scorpios, money and power are the two elements of a very basic equation. The more money you have, the more power you have. It's really that simple. In theory, at any rate! But the issue is often more complicated. Since Scorpio rules the eighth house of "joint finances" in the natural zodiac, Scorpios invariably find that acquiring wealth usually *does* depend on others — whether they be partners, spouses, stockbrokers or advisors — and regardless of whether their money comes from wills, inheritances, or even, sometimes, their in-laws!

Scorpios' intense desire to make money is usually accompanied by a tremendous inner faith that their endeavours will eventually succeed. Scorpios rarely lose sight of their inner conviction that they'll always win through, even when the skies look darkest, and they're staring financial disaster in the face. And provided they can conquer their twin bugbears — impatience and over-emotionalism — they nearly always win!

Scorpios' unwavering faith in a positive final outcome is one of their greatest financial assets, for it gives them the strength and staying power to achieve long-term financial goals. Scorpios will quite happily live within a stringent budget for literally years, whilst they're striving to build up a business or some other kind of moneymaking scheme. And it's this ability to postpone short-term gratification in favour of a far bigger, better "payoff" that yields the handsomest dividends in the end....

Scorpios' famous powers of intuition can also be a huge asset, provided, that is, that they've learned to trust them and follow them through. But even if the Scorpio doesn't listen to the "still, small voice within", and everything falls apart, sooner or later they'll always find a way of coming back, and rising like the phoenix, from the ashes of their former prosperity into a whole new cycle of financial wellbeing...

It's undoubtedly the case that making money occupies a larger percentage of Scorpio's waking energies than of those of most other signs. Investment adviser Dan Pallant notes that over the years, his client list has contained a particularly high number of Scorpios — all seeking to make a killing on the stock market! "There's something about a strong Scorpio balance in the horoscope that gives an almost fanatical drive for great wealth. Combine it with other factors in the chart and you may end up with the kind of person who will stop at nothing to make money", says Dan. Happily, though, the stereotype of the "ruthless Scorpio" who's ceaselessly trying to manipulate circumstances to their advantage, is rare indeed, and you're more likely to encounter Scorpios who use their wealth for positive ends.

Scorpio is the sign of the "spiritual businessman" par excellence, but this doesn't mean that Scorpio entrepreneurs need confine themselves to producing crystal balls, Tarot cards or even meditation books! Using wealth wisely to help heal and transform the planet can take many, many forms. Many Scorpio businesspeople quietly donate a percentage of their time and money to charities. Others practise the ancient prosperity principle of tithing, which involves giving a proportion of their earnings to individuals or organizations which are contributing to spiritual education, or even, these days, to the quality of life on the planet. Tithing is an excellent financial exercise for

Scorpios, too, since it's a constant reminder that wealth comes *through* them, rather than *from* them. It also helps them to be more generous and to practise "letting go"!

On a day-to-day financial level, Scorpios are usually extremely adept at handling their own accounts, both business and domestic. Their eagle-eyed attention to detail means that they're totally clued-up on what's being spent and where. Their mental focus, self-discipline and long-term approach mean they're also good at making budgets and sticking to them, too (bar the occasional bout of excess), and unless their Sun is afflicted by spendthrift Jupiter, they're highly unlikely to squander the rent money at the racetrack. Scorpios never take anything at face value, so they always check their bills and bank statements with the utmost rigour. Nothing, but nothing, escapes their scrutiny, and they'll never stand for being overcharged.

Though Scorpios are usually quite loath to part with their money, and can often drag their feet when it comes to paying the bills, they're keenly aware of debt, and always take it seriously indeed. Pluto, their ruling planet, also governs taxes and indebtedness, and Scorpios always honour their obligations to the letter − even if it takes them a lifetime to do so. So if a Scorpion owes you money, never fear. You're certain to see it repaid. If you owe *them* money, however, then you *do* have a problem − especially if you can't pay. Scorpios aren't noted for their patience, and if you stretch their reserves of tolerance too far with stories and excuses, they'll have no hesitation in suing you so that they can promptly recover their cash. The link with taxation is an interesting one, for it's a fact that many celebrity Scorpios — jockey Lester Piggott and comedian Ken Dodd, to name but two — have been accused of cheating on their taxes! (Piggott was convicted, whereas Ken Dodd cleared his name) The only real pitfall that Scorpios tend to encounter in the arena of household finance is their tendency to "take over" and insist on controlling the purse-strings. If the Scorpio lives with one of the more easy-going signs — an Aries, say, or a Libra or Gemini, they are probably quite happy to let them. But if they've chosen a partner like a Taurus or a Leo, who also has strong ideas about how the money should be spent, then sooner or later, sparks are bound to fly.

Separate banking accounts may provide a solution up to a point, but it's better to have at least one "joint account", so that cohabiting Scorpios can learn to share money as well as resources. Another problem here is that famous Scorpio secrecy — for Scorpios are often highly reluctant to reveal their true financial position. Unlike Leos, who love to flaunt their wealth, the average Scorpio will go to considerable lengths to conceal it. It's as though they're afraid that if someone knows the truth, that person can then take advantage! So a Scorpio may often have a dozen or so different bank accounts all held in different places, so as to prevent anyone — especially their partner — ever knowing how much money they have.

Financial problems can also sometimes arise in relationships, because Scorpios aren't that keen on financially supporting their partners, should the need or occasion arise. If the partner is in dire straits through no fault of their own, then all's well and good — for no-one's more generous than Scorpio when the chips are really down. But if Scorpios feel the errant partner could have done more to help themselves, they'll probably be less than helpful. Weakness is something that Scorpio doesn't tolerate too well, and that includes financial weakness, too.

At some point along life's journey, Scorpios' destiny usually involves learning to be more open in their daily financial dealings. What every Scorpio really wants, above all else, is to merge with another person in an intimate relationship, and in order for this to happen, they need to share their finances too. Scorpios who learn to share and cooperate with their partners over the years will often find that money gradually comes to matter less and less, as their reserves of happiness and contentment grow correspondingly greater! At the end of the day, most Scorpios benefit greatly from living with a partner who's keen to share the financial obligations rather than leaving them solely in charge. Compromise and cooperation are always better than control − as many a Scorpio usually eventually comes to learn! Incidentally, Scorpios often tend to become more relaxed about finance in the second half of life, when their Sun has progressed well into the "lucky" sign of Sagittarius. That's often when Scorpios tend to benefit from wills, become more prosperous and assume a more "laid-back" approach to money. Stock market investment may prove lucrative at this time, along with foreign investments and ventures with foreign partners, such as import-export businesses.

♏ The Spending Style Of Scorpio

With their penchant for accumulating money, rather than circulating it, the typical Scorpio is rarely a big spender. Paradoxically, for a sign that's frequently so set on "making a stash", the Scorpio lifestyle is often quite simple. Their houses may be furnished in a style that's almost spartan, and they may well wear the same pair of black leather trousers month in and month out. But then, just once in a while, when a passing planet touches off Jupiter in their horoscope, they'll go on a spending spree that would make Imelda Marcos look like Old Mother Hubbard! For this is a sign of extremes, and Scorpios can either be very, very lavish, or very, very careful. More often, however, they tend to be the latter.

Scorpios are sometimes accused of being stingy, but in my experience they can be hugely generous — especially when there's money in the bank and they're relaxed and at peace with the world. But when Scorpios are focused on a particular financial goal, such as buying a house, for instance, or perhaps a new car, they can display a talent for economy that even a Capricorn would pause to admire. All Scorpios loathe waste, and they often practise recycling with an almost missionary zeal.

Scorpio's spending style is firmly ruled by their feelings, and their spending patterns are fixed and set quite early on in life. Scorpios who've been emotionally damaged in childhood can end up with spending disorders that range from freeloading to the opposite extreme. Scorpios can sometimes be spendaholics, too, endlessly spending and creating debt to feed their inner emptiness — and naturally, often in secret! Midnight sessions in front of the home shopping channel will aggravate the misery, not assuage it, and Scorpios who've fallen prey to "consumer addiction" should seek help quickly, before the ever-growing debt-load deals their self-esteem a fatal blow.

So what does the typical Scorpio (if such a creature exists) enjoy spending money on? Surprisingly, books, books and more books head the list, way above the whips, leather gear and sexy undies that conventional wisdom assumes comprise the bulk of their purchases. Scorpios may well believe that "money is power", but knowledge comes a close second. Scorpios love to learn and explore, and the quickest way is through the printed word. So however sparsely their apartment or house may be furnished, there'll always be plenty of books. With their perennial interest in the occult, Scorpios love books on astrology, Tarot, the I Ching and the paranormal, and they also enjoy a really good detective story, too... Like all water signs, Scorpios are also great music-lovers, and they often have extensive sound collections to suit their every mood. Music is like therapy to Scorpios, and few things can soothe and heal their spirits like a Sibelius symphony, say, or a gentle snatch of Debussy.

Being great sensualists at heart, Scorpios love good food and wine. Small, intimate dinner parties are their favourite way of entertaining, but they enjoy eating out sometimes, too. Like their opposite sign, Taurus, they place a premium on "value for money". So they're particularly pleased when they discover a restaurant where the food is superb, but the price-tag happens to be modest. Decor matters little, unless they're entertaining a new lover or client — in which case, they'll make a beeline for the sleekest joint in town. Occasionally, the excesses of their epicurean tastes will catch up with them, and they'll head firmly in the opposite direction — straight to the health resort!

Scorpios like to stay in shape, so their budget often includes a subscription to the local gym or health club. They rarely bother keeping up with fashions, though: they prefer to wear classics and stay firmly in the background. It must have been a Scorpio who invented the fashion for black, black and more black, and Scorpios often wear their outfits till they fall to pieces on the hanger. Scorpios also adore leather — whether it's to wear, or to sit on — and you're practically guaranteed to find some sexy leather gear in their wardrobe. Affluent Scorpios love to lash out on leather sofas or chesterfields — though if Venus is strong in their birthchart, it may well be pink — or baby blue!

Taking time out is important to Scorpios and, if it's financially possible, they'll often have a second home or time-share by the sea. They like to travel in comfort, too, and will buy the very best car they can afford: a smooth, purring Jaguar would possibly be their ideal! Holidays that involve an element of danger or mystery as well as the obligatory "lying on the beach" appeal greatly to Scorpio, and they love vacations where they can learn a new skill, such as deep-sea diving or even swimming with the dolphins.

♏ Scorpio: Saving and Investing

With their highly-developed instinct for security, and their future-oriented outlook, most people born under Scorpio find it relatively easy to save. Scorpio is also a fixed sign, so if the habit of saving is established early in life, it's one that they rarely abandon. Scorpios enjoy saving their money in a range of different accounts. It's a way of keeping their financial options open, and also means that if someone discovers how much money they have in one particular account, there are always six more they don't know about! For Scorpios love to save in secret. Moreover, they're often pretty secretive about their financial dealings in general, and will often erect a smokescreen to conceal their true financial status. When you meet them on Friday, they may tell you that they're broke, and you'll believe, for all the world, that they're only one step away from the breadline. But then you'll see them the following week driving around in a brand- new car − purchased with the contents of one of their secret savings accounts, of course!

Investment-wise, most Scorpios like to divide their money and energy between making 'fast bucks', on the one hand, and pursuing a longer-term strategy on the other, one that will hopefully lead to the attainment of their most cherished goal, namely complete financial independence. The world of corporate finance is Scorpio's natural domain, and most Pluto people enjoy investing in the markets. Whenever new shares are announced, Scorpio speculators will always check them out to see if they're worth investing in − and their methods of market analysis are often novel, to say the least. The investment strategy of most Scorpios is firmly governed by their intuition, and although they'll read all the latest market reports and intelligences, they're capable of flying in the face of every expert and analyst in town and acting totally against all the apparent trends, if that's what their instincts tell them to do. What's more, they're very often right! Many Scorpios also use some of the more unusual methods of financial forecasting, such as financial astrology, which combines their passion for making money with their fascination for the occult.

Scorpios have a considerable drive to accumulate wealth, but sometimes they can over-extend themselves by taking on more investments than they are truly able to handle. They are prone to keeping too many projects on the go at once and spreading their resources far too thinly. There are several reasons for this Scorpionic trait... They hate to reveal their true position (even their broker may be unaware of their real financial standing) and they always want to keep their options as open as possible. So, when new opportunities present themselves, Scorpios hate to say "No". This diffuse mode of operating might appear, superficially, to serve their best interests, but in practice it usually makes it far harder for them to optimise the return on their myriad investments. It's generally most profitable for Scorpios if they try to focus on just one area of investment at a time. Another problem lies in the fact that Scorpios can develop such highly charged emotional attachments to particular investments, they blind themselves utterly to the actual financial reality. So, canny though they undoubtedly are, it's best if they seek professional advice before parting with their money.

Since this is the sign of joint and shared resources, Scorpios often make good profits investing in their partner's business. They usually do best when they choose investments which also benefit others, for example, ethical funds. Since this is, above all else, the sign of transformation, the real financial challenge for Scorpios lies in finding the best way to use their money to heal the planet.

With their long-term outlook, property is another investment "natural" for Scorpios, and they often like to buy larger-than-average properties that can provide additional rental income, as well as a family home. And although their tastes are often quite spartan, you'll occasionally meet Scorpios indulging their taste for luxurious, exotic furnishings by investing in Persian carpets!

Pluto's connection with the underworld means that Scorpios can also profit by investing in precious stones, such as diamonds and emeralds. Other good business opportunities for Scorpio can be found in the funeral business, mining, oils, minerals and prospecting, and corporate finance. Other potentially profitable areas include occult publishing, recycling plants, mass media concerns, research agencies, medical research, detective agencies, the salvage business, security systems and alarms, locksmithing, nightclubs, debt collection agencies and insurance claims investigation.

♏ The Earning Power Of Scorpio

As might well be imagined from considering the planet Pluto and its link with financial power, Scorpio is a highly ambitious sign — although the Scorpio drive to "go places" is often concealed from public view. But despite appearances to the contrary, there's one thing you can be sure of with Scorpios. No matter what their chosen calling, in order for them to succeed, they must be totally, intensely and passionately involved at all times in their work.

Life is a serious business for Scorpios, and just like everything else, they take their work very seriously, too. They need to feel that their work is making a worthwhile contribution and that it has some sense of purpose. Ideally, it will be the thing that infuses their life with meaning, the mysterious activity that makes their blood sing and their heart dance as they leap out of bed in the morning! And if it doesn't, they may as well not bother to do it at all. Their time would be far better spent looking for something they *can* do that they love... For, above all else, Scorpios need a sense of passion about their work. Many outstandingly successful and creative people have been born under this sign and they all had certain qualities in common: a sense of purpose, a sense of mission and a great challenge to overcome. The young Picasso practically starved in the proverbial artist's garret until his work began to sell, but he refused to yield to despair. His trailblazing, innovative approach was a seminal influence on modern art and can truly be said to have transformed it — the classic Scorpio hallmark. In our own day, HRH the Prince of Wales has shown himself to be a quintessential Scorpio. Despite the fact that he's essentially a monarch-in-waiting, he has given purpose to his life by striving to change the face of modern architecture, and has largely succeeded, in Great Britain at least! Scorpios also excel at helping people to connect with their potential and, through his work with the Prince's Trust, Prince Charles has helped many young people to discover a new sense of purpose in their lives — and this has helped, in turn, to give new meaning to his own.

When Scorpios connect with their inner sense of vocation, their total single-mindedness and air of focused intent is quite impressive to behold. It's as though they've suddenly pressed the right computer key and accessed Pluto's secret powerhouse of energy, for they will work all hours and overcome all obstacles to get wherever they want to go. And if their goals also encompass a spiritual or transformational dimension, they're more than likely to succeed.

For all Scorpios, then, life must have a Great Plan, otherwise it lacks meaning, focus and direction. Without a blueprint, Scorpios can also fall prey to the demons of depression. Young Scorpios who haven't found the right channel for their gifts and abilities will sometimes drift from job to job, growing ever more cynical as the years go by. Another problem Scorpios often run into arises from their tendency to do too much at once. Given their many talents, it's all too easy for Scorpios to get caught up in working in business during the daytime, doing up property in the evenings, and then trying their hand at some writing, etc. It's as though they fear that doing what they really want, or focusing on just one thing, will make them more vulnerable to disappointment and rejection. But without a single "special focus", little can ever be really achieved.

Scorpio's way of working can be extremely intense. People born under this sign have formidable powers of concentration, and often work with sharp, concentrated bursts of energy. Then they'll withdraw to ponder, reflect, draw some inspiration from their subconscious depths, and then plan out the next steps in their game-plan.

The combined rulership of Mars and Pluto makes Scorpios a law unto themselves, and they're always bound to be happiest when they can call the shots and, hopefully, make the rules. Their love of being in control and running their own show means that they're ideally suited to the life of a freelance professional — with all its Pluto-style ups and downs. Scorpio freelancers like feeling independent and being able to come and go — and their excellent intuition will usually guide them to their next post or contract. Their long-term approach and natural executive ability mean they often excel at running their own business, though they should always be prepared for plenty of drama along the way. Another constructive option is to start up in business with their partner, for with their eighth-house emphasis on "shared and joint resources", moneymaking with their spouse can be a source of mutual delight!

Scorpios' fixed nature means they're rarely inclined to give up, but sometimes their determination to make things work can unfortunately backfire, and they end up stubbornly clinging to a project or business that should really have been released long ago. Scorpios really come into their own, however, when they're charged with the task of rescuing a moribund business or project. The influence of Pluto gives them the ability to breathe new life into businesses or projects that are dying and bring them back from the brink. Equally, when the world has collapsed around them, and Scorpios find themselves jobless or bankrupt, they'll just shrug their shoulders and start again from scratch ...phoenix-style!

Scorpios often rise to key positions in organizations because they are as catalysts for change in the business, and nobody quite knows how. Counselling and mentoring roles bring out their finest qualities, too, for they're highly adept at helping others to realise their dreams. At their best, Scorpio, often act as "transformers" for their colleagues, helping them to heal and empower their own lives, clearing away the dross to connect with their own true inner essence.

Scorpios are usually very thorough and conscientious, but they're rarely the easiest of workmates. They tend to be very "high-voltage" people, and can be intolerant of lesser souls who can't keep up with their schedules. Neither do they "suffer fools gladly". Scorpios are also constitutionally incapable of taking anything at face value, and will constantly dig and probe to discover the hidden meaning of all that's going on at work — even their workmates' love lives!

Even when Scorpios are totally immersed and involved in projects they deeply care about, they can be challenging to work with — and, truth be told, they're often happiest working alone. That's when they can do their deepest thinking and let their powers of concentration flow unimpeded — undisturbed by the social niceties that go to make a Libran worker's day.

Office chitchat and small talk just isn't Scorpios' thing and they hate being bothered when they're working. Open-plan offices simply aren't their style: nor do they care for jobs that involve a great deal of contact with the public. They'd far rather beaver away behind the scenes at their own sweet pace — which, needless to say, is very often prodigious!

Remember, however, that this is a sign that *always* holds something back. No matter how much of themselves they give to their work, there's a mysterious, hidden side of the Scorpio nature that no boss or co-worker will ever, ever see. Scorpios aren't going to broadcast the fact that they went for an astrology reading in their lunch-hour, after all, or that they're studying spiritual healing in the evenings ...and the wise workmate or employer will always respect their privacy.

♏ The Scorpio Boss

Since Scorpios infinitely prefer giving orders to taking them, they're happy to be the boss, despite their aversion to being in the limelight. Scorpio executives rule the business from their eagle-like eyrie, and rarely need to be briefed about what's really going on. They have a psychic sixth sense about people and situations: it's what got them to the top and they usually use it to keep them there!

Scorpio leaders are superb in a crisis, and the expression "grace under pressure" might have been coined with them in mind. Think of the way Prince Charles remained so cool when a starting pistol was fired at him in Australia — or how Margaret Thatcher (Scorpio rising) emerged, all cool and collected, from the ruins of the Grand Hotel in Brighton, just moments after an attempt on her life. Scorpio leaders stay cool and act decisively. They're sympathetic and understanding to their employees' problems and fiercely loyal and protective. There's just one thing that they'll never, ever tolerate, though, and that's the merest whiff of disloyalty. Any thoughts of shafting a Scorpio boss or even a Scorpio workmate are, shall we say, ill-advised! For at the very first hint of betrayal, would-be perpetrators will find themselves out on their proverbial ear.

♏ The Scorpio Employee

Scorpio employees feel strongly about loyalty, too, the only difference being, their primary loyalty is always to themselves! Scorpios' game-plan for their future career will always be what matters most, and they'll have little hesitation in changing jobs when their feet begin to get itchy. After all, they want to be the one giving the orders one day, so they can't let the grass grow under their feet! Scorpios generally make excellent employees in the meantime, though, and if they respect the company's visions, no-one will work harder to achieve it.

There are just a few ground-rules to remember, however, for bosses who want to keep their Scorpio workers happy. Ask them to do things, *never* order; never criticise them if you can help it (even in private); and, above all, *never* make them a target for your jokes. Scorpios' pride is as legendary as their memory, and if you make them look foolish, they'll always find a way to pay you back — even if it takes a decade. It's more likely, however, that they'll simply set about quietly sabotaging your business, with all their usual efficiency. But if they're unhappy about something, you'll probably be aware of it, for Scorpios rarely suffer in silence. And since financial security is one of their main objectives in working, that they'll only really be happy if those pay-rises keep coming, too.

♏ Scorpio and Career

Given their formidable willpower and self-discipline, Scorpios can succeed at just about any career they put their mind to — provided, of course, they feel truly passionate about it!

The sign of Scorpio is strongly linked with big business, and, although you won't find the names of many Plutonians emblazoned across the fronts of offices (they loathe publicity), a high percentage become business leaders and managers — think of Scorpio Bill Gates, the richest man in America. Scorpio businesspeople often use astrology to help them make their way to the top, and business astrologers report that a great many of their "mega-rich" clients were born around Hallowe'en. Scorpio John Cleese achieved great success with Video Arts, a company that made business training videos, before selling out for a handsome profit. Scorpio Sophie Mirman also became a financial high-flyer with her company, Sock Shop ...which then underwent a painful Pluto-style corporate collapse!

The field of finance is a source of endless fascination to Plutonians, and banking, investment finance and financial forecasting are where many make their career. Handling wealth comes naturally to Scorpios and they adore taking risks with other people's money! Some

Scorpios yearn for political power, too, and often become the "power behind the throne" — like Scorpio First Lady Hillary Clinton.

Research work of all kinds is a natural outlet for Scorpio's talents, and you'll find Plutonians happily engaged in scientific and academic research, archive film work, and even the literal "digging" of archaeology. Some even delve into the depths of the earth itself, becoming geologists, seismologists, or mining engineers. Scorpios who feel strongly about the correct use of the earth's resources (another Pluto theme) and don't mind putting themselves in the firing line often get involved in environmental work, by working or campaigning for Greenpeace or Friends of the Earth.

Scorpios often choose careers that involve a certain element of danger, and one of the most famous spies of all time — Mata Hari — was born under this sign. Of course, I don't have any statistics to tell you how many Scorpios are currently involved in espionage, but a great many go into police work! Scorpios are natural detectives — think of Sherlock Holmes, or TV's Inspector Morse: both of these fictional characters are classic Scorpio types — for the Scorpio combination of observation and intuition is capable of solving even the most baffling of crimes.

Pluto's gifts of charisma and smouldering sexuality lead many Scorpio good-lookers to become film and television stars. And naturally, of course, they feel passionate about what they do. Scorpio Julia Roberts, one of the highest-paid women in Hollywood, says, "I do the acting for free, because I love it so much. I get paid all this money to put up with all the nonsense that goes with the job" — a classic Scorpio comment! Other sultry Scorpio stars include Jamie Lee Curtis, Demi Moore, Sally Field, Goldie Hawn, Linda Evans, Sean Young and Tatum O'Neal.

The world of the mass media is also ruled by Pluto, and many Scorpios find career satisfaction by working in film, radio, or TV. Other Scorpios express their creative gifts through the arts, and their work is invariably powerful and packed with familiar Scorpio themes — such as passion, sex and death. Think of the work of Picasso, a Scorpio superstar, and Auguste Rodin, the world-famous sculptor. Then there's Dylan Thomas, the poet, and the late lamented Sylvia Plath, whose Scorpionic despair drove her down the self-destructive road to suicide.

It's the process of understanding and unravelling that kind of despair that gives life meaning for many other Scorpios — namely, those who have chosen to devote their lives to healing and transformation. Scorpios have an acute awareness of human suffering and emotional pain, mostly gained through first-hand experience, and you'll find many Scorpios working as counsellors, therapists and social workers. Others work with healing the body, like the pioneering heart-transplant surgeon Christian Barnard, whilst the bravest of all help guide the dying through the Plutonian portals of death. Elizabeth Kubler-Ross, famous for her work with death and the dying, has Scorpio on the ascendant, and you'll find many Scorpios working in hospitals and hospices.

Scorpio is also a highly mediumistic sign, and many Sun Scorpios are gifted psychics, hypnotists and clairvoyants. Others express the more traditional link with the afterlife, by working as funeral undertakers, or even as obituary columnists!

♏ Scorpio: Keys to Financial Success

- DO be sure to focus and hone your willpower by setting clear financial goals, and never lose faith in your ability to achieve them.

- DO focus on one goal at a time — and keep your focus clear by regularly visualizing the outcome that you want. And read lots of inspiring literature to keep your spirits high! ...see the 'Recommended Reading' section at the back of this book.

- DO make a point of seeking regular advice from experts and professionals who may be more practical than you. Letting people in on your plans may actually improve your chances of success.

- DO stay away from any deals which are remotely shady. Don't be tempted into gambling by the prospect of "fast bucks", either — some Scorpios can get addicted, and it simply isn't worth the risk.

- DON'T rely on windfalls and/or inheritances to help you meet your financial targets. You know you have got what it takes to get you where you want to go — so regard these extras as bonuses!

♍ Rich & Famous Scorpios

Fyodor Dostoevsky	Georges Bizet
Niccolo Paganini	John Keats
Marie Antoinette	Bram Stoker
Pablo Picasso	Aaron Copland
Luchino Visconti	Albert Camus
Evelyn Waugh	Neil Young
Dylan Thomas	Sylvia Plath
Rene Magritte	Kurt Vonnegut
Bobby Kennedy	Grace Kelly
Bill Gates	Alistair Cooke
HRH Prince Charles	Calvin Klein
Auberon Waugh	John Cleese
Michael Winner	Katherine Hepburn
Joni Mitchell	Winona Ryder
Demi Moore	Mary-Elizabeth Mastrantonio
Julia Roberts	Meg Ryan
Jodie Foster	Roseanne Arnold
Barbara Bel Geddes	Jodie Foster
Goldie Hawn	Jamie Lee Curtis
Whoopi Goldberg	Jaclyn Smith
Stefanie Powers	Charles Bronson
Jeremy Brett	Bob Hoskins
Nigel Havers	Robert Hardy
Danny de Vito	Nigel Dempster
Tina Brown	Billie Jean King

SAGITTARIUS
November 23rd to December 21st

As November draws to a close, and the scent of woodsmoke hangs in the air, we enter Sagittarius, and it's time to boogie! So stoke the fire and don those glad rags at the double: the "lucky" planet Jupiter rules this fun-loving sign, and there's little on earth that Sagittarians love more than a party. Apart from spending money, that is, for this is the sign of the zodiac's "big spender". And sometimes it's the sign of its "biggest earners" too....

Were you to conduct a random poll amongst astrologers and ask them which sign they would *choose* to be born under, I'd hazard a guess that many would plump for Sagittarius — or Sag (pronounced Sadge), as it's often known for short. Jupiter, the ruler of Sagittarius, was known to astrologers of old as "The Greater Benefic" and despite the fact that *every* sign has its drawbacks, the notion that it's the sign to be has stuck firmly to Sag ever since. The good humour, bonhomie and cheery spirits of Jupiter's children are legendary, and there's a general consensus that it's a singularly fortunate sign.

Over the centuries, Sagittarius has come to be thought of as one of the luckiest signs of the zodiac, and experience shows that fortune smiles on these people with uncanny regularity. This is partly because Sagittarians are great self-promoters, of course, who always give themselves the most PR. But good things happen to Sagittarians for the plain and simple reason that they always *expect* them to happen! You can call these people Pollyannas if you wish, but the Sagittarian tendency to think that good things are just around the corner, even when the skies are darkest, is an attitude that usually stands them in good stead — and also has the strangest way of coming true...

In ancient mythology, two figures are linked with this sign — the first being King Zeus. Zeus — or Jupiter — as the Romans usually called him, — was the king of the gods and ruled the roost on Mount Olympus, and his majestic, kingly ways tell us a lot about Sagittarius. On a good day, generally speaking, he was magnanimous, kind and generous. But if you dared to cross him, then he'd fill the skies with lightning! That's par for the course with latter-day Saggies too — try criticising one and just wait and see what happens. The heavens will erupt with fiery epithets, not to mention a few choice insults! Five minutes later, though, all will be forgotten — and more than likely forgiven, too, for Sagittarians rarely nurse grudges. Zeus would also "change shape" to get what he wanted — which, more often than not, was an amorous conquest. In a similar way, Sagittarian men and women can be brilliant actors, too, adept at playing the roles that they think will get them what they want. In fact, their acting skill is so great, it can even win them Oscars — think of Bette Midler and Jane Fonda, two award-winning Sagittarians!

The second mythic figure that's linked with Sagittarius is that of Chiron the centaur — or the archer, as he's sometimes more commonly called. Half-man, half-beast, Chiron's like all those Saggies who have their "head in the clouds" on a pretty permanent basis, but also need their feet on the ground as well. Just like Chiron, whose arrows sometimes went astray, Saggies need to pay attention to whatever task is in hand. Sometimes, alas, though, they find that awfully hard. That's because their eyes are firmly fixed on the far horizon and the very next rainbow. And no sooner have they fired an arrow than they're reaching for the next...

Physically, Sagittarians can quite easily be spotted, for they're usually head and shoulders above nearly everyone else in the room. Both the men and the women tend to be built a bit larger than average; just like their nature, their frame is pretty generous. You'll sometimes find the odd Sagittarian who's somewhat shorter than average, but this is definitely an exception rather than the rule. Many archers have a long, fine-featured, slightly horsy look about them, along with a telltale habit of forever flicking back their hair. With their bounding walk and lolloping stride, archers are great "outdoors" people, too. They're always at their best when they're striding or riding the landscape, and it's exactly what suits them best. And provided they get sufficient fresh air and exercise, you'll usually find the archer very, very rarely gets ill.

Many of the traits of the Sagittarian adult can be observed even in childhood. All the world's a playground to Sag, and there's a sense in which they never lose touch with their precious "inner child." Even Saggie youngsters are fiercely independent, and the smallest Sagittarians still need plenty of space to roam. For their own sake, do set some boundaries and enforce them — so your little Sag will grow up knowing that even *they* must submit to a higher order sometimes — not to mention a system of rules! Needless to say, though, it will probably go against the grain!

One of Sagittarius' greatest assets is their truly positive outlook. Archers rarely succumb to depression or despair, and even when they suffer quite serious reverses in their lives, they're always quick to bounce right back. Sagittarius is the sign of the incurable optimist, and the phrase "Something's bound to turn up" is never far from their lips, even in times of relentless adversity — rather like Mr Micawber, that much-loved figure of Charles Dickens' creation. There's no denying, indeed, that their tireless trust in the outworkings of fate goes a long way towards creating positive results, for life has a curious way of rewarding their faith — and, very often, tenfold.

But there's a downside to all this bright-eyed enthusiasm, too, for the archers' pressing need to have everything work out their way can occasionally cloud their judgement. Rather like their fellow fire sign, Aries, Sagittarians act on intuition, rather than cool, deductive logic. Since they often grasp the essentials of a situation in a mere split-second, their judgement, though speedy, is very often correct. But Sagittarians rarely see the drawbacks of any scheme they like the sound of, and their optimism, if unchecked, can lead them down some pretty dark "blind alleys".

No matter how gloomy the business forecasts, though, there's nothing that a party can't cure, and like their opposite sign of Gemini, most archers are wildly sociable. There's little they like more than going out — with the exception of partying at home. You'll always find Saggies aplenty vying for the limelight at the latest bar or bistro, art, film or theatre preview — and usually long before the rest of the "in-crowd" gets there. Sagittarians always like to be right where the action is, and this can sometimes make them elitist. So if you're planning on mixing with the archer, make sure you're au fait with the latest books or, better still, the latest Booker Prize winner ..for archers love mingling with celebrities and media stars almost more than anything else.

Sagittarians are inveterate globetrotters, especially in their youth, and until they've explored the planet, they're often afflicted with chronic wanderlust. These are the sort of people who always keep a suitcase ready-packed in their closet — and who'll jet off to Mexico or Delhi at merely a moment's notice. Bold, fearless Sagittarians are the free spirits of the zodiac, and few things are more precious than their freedom. They usually design themselves a lifestyle that gives them plenty of space to travel, along with a partner who likes travelling too. Or they choose partner who'll "keep the home fires burning", whilst they, by contrast, keep moving ever onwards. Rather like Libra, Sagittarius is one of the zodiac's Great Romantics — but unlike the classic Libran, though, most Saggies are slow to wed. Many remain free-spirited travellers and diehard bachelors their whole life through — or at least until they reach midlife, when coupledom may start to appeal.

Sagittarius rules the ninth house in the natural zodiac and is the sign of "long journeys", both inner and outer. So Sagittarians love to traverse the worlds of the imagination and the intellect too, as well as the outer world of travel. All Sagittarians are philosophers at heart, and there are few archers who don't have a sense of a Power greater than themselves — even if they rarely express it in words. Sagittarius rules the church and also religion, and although you'll find many Sagittarian preachers, not all archers believe in going to church. Sagittarians are just as likely to experience God whilst they're walking their dog on a windy hilltop, or gazing out on a glorious sunset. Spending time amid the glories of the natural world or the animal kingdom is often the Sagittarian way of worship, and their belief that God is everywhere — and in everything — has much in common with ancient religions.

Sagittarius' large-hearted nature means they also loathe injustice and you'll often find them fighting battles or "crusades" of a political nature. Sagittarians usually like to tackle the larger issues of the day. Remember Jane Fonda and her Vietnam campaigning? That combination of actress-turned-crusader is pure Sagittarian fire. Sometimes the archer's "battles" turn into legalistic ones, for the more extreme kind of Sag has a chronic "know-it-all" streak. They'll never, never admit that they're wrong, and will often go to court to prove it. More often than not, though, their disputes and disagreements blow over and are usually forgotten long before they ever get that far...

Traveller, adventurer, partygoer, actor and diehard optimist — Sagittarians can be all these things, it's true, but they're also romantics and dreamers — and no-one's dreams are bigger than theirs. This is the sign of the Grand Plan, the Great American Dream and the Big Adventure. The stuff of other people's fantasies is Sagittarius' staple diet, and to the archer, life without it would be meaningless. Think of that great archer, Walt Disney, and his dream of producing *Snow White* — the first-ever animated feature film? Where would the world of children's films be now if Walt hadn't dared to dream his "impossible dream?"... Sagittarians are the great risk-takers of the zodiac, and when their dreams come true, they can change the course of history — provided they keep their feet on the ground long enough to make them happen. Not long enough to let the grass grow under them, of course. No one, not even the archers' worst enemy would wish *that* fate on them — just long enough to get the job done. Finding and keeping a creative balance between their own precious dreams and the practical side of life is probably the archers' greatest challenge — and it's a task that can keep them thoroughly occupied for a lifetime!

On my astrological travels, I've noticed that Sagittarians often have a passion for astronomy, and you'll frequently find a rather expensive telescope set up in the archer's backyard. It's an essential tool for

Sagittarians' life journey, if you think about it — for their favourite occupation is usually looking at the stars. That's where they're aiming their arrows, after all. And you know the funniest thing? They very often get there too...

✗ Sagittarius and Money

Putting it as plainly as a Sagittarius well might, this is a sign that, quite simply, *loves* money. Archers are aware, even from the tenderest age, that money can buy them fun, plane tickets and great new comic books, as well as a whole host of other things that make them feel good, too — and that most definitely means that money is a seriously good thing! Sagittarians don't fret or worry about money like some of the other signs of the zodiac, though, and they also believe that they're entitled to have as much as they want. That's not so surprising when you think about it, really, for what else would you expect from a sign that's ruled by Jupiter — the undisputed planet of prosperity, wealth and plenty?

Despite the fact that Sagittarians are so fond of money, though, and often end up amassing a considerable store of wealth, this is not the most money-minded sign that you could ever hope to meet. Money for its own sake means little to the archer. No, Sagittarians value money first and foremost because it's their passport to freedom and independence, and these are the things they value way and beyond mere money in the bank. Sagittarians use money to broaden their horizons, but never to make themselves "safe". To the archer, security resides not in things or their bank account, but in ideas and philosophies — and the power to dictate their own destiny. Security, to a Sag, is the ability to jet off to Katmandhu or the South Pacific whenever they feel like it, or to take six months off and just sit down and write a novel. And that's why they like making money — over and above the "treats" it can buy them. Stacking up a bulging deposit account, or endlessly investing in land and property, quite simply just isn't their scene...

Down the centuries, Sagittarius has acquired the reputation of being just about the luckiest sign in the zodiac, financially speaking, and observation shows that this link is quite well-founded. Despite the fact that money has a habit of running through their fingers, rather than gathering interest in their deposit account, it also seems to turn up just when the archer needs it most. This is the kind of person who'll be down to literally their last penny, and then wake up one morning to discover they've won the Lottery ...or a horse race ...or a competition they entered months ago on the spur of the moment because they "had a feeling that they should".

If the truth be told, Sagittarius' financial "luck" stems largely from their positive attitude. Good things happen to these people because they think good things will happen. Sagittarians rarely lie awake at night worrying if they'll have enough money for their bills, expenses and school fees. They focus far more strongly on the *solutions* to their money problems, rather than the problems themselves. And because they tend to assume that any problems are strictly temporary, more often than not they *do* tend to go away... Money holds no fears for the archer. They expect to make it, they expect to have sufficient for their needs and more besides, and because their financial activities are all backed up with such sunny optimism, very often they tend to pay off. Not that the archer's financial ventures *always* pay off, of course. Exceptions do occur, and sometimes spectacularly so, because Sagittarians sail close to the wind. Very often, things may work at the very last minute ...and the archer will escape from the jaws of financial disaster in the nick of time. Once in a while, they don't quite make it, and they lose their shirt or go bankrupt. But even when things don't pan out, and the archer takes some losses, you can bet your bottom dollar that they'll soon be back with a brave new venture and the money-go-round will promptly start to spin again!

Investment consultant Dan Pallant has Sagittarius on the ascendant and, like all Jupiter people, he's "always looking for the really big deal, the big dream of a scheme that will put everything to rights". Pallant amassed a considerable fortune during the UK property boom of the 1970s, but lost most of it overnight when the market suddenly crashed without warning. Undeterred, he developed a keen interest in financial forecasting — who wouldn't, after such an experience? He then devised an astrological computer programme that helped him to build up another fortune in the stock market boom of the 80s! Such a riches-to-rags-and-back-again story is pure Sagittarius, but Pallant freely admits that he isn't all that interested in money. "I like having the money because it buys me plenty of time to do what I want", he claims. "That's what matters most — my freedom!" Pallant is also a great believer in the classic archer "hunch". Like other financial astrologers, he's noted that he and his fellow Sagittarians do best when they follow their intuition, which, generally speaking, is usually superb. Archers can be almost psychic when it comes to doing deals or choosing the right stocks and shares, and, so long as they follow their "nose", it will rarely lead them astray. Sagittarius is the sign of the speculator par excellence: they love to gamble and take risks, and their risk-taking often pays off. Archers also often use more esoteric methods of forecasting to effect, such as financial astrology, or even the *I Ching*.

Another key factor in Sagittarius' "money luck" is the fact that they're often so generous. Sagittarians enjoy making money, but they like to give it away too, and some of the greatest philanthropists of our time — like Andrew Carnegie and J.P. Getty — were born under Sagittarius. The latter may have been stingy with his house-guests (blame that on his heavy Saturn influence), but he certainly endowed a great many good causes. Few signs are quicker than the archer to lend money to those in need — and considering their shrewdness, they can often be quite a "soft touch" — especially when it's their friends or family who need help. But when people give freely, as archers often do, life usually returns the favour....

When it comes to managing their day-to-day finances, most Sagittarians cope pretty well. Their quick wits and sharp intelligence mean they're adept at juggling their funds to meet their obligations, and they're skilled at moving their money around to take advantage of special deals. They're often drawn to "get-rich-quick" schemes, and more often than not they succeed. At the end of the day, however, Sagittarians are usually happier when they're making money, rather than looking after it. Their innate tendency to focus on "the big picture", or to "see the forest, rather than the trees", means that they very quickly grow bored with dealing with minor financial details. Most Sagittarians have an irresistible tendency to round off accounts and figures, whether up or down, and to deal in generalities. The concept of "looking after the pennies" usually sounds rather dull to archers, who forget that if you *do* look after the pennies, then the pounds will take care of themselves! Sagittarians can rarely be bothered to check their invoices and statements and their lack of attention to detail can sometimes cost them dear indeed.

The best course of action — moneywise — for archers is to focus on what they do best (making money) and leave its management to someone else. It's usually best if outside professionals are employed for this task, rather than the archer's spouse or partner. Sagittarians have a habit of assuming that they're always right, and may all too easily question their nearest and dearest's figures! Calling in the professionals may involve some extra expense, but it will certainly make for a happier household in the long run. And since Sagittarians place a premium on domestic harmony, they'll probably wind up making far more money as a result.

Sagittarians excel at making money, it's true, but they're also very good at spending it. This is a sign that's well-noted for its extravagance, and many archers live well beyond their means — particularly if Jupiter, their ruler, is badly aspected in their horoscope. *These*

Sagittarians — and luckily, they're in the minority — are the most spendthrift people you could ever hope to meet, forever treating their friends at expensive restaurants, running up their charge accounts and playing the gaming tables. They often have real difficulty in dealing with financial reality, along with a total inability to deny themselves anything at all. All Sagittarians can create excellent budgets when they put their minds to it, and even the most hopelessly extravagant can stick within their limits when they really have to. But it's far, far better for them to do this out of choice — otherwise they'll end up being forced to by the bank! The thoroughgoing vagueness of archers about financial details and records means they sometimes run up debts without realizing, which can damage their credit-rating, too.

Archers can be vague when it comes to borrowing money — and also, as we've seen, when it comes to lending it, too. Generosity is one of their very great virtues, and most of the time they'll lend their money quite freely, or even give it away. Sagittarians rarely keep proper records, though, and are often quite forgetful about who they've lent to and how much. And, if they can possibly afford to do so, then, in true Jupiterian fashion, they will often turn their loan into a gift, instead. But once in a while, a more shadowy side of their nature rears its head, for in vivid contrast to their normal generosity, they can sometimes be most punctilious — like the man who lends you an umbrella and then asks for it back when it's raining! Lulled into a false sense of security, you're naturally very surprised to see the archer turn up at your door on the appointed date to collect the money that's due. And heaven help you if you don't have it, down to the very last penny.

There's a bit of a double standard in operation here, for lending an archer money *can* be a bit like kissing it goodbye. For when you call to collect a loan you've made them, you may find your archer friend has suddenly left town, or by a strange coincidence they're suddenly clean out of funds ...else their waiting for a cheque to come in, so they can't possibly pay you back until at least the end of next week. Yes, collecting a debt from an archer can sometimes be quite a challenge.

When archers find themselves in a tight financial corner, though, their faith in a positive outcome will usually pull them through. Rather than rushing around trying to hustle extra money, their best course of action is usually to still their conscious minds and tune in to their powerful intuition. For when they relax and let their "inner radar" do the work, the solution to their problems will come in a blinding flash, often in the form of a powerful, intuitive insight that clearly shows them their best path forward.

Despite any temporary shortfalls they may sometimes experience, archers have a way of always coming out on top — and usually to the tune of a handsome profit. They're supremely gifted at getting themselves out of tight financial corners, too, for they'll always ask for help if they feel they really need it. And most of the time they get it, too — for who, after all, could refuse the king of the gods?

✗ The Spending Style Of Sagittarius

Sagittarians can rank among the zodiac's biggest earners, but they're often way up there among its biggest spenders too. This is a fire sign, and money can sometimes burn a hole in their pocket — quite literally! The general rule with Sagittarius is, if you've got it, why not spend it? — and there's little they like better than going on a spree. It must be said, though, that archers are also generous to a fault — and although they enjoy nothing better than spending money at the very finest stores, they're bound to come back with lots of gifts for their loved ones, too.

Archers are renowned for their big spending and extravagance, but these habits stem primarily from their positive philosophy of life. Sagittarians love to spend money, because it's a way of demonstrating their deep-rooted belief in the abundance of the universe and their faith that there'll always be enough. And, more to the point, that there'll always be plenty more where the last lot came from. Since archers live so strongly in the present, they don't always stop to ask, "Can I really afford it?" — which means their charge cards and bank account do go overdrawn *very* easily. If overdrafts didn't exist, the archer would have had to invent them, along with credit cards and charge cards, too, all of which are essential to the Sagittarians' lifestyle. Debt never worries them — remember, there'll always be enough. The urge to overspend is observable even in childhood, and if the archer's parents are wise, they'll try to instil the importance of developing good money habits from the earliest age. This isn't always an easy task, though, for the archer's natural leanings are *always* towards excess.

The Sagittarian lifestyle is, ideally, quite luxurious — though I've known archers who live quite happily on a shoestring, provided, of course, that they've sufficient "inner freedom". Travel rates highly on the archers' list of priorities, especially in youth, when their feet are constantly itchy. They'll also spend freely on videos and cameras to record their many travels. Books and education rank high on the archers' spending lists, for the archer values mental journeys almost as much as those of the body. Sagittarian homes are invariably crammed with books from floor to ceiling, and they sometimes become "eternal students", collecting multiple degrees and diplomas, even when well into their forties when, at long last, they begin to think of settling down...

And when archers do "settle down", their attention usually turns to property. Here, as elsewhere, they like to think *BIG*, and archer homes are mostly elegant, high-ceilinged places, with bags and bags of space! The decor will probably be cosmopolitan in tone, with solid wooden furniture and lots of souvenirs of their travels.

Sagittarians love entertaining, too, and little delights them more than treating their friends at the latest new bistro. Should they wish to entertain you at home, though, never refuse the invite, for Jupiter-ruled people spoil their guests every bit as much as Leos. So you can expect the very best in food and wines, and also in party guests! Weather permitting, you'll probably dine al fresco, for there's little they like better than a barbecue. Extravagant, stylish, elegant — that's

Sagittarian style for you. It's a casual kind of elegance, though, for they hate to feel too stuffy and formal.

The Sagittarian penchant for low-key chic is also reflected in their style of dressing, which veers at all times between the extremes of "sloppy" and "smart". Archers love to shop for clothes, and designer casuals — often with an "ethnic look" — are always their favourite attire. Left to their own devices, they'd rather wear colourful sweaters, even to the smartest gatherings and functions — their closets are stuffed with them, knitted in every colour of the rainbow. They like sensible, functional footwear, like cowboy boots or brogues, and they adore wearing ponchos or capes. Top it all off with a wide-brimmed hat, and you've the perfect ensemble for a sporty Sagittarian. Since archers enjoy spending so much time outdoors, they also buy lots of sportswear, and usually from the very best stores. So, whether they're mounted on their horse or headed for their yacht, they'll always be superbly turned-out!

✗ Sagittarius: Saving & Investing

Astute readers may have guessed by now that, though Sagittarians are usually quite fortunate financially, they're not necessarily the biggest savers of the zodiac. Archers are often the big spenders of the zodiac, but it's very rare indeed for their savings to match the outflow. And the few archers who *do* excel at salting their pennies away will more than likely have a healthy dose of Saturn in their horoscope, too, or maybe even

Capricorn rising. That kind of combination can — and did — produce a financial giant such as J.P. Getty.

The greatest motivational force in Sagittarius' financial life is the ever-present urge to keep expanding their horizons. They see little point in keeping money for tomorrow if they can put it to good use today, and that's an attitude they tend to have even quite early in childhood. The archer's antipathy to saving starts young — even eight-year old Sagittarians will constantly overdraw their pocket money if you let them — and they'll only ever save if they feel there's a good incentive. Young archers may be coaxed into saving if there's a trip to Disneyland in the offing — but saving just "for saving's sake" will rarely ever appeal.

A similar principle operates with older archers, too. Sagittarians will save hard and fast for a round-the-world ticket, or a study course or classes. They may also slash their spending in order to finance their speculation or a business that's caught their interest. But since their attention span is so short, short-term savings goals of a year or so at most are usually the only kind they favour.

Investment-wise, most archers have a similarly short-term outlook. The Sagittarian investment motto is "Get in fast, get out faster!", and, as with all their financial activities, they invest on the basis of what their intuition is telling them. This, it must be said, is usually excellent. Since archers hate to feel restricted or tied down in any way, they usually steer well clear of long-term investments like pensions and insurance. Spouses and partners may find that they're left to sort out these arrangements for themselves, since the archer finds it hard to focus on maturity dates so far in the future. This attitude sometimes changes, though, when the archer reaches midlife and looks at investment in a more down-to-earth way.

When it comes to speculation, though, it's a totally different story. Sagittarians have a real "nose" or "sixth sense" for knowing exactly which companies and enterprises will prosper — which means the stock market is often one of their most fruitful fields of investment. With their split-second judgement and frequent "lucky hunches", many Sagittarians do so well in the markets that they even become brokers themselves. Archers enjoy the exciting, volatile buzz of the market, with its thrilling ups and downs and its potential for huge returns and making fortunes overnight. There's also the chance of losing them, too, but most archers' fearless outlook means they're better equipped to handle risk and speculation than just any other sign in the zodiac.

The stock market is a short-term, high-risk, high-return vehicle — and that suits most archers right down to the ground. Problems may occur, though, if they're too impatient for a stock to reach its peak — a classic archer failing — or if they fall into the trap of thinking that a particular investment will rise forever. When this happens, they're likely to fall to earth with a crash. But, naturally enough, they'll always bounce back. The stock market will often be the archers' happiest hunting-ground, but they can also fare well with foreign investments and businesses with foreign connections, such as import-export and the travel trade. Sagittarians often find their greatest profits come from overseas ventures, so Sagittarian investors should pay particular attention to large, promising-looking corporations with lots of foreign outlets or overseas subsidiaries.

Investing in airlines, motor car firms and railway transport can be lucrative for archers, along with air and ocean cargo, cruise lines, and any form of long-distance travel and communication. Educational ventures, such as schools and colleges, can also be lucrative, along with career guidance agencies, leisure resorts and casinos. Publishing — especially self-publishing — is traditionally a profitable area, as are newspapers, magazines, journals and periodicals. Finally, many Sagittarians profit handsomely from investing in bloodstock or sport in all its guises.

↗ The Earning Power Of Sagittarius

The French Surrealist poet Francis Picabia once said, "If you want to have fresh ideas, you should change them as often as your shirts" — and that little phrase sums up the archer's approach to earning. Ideally, Sagittarians like their work to be just the way they like everything else in life — bold innovative, and supremely varied! Like their fellow fire signs, Aries and Leo, Sagittarians view work as a quest and a challenge — but, above all, a great adventure. To archers, work is far more than simply a means of financing their lifestyle, which, as we've seen, often takes some financing. It's also a wonderful way to explore the world, broaden their horizons and develop their own theories on the meaning of life. So whether you find them working as preachers, teachers or even bartenders — all classic archer occupations, they'll usually find a way of doing just that.

All Sagittarians firmly believe that they were born to lead. But, despite their natural tendency to assume an executive role whenever possible, they aren't always wildly ambitious — despite the fact that they always "aim high". This may sound like a contradiction in terms, but ambition simply isn't the most relevant concept here. That's because Sagittarians rarely set out with any fixed goals in life. Sagittarians prefer their goals to evolve from day to day, or from year to year, as they canter along life's highway. That way they rarely get pinned down to anything — which suits them just fine, because they like keeping their options open. So, because the archers' goals are always so changeable, striving to reach them is often an irrelevance. Chances are, even when those goals do become reality, they may well have forgotten what they were in the first place! They've fired off a great many arrows since then, you see — so many that they've probably lost count.

Unlike their astrological neighbours, Scorpio and Capricorn, Sagittarians are rarely single-minded about their work. Nor are they ruthless enough to step on others toes on their way to the top — apart from those they happen to offend by their notorious lack of tact. Not that they view their working life as "climbing the ladder" in any case, for in the glorious cinema of their minds, they're already at the top — and have been for quite some time. To a Sagittarius, that's their natural birthright. And because they truly believe it, from the bottom of their generous hearts, they very often get there, too...

Sagittarians dream their dreams on a somewhat larger scale than the rest of humanity, for the archer's dreams are invariably *BIG*: like travelling round the world a dozen times or writing a best-selling novel. These are the fantasies they lull themselves to sleep with at night, the glorious visions that lie tucked away in their heads. But although they do like to see their dreams come true, they rarely get hung up about winning. Sure, it's nice to win — to clinch that deal or finance that new venture. But win or lose, archers know that something else will always turn up. And they also believe that it's "better to travel than to arrive" ...and as long they're having fun, well, that's all that really matters.

When Sagittarians choose a career, money is rarely their prime criterion. Freedom, flexibility, and the ability to exercise their theories are far more important than money in the bank, and they're likely to trade a well-paid, boring job for a lower-paid one that's more exciting. But of course, if there's any way they can command a six-figure salary, a lavish expense account *and* all the challenge and excitement that their fiery heart desires, well, so very much the better. Steven Spielberg's hero, Indiana Jones, is the classic Sagittarian role-model, and a career such as Jones's, offering foreign travel, danger and unusual assignments in abundance, is surely every archer's dream...

Sagittarius is the sign of the "higher mind", and most archers you'll meet are simply brimming with ideas: in fact, they're happier working with ideas than with things, or even, in truth, with people. That's why you'll find so many archers working in law, academia and business consultancy. Dealing with the nitty-gritty of a production line or supervising a building programme really isn't their scene. They'd far rather spend their time theorizing, hypothesizing and expanding the mental boundaries in their chosen field of endeavour.

Along with boundless optimism and a cheery, heartwarming manner, archers are blessed with an ability to see the "broader picture", and sometimes even the future, too: for often they have a very bankable talent for sensing future trends. Some archers know exactly what people will want to see, hear, read or wear several years in advance, and when this intuitive ability is combined with entrepreneurial flair and their Jupiterian penchant for talking others into backing their ideas, it can be the stuff great fortunes are made of.

Sagittarian filmmaker Steven Spielberg, whose glittering career ranks as one of the great success stories of our time, provides a superb example of an archer who persuaded others to put money on his dreams. Even as a child, growing up in middle-class America, Spielberg dreamed of directing feature films. Spielberg possessed the classic Sagittarian qualities of optimism and enthusiasm in abundance — he ate, drank, slept and dreamed movie-making, and he never entertained the thought that he could ever possibly fail. At the age of 17, he sneaked on to the sound stages at Universal Pictures and spent a whole summer hanging around the film lots. Many months later, he was finally given a job! Spielberg went on to make some of the highest grossing feature films in history — *Jaws, Close Encounters of the Third Kind* and, of course, *ET* — thus proving once and for all that if you do what you truly love, the money will usually follow — and sometimes in truly vast amounts!

Not that Spielberg didn't make the odd mistake: some of his films, such as "1941", were major flops, and in the movie industry, a flop costs millions. But in true archer fashion, Spielberg always bounced back, usually with yet another high-grossing idea drawn from the treasure trove of his childhood. For, like most Sagittarians, he's never lost touch with the magic of his early years. That's the essence of his work, and also the secret of his success.

Not all archers succeed in carving out a dazzling niche for themselves in the glitzy world of the motion picture industry, but even those who content themselves with a less glittering career always need certain qualities in their work in order to feel fulfilled. Firstly, it should be flexible: archers are easily bored, and find a strict routine is anathema. Archers always like to feel that they're in charge of their own destiny, even when they're working for someone else. Ideally, they'll have the freedom to dictate their own work-schedule: to take a long lunch-break one day and work later the next.

Intuition, optimism and insight are the great gifts that Sagittarius brings to the workplace and they should never be underrated. But sometimes, archers get so preoccupied with "the big picture" — or the broader brush-strokes of the job — that they totally neglect other aspects of their work.

Looking at the sport of archery can provide some useful insights into Sagittarius' work habits, and the precise kind of lessons they usually need to learn. As every archer knows, hitting the bull's-eye isn't just a question of aiming your arrow any old how and shooting it off into the wild blue yonder. Striking the target requires focus, concentration and presence of mind — and these are qualities it takes years to acquire. Sagittarians sometimes lack these abilities, and it causes them all sorts of problems. They can have trouble feeling committed, or forget to stick to deadlines — but the biggest problem is "taking care of the details" — or even, just finishing the job. Sagittarians are superb at dashing off a management report, a painting, or the first draft of a novel, and in record time, too. But they seldom enjoy the process of refining and perfecting their work. This needn't be a problem if they're working with more practical signs, like Virgo. But if they're left in *sole* charge of a project, then disaster can sometimes ensue...

Here's an example of the kind of thing that can happen when archers omit to prepare or finish their projects. A publisher friend of mine once commissioned a book from a Sagittarian author — a work about a spiritual guru, as I recall, a favourite archer topic. (Sagittarians *love* gurus or spiritual masters — they're among the few people on this earth who they think have anything to teach them!) The manuscript was duly handed in on time, and all seemed well at first. But when it came to editing the book, well, then the trouble started. The author considered his book was *perfect*, and not a comma should be changed, but in reality, however, it left much to be desired. Letters began to fly like snowflakes, but then an even bigger faux-pas came to light. Sagittarians always initiate projects in a huge flurry of enthusiasm, and this author was no exception. Other writers might have sought permission before beginning a biography, but this fellow felt he was above all that. Of course the guru would like the book, simply no question about it! In the midst of the editorial wrangles, however, he suddenly had a bright idea. Why not send the manuscript to the guru, get his seal of approval and silence those publishers once and for all? But much to his chagrin, word promptly came back that No, the guru *didn't* like the book — and besides, no-one had asked him if he wanted it written in the first place! Result: one red-faced Sagittarian author, who's learned the hard way that it pays to do the groundwork first.

This cautionary tale illustrates the kind of lessons that many Sagittarians are faced with when their sun progresses into Capricorn and they come down to earth with a bump! Higher education is very helpful here, for it teaches archers to be more logical in their thinking, as well as how to work steadily — and how to meet those deadlines. Happily, many archers *do* learn to be more grounded during their Capricorn progression, and go on to achieve great things. Earlier on, though, they often promise things they can't deliver and take on jobs and projects that are way beyond their abilities. Sooner or later, most Sagittarians learn to temper their dreams with realism — although they still need to have one or two wildly impractical fantasies tucked away somewhere that they can dream about at night — for a world without dreams would be a lacklustre place indeed!

✗ The Sagittarian Boss

By and large, Sagittarian bosses are happy to rule the roost, although their need to move around a lot means they're seldom to be found in the office! As executives, they can be patriarchal, generous and kind — but also blunt, authoritarian and even tactless on occasion. They're great at boosting morale and raising the company's spirits when things look bleak — and their optimism, along with their hunches, has the strangest way of paying off. They *are* lucky, there's no doubt about it. There's just one thing to remember, though: never, never tell them lies. They'd far rather hear the truth about something, no matter how ghastly it is!

✗ The Sagittarian Employee

Sagittarian employees like to keep on the move, too, and you'll find a great many archers "working their passage" in various cities round the world, often as waiters and bar-staff. Their cheery personality ensures they're always in great demand, and they ooze self-confidence at interviews. Be aware that they are prone to promising more than they can deliver, though, or you might find you've hired a "bilingual secretary" who can speak only pidgin French and types with two fingers! It's also good to be aware of the archer's work preferences and allot tasks accordingly. A Sagittarian will rarely feel at home with fiddly tasks like bookkeeping or copy-editing. Far better to employ them in sales or marketing, since their sales pitches are second to none and they can talk just about anybody into buying whatever they're selling! But watch out for their tendency to give away huge discounts, or the company's bottom line could very quickly suffer!

♐ Sagittarius & Career

Sagittarians relish any kind of career or profession that allows them to expand their horizons, either inwardly and outwardly, and that allows them to express their flamboyance, or simply to act and talk "big". Many archers broaden their horizons in a literal sense by working in the travel industry. They'll work as airline pilots or stewardesses, or even in a desk job — just so long as they can travel. Freedom means far more to them than money, so any job that keeps them mobile is bound to hold great appeal. These can include journalism, broadcasting, or sales and marketing.

Our modern word "jovial" actually comes from the Latin word for Jupiter, and with their ribald sense of humour, Jupiter-born people have a talent to amuse. Think of flame-haired comedienne Bette Midler, with her wisecracks and bawdy humour — as well as cartoonists James Thurber, and Terry Gilliam, of Monty Python fame. The world of showbusiness is packed with Sagittarians, and more comics, singers and rock stars have their sun in this sign than almost any other. There's Tina Turner, Billy Connolly and Pamela Stephenson, Frank Sinatra, and the late Noel Coward. With its irresistible combination of grand visions, large budgets and huge egos, many archers are also drawn to films and TV. And whilst not every archer attains the fame of Steven Spielberg, a great many *do* succeed in making it to the top. Think of Walt Disney, Terry Gilliam and Woody Allen — as well as the thousands of lesser-known archer directors and producers calling the shots in studios all over the world.

Sagittarians are justly famed for their intelligence and insight, and many find their niche in teaching, lecturing or the law. Although this sign is traditionally associated with higher education, religion and philosophy, most archers have such a love of giving advice that they'll teach anything from sailing to Greek! A great many Sagittarians also work their way up through the legal profession to eventually sit on the judge's bench, where they can exercise their talent for "taking the broader view." Before they can aspire to such lofty heights, however, they'll need to polish their listening skills. For although they love to teach and preach, Sagittarians aren't always good listeners! Others are drawn to religion and the ministry, where they can inspire and uplift their "flock" on a regular weekly basis.

Sagittarius is also a highly creative sign, and many archers make their career in the arts. Some of the greatest authors in history, from Jane Austen to Mark Twain, were born under this sign. Archers like Arthur C. Clarke have used their gifts to explore the imagination; others, like Andrew Carnegie used them to write about positive thinking. Many other archers find a home in the world of publishing — which, with its speculative nature and potentially high returns, is a classic Sagittarian profession!

With their love of the great outdoors, many archers excel as sportsmen. Top cricketer Ian Botham is well known for his archer style outspokenness, as well as his sporting gifts. Other Saggies work in sports and leisure centres, run farms or nursery gardens, or even work as forest rangers! Most Sagittarians love the animal kingdom, too, and a great many of their number are drawn to veterinary science. Others combine their love of animals and gambling by working as tipsters or on the turf. And even if they don't work with animals for a living, you may well find an archer manning the phones or at your local animal shelter come evenings and weekends. The one animal centre where you *won't* find many archers working is down at the local zoo: they hate to see creatures confined and restricted and, deep down, they'd love to send them all back into the wild!

In centuries gone by, the most natural occupation for a Sagittarian would surely have been as an explorer, forever heading off in search of pastures new. But these days, few places on the planet remain unexplored and uncharted, with the exception, perhaps, of the world of the paranormal. So maybe that explains why so many archers are astrologers, mediums and healers. These occupations allow them to explore the "inner worlds", to look into the future and to be as eccentric as they like! Prophetic visions, ethnic gear and flowing silk scarves are all totally *de rigeur* in the soothsayer's tent and that suits the archer just fine...

✗ Sagittarius: Keys to Financial Success

- DO try and curb your natural tendency to "round everything up" when you come to balance your chequebook. Watch those pennies, and you'll soon have more pounds than you know what to do with...

- DO remember that when you have major financial decisions to make, your intuition is always your best friend. So listen to it!

- DO be ruthlessly honest with yourself about your real-life strengths and weaknesses. Take the stuff you don't like, which probably includes bookkeeping and balancing your chequebook, and delegate it to someone else.

- DO remember that words have power, and always think before you speak. You can lose valuable friends and contacts through your occasional outbreaks of "foot-in-mouth" disease and it really isn't worth it.

- DO think big, and dream even bigger — but always remember to stay grounded, too. Think of your long-term financial future and open a "Financial Independence Account" today.

Rich & Famous Sagittarians

Nostradamus
Ludwig Van Beethoven
Toulouse-Lautrec
William Blake
Winston Churchill
Frank Zappa
Frank Sinatra
Laurens Van der Post
Edna O'Brien
Christina Onassis
Lord Forte
Andrew Carnegie
Walt Disney
Steven Spielberg
Terry Gilliam
Kim Basinger
Jimi Hendrix
Sammy Davis Jn
Joan Armatrading
Jose Carreras
Christopher Plummer
Christopher Cazenove
Kiefer Sutherland
Kirk Douglas

Mark Twain
George Eliot
Jane Austen
Madame Tussaud
Edith Piaf
J.P. Getty
Fritz Lang
Otto Preminger
Quentin Crisp
The Aga Khan
Uri Geller
Alexander Solzhenitshyn
Keith Richards
Woody Allen
Jenny Agutter
Ellen Burstyn
Tina Turner
Dervla Murphy
Jane Fonda
Bette Midler
Lee Remick
Kenneth Branagh
Don Johnson
Richard Pryor

♑

CAPRICORN
December 22nd to January 20th

As Christmas approaches, there's a subtle, but unmistakeable, shift in the atmosphere. The days are at their shortest now, in the northern hemisphere at least, and the party-loving ambience of Sagittarius suddenly gives way to a more sober, introspective mood. Along with this newfound seriousness comes a corresponding shift in financial attitudes too, for in contrast to the happy-go-lucky approach of Sagittarius, few signs handle their money as cleverly as Capricorn.

Capricorn's season is also the great turning-point of the year — the time when we take stock and review the last twelve months: what we've achieved and where we're going... It's a time for looking back, but also a time for looking forward and setting new goals on every level: work, relationships — and, of course, our finances

"But hold it a moment", I hear you say, "...why so serious?" Isn't Christmas the party season too? Yes, of course it is — but those Christmas get-togethers proper that we know and love so well usually have far more to do with duty and family obligation than those rip-roaring office parties that happen earlier in the month. The keywords here are "ought to" and "should", rather than "want" or "like", for Christmas is a thoroughly Capricornian festival. We may not feel like giving presents, exchanging cards, or stuffing the turkey, but we do it anyway, for Capricorn has a lot to do with discipline and even self-denial; with keeping our loved ones happy instead of just having a jolly good time.

But please don't assume that Capricorns are kill-joys, for they can also be thoroughly abandoned when the mood or fancy takes them. Long before the birth of Christ, the old pagan feast of Saturnalia was celebrated at this time and, in ancient Rome, it was *the* great party of the year; the time when the class system went out of the window and masters and slaves caroused together. Drinking, eating and merrymaking were the order of the day and all and sundry just got down and boogied. That old pagan heritage can still be glimpsed at times, for few signs can let their hair down as well as Capricorn — provided they're in the mood, that is... Most of the time, though, they stick to the straight and narrow — that steep little path that leads right to the top of the mountain!

Capricorns have come in for a great deal of bad press over the centuries, owing largely to the fact that they're ruled by the planet Saturn. In ancient myth and early astrology alike, Saturn was regarded as the "baddie" of the cosmos, and to be born under his so-called "malefic" influence was generally regarded as pretty poor luck. Saturn-ruled Capricorns were invariably said to be in for a life of struggle and suffering, not to mention hard work. These days, however, astrologers take a far more enlightened view. Saturn is regarded more as the great teacher of the zodiac, valued for his wisdom, learning and insight — all gifts that Capricorns possess in abundance — once they've scrambled to the top of their mountain. To Capricorn, hard work and self-denial are often second nature. This is a sign that's born to work, to strive, and ultimately to overcome adversity, and Capricorn's deep, dark secret is that they wouldn't have it any other way!

Capricorn's animal symbol is the hardy mountain goat, and this also tells us much about the sign. Tough, hardy, independent and wily, goats can survive on next to nothing whilst they're headed for the top of the hillside, which is where Capricorns like to be most of all. They like the air up there — it feels so cool and clear — and being that high up makes them feel thoroughly in control. Wherever they find themselves, the goat must climb ...and so too must Capricorn, if they're to find fulfilment and happiness in life. If goats find obstacles in their path, like tin cans, hedgerows, or thistles, they'll munch their way through them! Human Capricorns are rather like that too, for although problems and setbacks may hold them up and slow them down, they'll rarely be stopped for long, and they'll certainly never think of giving up once they've set their sights on a goal.

The goat's determination in pursuing their aims is second to none, and when success depends on endurance and perseverance, they usually win out over all the other signs — even over Scorpio, traditionally regarded as the most persistent of souls. That's because Scorpios can get caught up in their emotions when they encounter too many problems — but a Capricorn? Never. They just battle on regardless, because they know full well that just like the tortoise in the children's fable, "slow and steady wins the race"...

Determination, patience and perseverance, then, are Capricorn's great strengths. But curiously enough, they're often pretty cautious too. Capricorn's measured, quasi-suspicious attitude to life, the universe and everything, is often quite all-pervasive, and can usually be traced back to childhood. Rather like Leo, the average Capricorn has usually had a somewhat difficult relationship with the father, who may have been absent physically, or simply just emotionally. Alternatively, he may have been a harsh, forbidding figure who withheld praise and encouragement, and left the little Capricorn with an insatiable need for approval and love: when Capricorn grows up, that need sometimes gets translated into an incredible longing for material wealth.

Because their early life is usually quite tough on some level, Capricorns grow up with an internal idea that that's just the way life is. Tough. So, because they *expect* life to be difficult, life usually obliges them by being just that — until they hit the age of thirty-five or forty, when a delightful change begins to happen. By this point, the Capricorn man or woman will usually have made their mark in terms of the things that really matter to them — career, home and maybe family — so they start to relax a little and let life begin to flow... This is often the point at which Capricorns begin to reap the rewards they've been working for so long — whether it's a seat on the board, a college lectureship, or even a partnership in the family firm. And since there's little that goats love more than being acknowledged for their achievements, it usually marks the start of a far happier phase of life.

Personality-wise, Capricorns are usually quite reserved, so they can often be quite hard to recognise in a crowd. Look out for people with stunning bone-structure — Saturn rules the skeleton and the typical Capricorn profile is truly to be envied. Think of Marlene Dietrich, Dame Maggie Smith, or David Bowie — all born with the Sun in Capricorn. The typical Capricorn complexion is often quite sallow, and even Capricorn blondes have a kind of special "dark" quality about them — think of Bowie again, or Eurythmics songstress Annie Lennox. But although goats can be quite shy and retiring by nature, and often prefer work to play, please don't think that they never go to parties! The typical Capricorn enjoys scaling the social ladder every bit as much as the corporate one, and since success, status and authority are so dear to them, they like nothing more than to hobnob with the rich, the famous and the powerful. So next time you're at a society bash, check out the well-dressed man or woman standing on the sidelines, slowly sipping their martini, and sizing up the gathering long and hard before "working the room"... Chances are they're a Capricorn. They'll probably find it hard to introduce themselves, since goats often suffer from a chronic lack of confidence.

But since a Capricorn will never pass up an opportunity to better themselves, either, then, sooner or later, they're bound to take the plunge.

Once you've gained a Capricorn's confidence and they trust you enough to tell you their age, you'll probably also be struck by the curious "ageing twist" that Saturn gives these people. Capricorn babies are the classic "little old men" types; they arrive on the planet looking wizened, wrinkled and serious, as though they know full well all the hard work that's in store for them. As children, teenagers and young adults, Capricorns often look old beyond their years, and seem to suffer from a kind of Atlas Complex, as though they're carrying all the worries of the world on their bony shoulders. But then, once they hit the age of 29-30 (known as the Saturn Return, or astrological "coming-of-age"), life begins to turn the clock back, and they look younger each year, instead of older. And the gift of looking ever-youthful as the years pass by is surely one to be coveted!

Capricorn children often seem grownup way beyond their years, preferring the company of adults to that of their peers, and taking on responsibilities at a very early age. Parents of Capricorn children generally have few problems getting them to do their homework or go to bed on time (Capricorns love routine), but they should aim to nurture their fragile self-esteem as much as is humanly possible. Self-doubt is Capricorn's middle name, and anything a wise parent can do to dispel it will be helpful in the extreme.

Astrologer Liz Greene points out how Capricorns often seem to take on a kind of self-imposed "hair-shirt" of denial or self-restriction, often in the shape of a family obligation. One Capricorn I know gave up a promising career in the theatre to marry and support his pregnant girlfriend, because he felt he should "do the right thing". Other Capricorns often end up spending many of their "best years" tending a sick or infirm parent, or sacrificing their own ambitions to work in the family business.

Like the proverbial mountain goat, Capricorns are usually robustly healthy, and people born under this sign often live to a ripe old age, provided they can overcome their number one health hazard — pessimism! Although they prefer to think of themselves as "practical" and "realistic", even the cheeriest Capricorn can be guilty of gloomy and negative thinking, which, if unchecked, can lead them deep into the swamps of depression. In the Middle Ages, astrologers called Capricorns the "melancholic" sign, and even their sense of humour tends to be somewhat wry and satirical! Think of Rowan Atkinson and his uniquely "sourpuss" wit.

But there's a wonderfully serene and peaceful side to Capricorn, too, and their calm, methodical nature and instinctive awareness of the rhythms and cycles of life are often seen at their best in the great outdoors. The great goat-god Pan is linked with this sign, and he usually makes his presence felt through a profound love of nature. Capricorns are often passionate gardeners: they have a real feeling for the earth, as well as a genuine talent for nurturing trees, plants and flowers. Given the opportunity, they also love to grow their own food. This side of Capricorn is rarely glimpsed before midlife — and certainly not before goats have achieved their more worldly ambitions.

The idea of Capricorn "returning to nature" may sound paradoxical, but as earthy and practical as they undoubtedly are, goats are also much given to visions, magic and mysteries. Capricorn is the sign of the millionaire, but it's also the sign of the mystic. Many great spiritual teachers and writers, such as Krishnamurti, Gurdjieff and Carlos Castaneda have been born under Capricorn's influence and the spiritual ambitions of this sign can be as lofty as the more mundane ones. As an astrologer, I've known Capricorns who spent the first part of their lives busily acquiring wealth, status and property, and were then seized by a strange sea-change of attitudes that made them totally rethink their priorities. They then spent the next few years just as busily dismantling the empire of money and possessions they'd built up, in a wild revisionist urge to free themselves of all their possessions! Such is the paradox of Capricorn. For despite their worldly longings and high-flying ambition, deep in the heart of every goat dwells a monk-like, hermit figure who's really quite content with very little indeed...

♑ Capricorn and Money

When it comes to earning, handling and making money, few signs have the edge on Capricorn. This is the sign of financial acumen par excellence, and no-one, but no-one, with the possible exception of Taurus and Cancer, both of whom are equally "green-fingered" in the monetary sense, can match the goat's skill and expertise in the financial domain. Watch and learn the goat's money tricks and secrets, for this is a field where they really come into their own.

Just like Taureans, Capricorns adore money, but for a totally different set of reasons. Taureans love money because it allows them to feel secure and indulge in the delights of the senses, but Capricorn's liking for cash has little to do with the pursuit of pleasure. The typical goat seeks dominion over the things of the earth not because it makes them feel good, but because it makes them feel strong ...and when they feel strong, they're better-equipped to scramble their way to the top of the heap, and more to the point, to stay there. To Capricorn, money stands for mastery, and that's why they value it. Equally precious is the fact that it also allows them to control their own destiny, and retain their independence. And since money is such an important social signifier, in Western society at least, owning it also affords them status and social standing — two other things that they happen to prize quite highly.

Astrological observation has revealed that there's often a very clear-cut pattern to Capricorn's financial development. Many goats are born into poor or less well-to-do families, and this often provides the spur that pushes them to break away and build a more prosperous life for themselves. In many cases, the goat's background of poverty is made worse by the fact that they also have an unhelpful, unsupportive father. A case in point is the Capricorn billionaire, the late Aristotle Onassis, who became head of his family household at the age of 16 when his father was thrown into prison. The young Onassis supported his family by smuggling liquor to the Turkish army, which helped to build his budding business skills in a most unusual way! On his father's release from prison, Onassis was given no recognition for supporting the family in his father's absence, and, following a major family quarrel, Onassis left to find his fortune in South America with a mere $450 in his pocket. But he also took with him a burning desire to show his father how well he could manage without him. After scraping a living with a variety of menial jobs, he began to build his fortune in the tobacco industry. The rest is history — but Onassis claims that without such a difficult beginning, he'd have lacked the incentive to "make it" on his own. Capricorns often have a tough start in life, and this usually means that money ends up very high on their list of priorities. That's because money means survival: with it, you eat, without it, you starve. The equation of money and survival is usually well ingrained in the goat's value system by the time they reach adulthood, and if they succeed in business, as so many goats do, their fondness for money may just grow and grow and grow...

For the typical goat, the first part of life is generally taken up with the task of building a measure of financial stability and independence. Goats excel at financial planning, and they always look far into the future. The need for security is never far from their minds, and they like the future to be assured, before they'll even think of relaxing. In the Capricorn scheme of things, money comes from hard work and hard work alone, so the best way to ensure there's plenty of it is simply to keep on working!

The goat's financial philosophy is one of pure, unadulterated realism. Capricorns know you need money to live in the world, so they *always* take care of that first. Once the mortgage has been paid off, however, and there's a tidy sum tucked away in the bank or their pension fund, then they begin to ease off a little, and spend more money on the creative things in life, like painting, gardening, or even a little travelling.

Essentially, though, the Capricorn approach to money is cautious to a fault. Before committing themselves to any investments or major financial decisions, goats will always consider all the options several times over, and they'll never allow themselves to be rushed. They like to have plenty of money in reserve for the "bad times", so they'll always have a sizeable "nest-egg" tucked away in a high-yield deposit account. Unlike Sagittarius, say, or Leo, they never, never expect to receive money from windfalls, and they're always extremely surprised when they do. "Get-rich-quick" schemes or gambling simply aren't the Capricorn way. Money comes from hard work, remember? Certainly not from luck — or even from the Lottery!

Capricorn also have an instinctive sense of economy, and the goat's frugal nature sometimes verges on the spartan. It's often said that even Capricorn MDs take their sandwiches to work in a brown paper bag, for no Capricorn likes to spend money if it isn't strictly essential. Indeed, I know a Capricorn lady executive who always takes a packed lunch, and defends her actions thus: "I never have time to leave the office when I'm working. And besides, why should I pay three times the price for a sandwich in a cafe, when I can make and take my own?"

The great thing about Capricorn's talent for household economy, though, is that when they *do* feel like splashing out, they've always got plenty in reserve! Mostly, however, goats are masters at self-denial. But being ruled by the planet Saturn, they are sometimes prone to depression. Happily, the astrological remedy for that particular malaise is a good, healthy dose of Venus — aka the pleasure principle, which could take the form of going out for a nice meal, buying some new clothes or perfume, a new music CD, or even getting a massage.

On a day-to-day financial level, Capricorn's performance is usually first-class. Counting the pennies is one of the goat's major talents, and most Capricorns always know how much money they have in the bank, usually down to the last cent or penny.

Most Capricorns, though, are glowing role-models of financial self-discipline and good behaviour. Goats take their responsibilities very seriously indeed, and they'll always make sure they pay the bills and mortgage on time, as well as contributing regularly to their pension. Yet it must be said, they're rarely the best people to approach for a loan. Goats hate debt: the very idea of indebtedness worries them, and, aside from mortgages and essential items like cars or furniture, they rarely buy anything on credit. They naturally expect their friends and family to do the same, and although they'll certainly help out if circumstances are sufficiently pressing, they usually make it abundantly clear that they don't expect to be asked again. They'll expect the loan to be repaid promptly, of course -and preferably with interest!

In an ideal world, Capricorns prefer to be left in sole control of the domestic finances, and, skilled though they are at the art of financial management, their urge to control the purse-strings can sometimes get slightly out of hand. When it comes to money, Capricorns usually assume they know best, and unfortunately, they'll expect the rest of the family to go along with their financial decisions. That's when you get the Capricorn who's decided that the family simply must move to a bigger house in a better suburb — which means no holidays, new clothes or fun for months, if not years, to come — and makes the decision to move without consulting anyone else.

Some Capricorns can also be financially withholding, too, denying their children financial assistance on the grounds that "struggle is good for them" — which only serves to perpetuate the pattern that marked their own development. I'm reminded here of Samantha, a filmmaker friend of mine, whose father became very upset when she gave birth to a child out of wedlock. (Capricorns revere the sanctity of the family almost as much as they revere money.) Her father refused to give her any financial help, despite the fact that he could amply afford it, for the simple reason that he disapproved of her actions. One Christmas, while she was still struggling to survive, he presented her with a Gucci wallet — but although the wallet cost £150, unfortunately it was empty! "I'd far rather have had the money, and he knew it", said Sam. "But giving me a status symbol, something he'd have valued himself, was just a way of keeping me in my place."

Sam's dad is an extreme case of how Capricorns can behave towards their families — the emphasis here being firmly on the word "extreme". At the other end of the spectrum, there are many, many Capricorns who, having realized their personal ambitions, set about helping others with as much zeal as they previously helped themselves. Some Capricorns become great philanthropists later in life, giving huge amounts of money to charitable foundations. More commonly, however, you'll find them endowing educational scholarships and bursaries, since they often prefer to give help on an individual basis.

There's a strange quirk that marks the Capricorn's money manners, however, and it's worth mentioning, in case some readers live with a goat, and can't relate to what I've said. Don't forget that Capricorn's opposite sign is Cancer, and these two members of the zodiac, though both gifted financially, are also the astrological symbols for parent and child. Capricorns tend to act out one or other of these roles in a financial partnership, and though they usually opt for the role of parent, they sometimes play the "child" role, too. But even in the rare case of the feckless goat who leaves all the bills and money management to their spouse or partner, you'll usually find they've chosen a companion with a strongly Saturnine chart themselves, as an instinctive way of keeping their financial house in order!

Capricorns love to set and achieve financial goals, but one thing that sometimes holds them back is their tendency towards negative thinking. No-one works harder than the goat, and they fully deserve the fruits of their success, but their early conditioning can sometimes make them feel fated to fail. When hard times come, goats can be a little too quick to see themselves as "poor", rather than "broke" — but in actual fact, it's a vital distinction. "Poor" suggests a permanent state, whereas "broke" sounds strictly temporary and incorporates the notion that the bad times will surely pass.

To combat their tendency to pessimism, Capricorns would do well to put themselves on an Anthony Robbins-style "Mental Diet", as described in Robbins' book, *Awaken The Giant Within*. Basically, this means that for a period of seven, or even ten days, if possible, Capricorns should carefully monitor their thought and speech, and stop themselves whenever a pessimistic or negative thought enters their mind. They should then allow themselves two minutes to change those negative thoughts to positive ones! It's not the easiest of exercises to carry out, as negative thinking is so often the habit of a lifetime. But there are few better ways of removing the mental dross of the past — and once a Capricorn has set their mind to it, they're surely bound to succeed!

♑ The Spending Style of Capricorn

In keeping with their natural sense of prudence and economy, the spending style of Capricorn tends to be very cautious. Unlike the neighbouring sign of Sagittarius, who rarely stops to count the pennies before rushing out to shop, Capricorns will count and plan, count and plan, and count and plan again, before committing themselves to any purchase, be it major or minor...

Capricorn's natural caution and reserved attitude to spending is frequently interpreted as "penny-pinching", but their hesitant ways rarely stem from genuine meanness. It's just that Capricorns are careful spenders par excellence, and generally speaking, they prefer it that way, too. Many Capricorns shun credit cards, preferring the old-fashioned financial discipline of saving up for what they want *before* they buy it, rather than after! Those Capricorns who do use credit for business or personal expenditure will always make the facility work for them by paying off the balance at the end of each month!

Capricorns take money very seriously indeed and, when it comes to spending it, they want to be sure of getting good value. When Capricorns go out to shop for clothes, for the home, or the family, they want the very best quality that money can buy. So, although the goat can rarely be accused of extravagance, you'll always find them wearing good labels, expensive shoes and perhaps a beautiful cashmere coat that will see them through several winters. Goats have a major investment in looking good, and they'll always spend the most they can afford.

Although Capricorns love quality, they love a bargain even more, and what they love most of all is topnotch merchandise at knockdown prices. Goats buy wholesale wherever possible, and when they can't, they'll frequent the very best stores at sale time. You'll find many well-dressed lady Capricorns ransacking the dress rails of Harrods and Harvey Nichols in January or July, where haute couture ensembles can be had at a fraction of the original price. Chances are they picked out the outfits they liked at the beginning of the season and then waited patiently for the sales! The typical goat can also spend many a happy rainy afternoon combing factory outlets for cashmere or linen seconds that look every bit as good as "firsts". Capricorns covet designer labels more than almost any other sign and, if they can be had cheaply, well so very much the better! Contrary to popular opinion, the goats *will* lash out on gold jewellery, handmade shoes and designer clothes — but only if the price is right, and their budget can stand the strain.

Capricorns will sometimes spend for status rather than pleasure, and they always choose their purchases with a keen eye for how they'll look to others. This is the sign that likes to "keep up with the Joneses", so buying a house in the right part of town and sending their children to the right private school are all major items on the Capricorn budget. So too are large comfortable cars — Volvo is one of their favourite makes — as well as riding lessons, ballet classes and subscriptions to country clubs. Anywhere they can be sure to rub shoulders with the top echelons of society!

Goats usually see their houses as investments as well as homes and they'll rarely stint on domestic improvements. Spending money on the home represents a major part of Capricorn's budget; Capricorn homes are usually impressive places and often quite large and beautifully furnished. Goats favour traditional decor over modern, and often go for a "period" look, with polished wood floors, antique or repro furniture, tapestries, hangings and rich, embossed wallpaper. Goats aren't the most food-minded of people — they're often too busy working, and regard eating out as extravagant. But they *do* love to entertain their business clients at home, so the typical Capricorn dining room is quite swish and well-appointed.

Capricorns will also spend freely on anything they feel will help them make progress in their chosen career or business, and that includes anything from clothes, shoes and the right hairdo (Capricorns often have hard-to-manage hair), to office furniture, a top-of-the-line lap-top computer, or an expensive leather briefcase! Incidentally, work-related gifts are often the ones they appreciate most...

With their innate respect for learning, goats often spend their limited free time reading. Biographies of the rich and famous are among their favourites — it's always comforting to read how hard other people had to struggle to get to the top — and they also love books on self-improvement and getting ahead in business! Capricorns find it hard to switch off from work, and don't particularly enjoy taking holidays, unless they can squeeze in a business call or two! The only exceptions are historical or cultural tours: goats love to improve their minds and enjoy visiting galleries, museums and historically important sites.

♑ Capricorn: Saving and Investing

As a general rule, Capricorns prefer saving money to spending it, and it's a habit that usually begins way back in childhood. Little goats often have well-stocked piggy-banks and pleasingly plump savings accounts, and parents are more likely to encounter resistance if they encourage their Capricorn offspring to dip into their savings, rather than to add to them! So, if you have Capricorn children, it might be as well to teach them how to let go sometimes, and just enjoy the experience of spending. And also how to have fun, safe in the knowledge that there's plenty more in the universe where the last lot came from ...well, that's the theory, anyway.

Since all Capricorns have a strongly cautious nature, they always make a habit of 'saving for a rainy day'. Their long-term perspective and dislike of risk-taking naturally inclines them towards high-yield, low-risk savings schemes where their money may be tied up and inaccessible for long periods, but where the eventual yield or pay-out is high. Favourite Capricorn methods of saving include high-interest building society accounts, pension plans and life policies. Capricorns should be careful not to tie up too much of their current income in long-term savings plans, however, lest they leave insufficient disposable income for their immediate spending requirements. Many goats plan their finances as though they intended to live forever, but there's little use in storing up huge reserves of wealth for old age if they may not have the energy to enjoy it!

Capricorns also have a similarly long-term approach to investment, where their twinfold aim is to minimise risk and uncertainty, whilst obtaining the maximum return on their money. Being an earth sign, Capricorns like investments they can see and touch, and their all-time favourites are buildings, property and land. They usually make a point of paying off the mortgage on their principal residence as quickly as possible and may also acquire additional properties for rental purposes. This way they profit twofold: the capital value of the property will hopefully increase over time, while the rental provides them with a steady income, too. My Capricorn friends take great delight in pointing out how well rental revenues have stood up, despite the recent slump in property values. Recent surveys (1994) point to an increase in rents of around 65% over four years in the UK, which spells good news for domestic landlords, whatever their sun sign! Goats who invested in the commercial sector, however, may not be feeling quite so sanguine, since capital values have crashed, and properties have been hard to let — although goats who shrewdly bought at rock-bottom prices in the early 1990s may now, at last, be set to realise a return.

Few Capricorns major in intangible investments, such as the futures markets, as they see these kinds of investments as, quite simply, just too risky. There are goats that do play the markets, of course, but those that do will never speculate without fully analysing every factor that might influence the outcome. And that can take quite a while! Generally speaking, Capricorns prefer to speculate only where they have a high degree of personal control. For this reason, they usually restrict their risk-taking to their *own* business ventures, where they're sure of seeing things through to a successful conclusion. Another area where wealthy Capricorns may be drawn to invest is in political campaigning, especially where a successful outcome will benefit their business interests.

Property-related businesses, such as building and construction, can make good investments for Capricorn, along with market gardens, horticultural nurseries, old people's homes and farming. In the manufacturing sector, good Capricorn ventures include academic and financial publishing, and 'traditional' products such as classic clothing, foodstuffs and collectibles.

Capricorns may also profit from investing in diamonds, gemstones, precious jewellery and any business related to the products of mining. Oil and petroleum have fuelled many a Capricorn success story. Insurance is another area where Capricorns have traditionally long profited, but due to the volatile nature of this sector, prospective investors should evaluate the risks very carefully indeed before making a financial commitment.

♑ The Earning Power Of Capricorn

Capricorn rules the tenth house of career and worldly achievement in the natural zodiac, and work is frequently the most important thing on the goat's agenda. Home and family come a close-run second, but the need for recognition and worldly approval is *the* great motivating force that drives the goat ever onward and upward. Success is something they can rarely get enough of, and in order to find real happiness, they *need* to make constant progress.

Capricorns who are starting out on their workaday careers need to spend some time discovering where their real talents lie, and then set themselves some detailed, long-term goals. This long-range focus is extremely important for Capricorns, because goats positively need to plan ahead — 20 or even 30 years ahead, if need be — and then set their course accordingly. Without such a solid internal career structure, the goat can easily fall prey to those classic Capricorn bugbears of depression and despair. Although young Capricorns may change their jobs quite regularly, they're actually far better suited to staying in one place: too much moving around can make them feel rootless and unsettled.

It's often a phase they are destined to go through, though, for life rarely takes off for the goats until their ruling planet, Saturn, has returned to its own place in the horoscope at the age of 29 (astrologers call this the Saturn Return). For Capricorns are the archetypal "late bloomers" of the zodiac, and don't usually manage to "find themselves" till then. Capricorns in their twenties can sometimes come across as unmotivated and unfocused: after the magic age of 30 or so, a major piece of the jigsaw slots into place, and goats apply their excellent minds to the challenge of their career. Their greatest successes, however, usually lie a few years further on, as few Capricorns ever really "make it" before the age of 40.

There's a quietly obsessive-compulsive quality about the truly focused Capricorn, for once the goats have decided where they really want to go, nothing and no-one will stop them. Once Capricorns are satisfied that their goals are realistic, and really can be achieved, then there's never any doubt that they will be. Determination is Capricorn's middle name, and just like the mountain goat, they'll just keep on going till they get there, regardless of problems, setbacks and delays. It's this ability to just "keep on keeping on", no matter what, that is one of Capricorn's most valuable workaday assets. People born under this sign usually "live to work", and can often be workaholics. Work is the gateway to the things the goat loves most — success, status and power, not to mention money ...and for Capricorn, at least, "more" is usually "better"...

Capricorns are usually the most level-headed and methodical people you could ever hope to meet, and they're also among the most hardworking and conscientious too. Goats are natural leaders, and the corridors of management are their spiritual home. Capricorn's shoulders are among the broadest in the zodiac, so they often end up holding positions of considerable responsibility within large-scale organizations. I know a female Capricorn for instance, who sits on the board of a large international manufacturing company and heads up not one, but two, of their major product divisions. She's the only executive in the company to carry a workload of this magnitude, but she takes it all in her stride — and even sustains a "second career" as a writer and broadcaster. How do you do it? I asked her one day... Well, her answer was the same as many a high-flying Capricorn would give: apart from the normal breaks for meals, sleep and work-related socializing, she simply never stops working. Ever. Even her holidays all seem to take in a good many work assignments! But since she loves nothing more in life than her work, she's as happy as the proverbial sandboy. My Capricorn friend is a divorcee who lives alone, so her long working hours pose no threat to family life. But in the case of married goats, their devotion to work can leave considerable domestic stress.

Capricorns are not only supremely practical people, they also love to feel useful and needed. Their skills ensure that they're usually in great demand, and they excel at planning projects and making them come in both on time and on budget. Instinctively efficient by nature, goats also have a real talent for seeing where any system falls down, and they're brilliant at initiating subtle changes in a business which make everything far more efficiently. Capricorns' natural air of reserve means they're often far happier working with facts and figures, rather than people — unless, of course, they have a more outgoing fire or air sign on the ascendant. They excel at working with things they can touch, feel and quantify — like money, for instance, or in the manufacturing sector.

Unlike the neighbouring sign of Sagittarius, Capricorns seldom make any provision for "lucky breaks" in their career. There's no substitute for hard work, elbow grease and perseverance in their book, and they prefer to earn their promotions and pay rises the hard way, rather than by providence. I know a young Capricorn businessman in his early thirties called James, who helped "jump-start" a new information technology business from scratch. The company became very successful very quickly, thanks in no small part to James's sterling efforts, and he was promptly offered a seat on the board in recognition of his efforts. Interestingly, he turned it down because he felt he "wasn't ready" ...when the offer comes around again in ten years' time, though, I'm sure his response will be Yes! Like any self-respecting goat, James made sure the business was sound, though, before getting involved in the first place. He wants to be sure the company he's put so much work into will also be around in ten years, too, for, like any self-respecting goat, he has no time at all for airy-fairy schemes, or pie-in-the-sky ventures that are lacking in realism.

The goats' ambition is second to none, and there's nothing they like better than working their way slowly but surely up the corporate ladder. The classic tale of the girl who starts as a secretary and ends up as Chief Executive is pure Capricorn, and it happens more often in big business than you might be tempted to think. It's often said that "A Capricorn at the top is a happy Capricorn", and to a great extent I think that's true, for executive Capricorns are generally a good deal more relaxed than younger goats who are still clawing their way up the company.

Capricorns' ambition is one of their great driving forces, but in certain cases, it stems from a need for the approval that was singularly lacking in their childhood. Once the goat begins to give *themselves* that approval, by acknowledging their efforts and achievements, they often find that their work flows far more smoothly. And it certainly takes a great deal of angst out of whether they get that promotion! Capricorns who have set their sights on the top will sometimes resort to some pretty extreme measures to stay one step ahead of the competition. In its mildest form, this can consist of a burning need to predict the future, for despite their practical, down-to-earth image, the client lists of most astrologers I know boast a very high percentage of Capricorns! At the other end of the scale, there are the classic "ruthless" Capricorns, who'll stop at nothing to get where they're going. Luckily, these types are rare. And since they'll probably get there anyway, their fears are seldom justified!

Once they've actually reached the pinnacle of success, however, Capricorns often begin to display some of the finer qualities, as a different side of their nature altogether emerges. Having attained their goals, they turn round to help others reach theirs; and many high-flying goats are valued counsellors or mentors in big business, and sometimes also in their spare time.

Capricorn is also the sign of the empire-builder, and some of the richest and most famous businessmen of all time have been born under this sign. Aristotle Onassis, who for a time was ranked as "the world's richest man", not only had the Sun in Capricorn, but Capricorn rising too. He'd made his first million by the age of 25, and he then set about pursuing that other great Capricorn goal — finding a suitable spouse! He first married the wife of a rich shipping magnate and later wooed and wed the world's most famous widow, Jacqueline Kennedy. Conrad Hilton, founder of the famous empire of Hilton hotels, was also a Capricorn and had many classic Capricorn traits, including a passion for work that played havoc with his family life. After two unhappy marriages, however, he finally found married bliss at the age of 89 — it gets better as the goat gets older, remember? Other famous Capricorn millionaires include Howard Hughes, J. Arthur Rank, of Rank Cinema fame, and J.P. Getty, who had Capricorn rising.

This famous line-up proves the point that goats excel at running their own businesses, and there's little they enjoy more than running a company they've built up from scratch. Capricorns usually do extremely well as self-employed businessmen, since they're so hardworking, thorough and willing to put in the long hours that are necessary for success. The biggest obstacle they generally have to surmount is their own lack of confidence, as this can dampen their efforts to push their company to the fore. The answer lies in teaming up with a more sales-oriented sign — like Gemini, Sagittarius or Leo, for instance, who can take the business out into the world. That way, Capricorn gets to do the two things they love most — make money and stay at home to count it!

♑ The Capricorn Boss

Capricorns enjoy being in positions of authority, so it naturally follows that they're happy to be the boss. As employers, Capricorns are usually strict, but fair. They can sometimes be slightly hard taskmasters, owing to their deep-rooted streak of perfectionism. But if they're hard on their staff, they're always ten times harder on themselves — and although they've no time for shirkers, they're always very helpful should real personal problems arise.

The Capricorn boss has many assets. They're unswervingly loyal, provided nothing happens to make them feel their trust has been misplaced; they're also supremely gifted at taking minimal resources and stretching them to superhuman limits; and they're totally unflappable in a crisis. So whatever happens — whether it's a collapse in the exchange rate that sends the company's profits down the tubes, a breakdown on the production line, or simply an everyday office crisis, you can rest assured that few signs will ever handle it better than the executive goat.

♑ The Capricorn Employee

The assets that Capricorn displays as a leader are also to be found at lower levels, too, and generally speaking, goats make superb employees. They're hardworking to a fault, and will put up with all sorts of menial tasks if there's a job that needs to be done, without ever once complaining. They're unfailingly punctual, neat and tidy, and will never bring their personal problems to the office. The ideal employee, you might say, and you're absolutely right, but for just one thing... Capricorns are headed for the top, and they know it — and they'll never be happy to stay in a junior position for long, no matter how much the company needs them!

♑ Capricorn and Career

Capricorn people always like to keep their feet firmly on the ground, and career-wise, they excel at creating and maintaining the structures that hold the world together for the rest of us mere mortals — whether they be physical, commercial or even moral and ethical structures.

Many Capricorns find their forte in working with the physical environment, and a high percentage of goats work as builders, architects and stonemasons. With their unerring eye for precision and detail, some goats find their niche in graphic design, while others choose to work with a craft. Artists and craftsmen down the centuries have always known, as Capricorn knows instinctively, that beauty cannot be created without discipline, devotion and hard work. Not surprisingly, many great writers and artists have Capricorn strong in their horoscope. Rudyard Kipling, Edgar Allan Poe and Henry Miller all had the Sun in Capricorn, and the great sculptor Auguste Rodin had Capricorn rising.

The French psychologist Michel Gauquelin showed that there is a clear correlation between Saturn and science, and many great scientists have been Capricorns too, such as Sir Isaac Newton and Louis Pasteur. The goat also has a great respect for learning and tradition, and many Capricorns find fulfilment as researchers, publishers or university lecturers. Capricorns are also often strongly drawn to teaching, since it gives them a strong inner sense of authority and structure.

With their love of order and rule-based systems, Capricorns often gravitate to careers that involve the formulation and enforcement of social codes. They feel thoroughly at home within the rule-based systems of the law, tax offices and local government, particularly since these are also places where they can "work their way up", seeking promotion at every level — and needless to say, usually earning it, too! Some Capricorns also have a deep-rooted need to serve society, and more physically-oriented goats enjoy pitting themselves against the accidents and disasters of everyday life as firefighters and ambulance workers.

Capricorns are also natural businesspeople. We've already considered the impressive roll-call of male Capricorn millionaires; Elizabeth Arden and Helena Rubinstein are just two of the lady tycoons also born under this sign. Part of Capricorns' great secret of success that they're totally undeterred by the cut-and-thrust of company politics: they take it all in their stride and just carry on climbing. Many Capricorns start out in life as businessman or lawyers, but then move into politics — after all, isn't that where the *real* power lies? Martin Luther King, PW Botha and Richard Nixon were all born under Capricorn, not to mention Stalin and also Mao Tse Tung!

With their natural business acumen and instinctive head for figures, many Capricorns build thriving careers in the financial sector. Many begin their working lives as cashiers or bank tellers and go on to become bank managers, loan officers or independent financial advisers. With their cautious outlook and awareness of "what could go wrong", goats also excel in insurance — one of the few business areas, incidentally, where they relish working in sales. Other Capricorns succeed in turning their penchant for property into a lucrative career: property development, renovation and rental management are areas where they can find their niche.

Many Capricorns like to work with the earth in a more literal way, through farming, nursery gardening or landscape architecture. Capricorn also has a strong association with mines, earthworking and all the products of mining, and many Sun Capricorns make careers as diamond dealers. Alternatively, they may find themselves drawn to geology, and make their living as surveyors and prospectors.

Many Capricorns are fascinated by astrology and delight in putting their interests to a highly practical use. Capricorn astrologer Helena Francis combines her skill as a gardener with her occult interests by designing and creating astrological gardens! Some Capricorns work with nature by becoming healers: others work as herbalists or midwives; while still others pursue a classic Saturn calling as osteopaths and chiropractors.

Finally, don't forget that Capricorn has a thoroughly outrageous side too — more often than not, these goats work in showbiz! Some of the most outrageously unconventional entertainers of our time have been Capricorns, including Elvis Presley, raunchy Rod Stewart and the ill-fated Janis Joplin, whose tragic end through drugs and drink showed the shadier side of the goat-god Pan. Capricorn entertainers often hide their true selves behind stagey masks and personas: think of singer David Bowie and his ever-changing images of the Seventies and Eighties — that's classic Capricorn style!

♑ Capricorn: Keys to Financial Success

- DO focus on your successes, not your "failures". Keep telling yourself you're a success and, sooner or later, you will be! Remember, "It always gets better with every year that passes !"

- DO try adhering to a "Mental Diet" and banish all negative and pessimistic thoughts from your life. If you can't manage to think totally positively for a whole week, just try it for a day to begin with!

- DO learn to have more pleasure with your money in the present. Strive to achieve a balance between long- and short-term financial goals. Cultivate a sense of trust that "there'll always be enough".

- DO practise the art of taking calculated risks — especially when it's your own business that needs financial investment.

- DO stick to the golden rule of "Do as you would be done by". It may sound trite, but it's an age-old piece of wisdom.

♑ Rich & Famous Capricorns

Joan of Arc
Johannes Kepler
Joseph Stalin
J Edgar Hoover
Martin Luther King
Raisa Gorbachev
Conrad Hilton
Isaac Pitman
J.D. Salinger
Gerald Durrell
Edgar Allen Poe
Shirley Bassie
Joe Frazier
Humhrey Bogart
Marlene Dietrich
Joan Baez
Mary Tyler Moore
Dolly Parton
Mel Gibson
Anthony Andrews
Diane Keaton
Kirstie Alley
Annie Lennox
Patricia Highsmith
Princess Caroline of Monaco

Henri Matisse
Benjamin Franklin
Mao-Tse Tung
Woodrow Wilson
Albert Schweizer
Howard Hughes
Louis Braille
Al Capone
Henry Miller
A.A. Milne
Elvis Presley
Mohammed Ali
Floyd Patterson
Cary Grant
Marianne Faithfull
Victoria Principal
Faye Dunaway
David Lynch
Kevin Costner
Jon Voigt
Sarah Miles
Dame Maggie Smith
David Bowie
Rowan Atkinson
Mary Archer

AQUARIUS
January 21st to February 19th

The winter snows of January are an appropriate backdrop for Aquarius, for this is the sign that's noted above all for its crystal-clear logic and mental brilliance. That famous Aquarian brain power, though, is usually reserved for dreaming up ways to "save the world" — rarely, if ever, is it applied to the subject of money. For although Aquarius is often called the sign of genius, you'll travel a very long way indeed to find an Aquarian who's a true financial genius ...for those fine minds of theirs are invariably focused on the less earthly things of life...

Aquarius stands for the high point of mental achievement, so, appropriately enough, the sign has a human symbol: no goats, bulls or crawling crustaceans here! Instead, we find the waterbearer, pouring the waters of knowledge upon the masses of humanity from a suitably lofty height.

The sign of Aquarius is ruled by two planets — the sky-god, Uranus, and the more sombre planet, Saturn. Before Uranus was discovered in the 1780s, Saturn alone was the ruler of Aquarius. But these two planets aren't always the best of bedfellows, and in many subtle ways they give Aquarians a thoroughly uneasy time. Sun sign Aquarians may well find it useful to have a full horoscope drawn up, so that they can get a more accurate picture of which planet is influencing them most. If it's Uranus, they'll probably be far more restless and given to bucking the status quo: they'll also be less conventional, and more focused on new ideas. If Saturn is stronger in the horoscope, however, your Aquarian is likely to be a far more conservative fellow, with a keen awareness of authority figures and a regard for what people think.

Balancing the two energies of Uranus and Saturn in one body and one lifetime is no easy task, and it certainly helps to explain why Aquarians are often so restless. One minute, they're happy to settle down and just get on with their lives as usual. The next, however, they're seized by some wonderful new idea, and all they want to do is head off and see where it leads them. This is the sign of the visionary, the dreamer, and also, quite often, the genius — but keeping their feet on the ground is something Aquarians find far from easy.

It's an interesting quirk of astrology that whenever a new planet is discovered, conditions in the world at large will always reflect the new planet's nature. So it was with Uranus, the ruling planet of Aquarius. For in 1781, just as the astronomer Herschel pinpointed the planet in the heavens, a violent wave of rebellion erupted all over Europe — culminating in the full-blooded mayhem of the French Revolution! So Aquarius — and Aquarians — have been linked with revolutions ever since.

Aquarians don't just believe in revolution for revolution's sake, though, for this is the sign of the social reformer, too. Waterbearers are just as interested in creating new social structures as they are in tearing down old ones. The US Presidents Abe Lincoln and Franklin Roosevelt were also born under Aquarius, and both had powerful visions of a "new social order".

On an everyday level, Aquarians are easy to spot in a crowd. Magnetic, charismatic and usually quite good-looking, they're often tall in stature, with wavy hair and high, noble foreheads. It's the eyes that are the real giveaway, though. Aquarian orbs have a kind of "charge" about them, as though electricity, not blood, were coursing through their veins. Well, we astrologers do wonder sometimes... Think of Paul Newman, who has classic waterbearer eyes. Look out for the expression, too: Aquarian eyes are rarely focused in the here and now, but usually fixed on the middle or far horizon! Hence the famous Aquarian clumsiness, for these are the sort of people who'll often crash into you at parties. Some great idea suddenly came to them, you see, and for a moment, they just forgot exactly where they happened to be...

Aquarians often have an unusual dress sense, too, and that's usually an excellent clue to their zodiac orientation. Some Aquarians can't be bothered at all with what they wear: they'll just put on whatever's at hand in the morning. Look for the man wearing two odd socks, and with congealed scrambled egg on his sweater. You can bet he's an Aquarian. If his clothes are held together with safety-pins and string, he may be an "absent-minded professor" type. Or if he's sporting an electric blue blazer and a jazzy fluorescent bow tie, he may be one of the super-wacky Uranians. Uranian women can look pretty strange, too: they often opt for futuristic space-age clothes, like vinyl shifts and latex boots, all topped off with granny's lace shawl! They can still look a million dollars — think of Mia Farrow or Morgan Fairchild, for instance — but they're *definitely* not conventional. Physically, Aquarians often seem to exhibit a "sexual crossover" similar to Librans, but it's usually expressed through the body and not the mind. Aquarian men often have quite large hips, for example, whilst the women may have extra-broad shoulders. It's the sign of equality — and also of unisex!

Since Aquarians spend so much time in their heads, they often neglect their bodies. Their ceaseless mental activity makes them prone to nervous exhaustion, and they commonly forget to eat and take exercise as often as they should. "A healthy mind in a healthy body" is a slogan that should be pinned on their refrigerator door, and they need to connect with the healing energies of nature just as often as they can. Total rest, peace and quiet are also much needed from time to time, to help them recharge their busy little batteries.

As children, Aquarians can be easily misunderstood, and wrongly judged to be backward. Their lightning minds often grasp things intuitively, and sometimes they're at a loss to explain just exactly how they came by their answers. Their impatience with conventional learning methods can make them inclined to lose interest in school. Many an Aquarian who makes a major contribution to society in later life leaves school early, and with a poor report card, as well. Perhaps it's worth noting that Thomas Edison, the inventor of the electric lightbulb, fell firmly into this group! Aquarian youngsters are preoccupied first and foremost with their *own* ideas and visions, and they're often accused of "daydreaming." But if truth be told, that's often how they come up with their best ideas.

Even in childhood, Aquarians are just different from everyone else. They seem to march to a different rhythm from the rest of the world, and it's definitely the drumbeat of the future. Astrologers often say that what Aquarians are doing today, the rest of us will be doing in fifty years' time, and if you look through the pages of history, you can see that this holds true. I know Aquarians who were interested in the environmental movement and "green issues", fifteen to twenty years ago, long before these ideas became mainstream. Now that they're widely accepted, of course, the Aquarians have moved on to other concerns in the forefront of current social thinking, like how to get "energy for free", for instance, or creating an alternative to money.

Not only are Aquarians different from everyone else, but gather together any half-dozen Aquarians and you'll find they're also very different from each other. This sounds confusing, and it's an argument that sceptics sometimes put forward to try and disprove astrology. But if you explore a little further, you'll see that they *do* have some things in common. It's just that they like to *think* that they're very different from each other — and even that they're totally unique.

Being the odd one out is something which comes naturally to Aquarius, and it's why they're often labelled as cranky, odd, or just plain eccentric. This is also a sign of great extremes, for its two ruling planets, Saturn and Uranus, could hardly be more different. These extremes embrace all kinds of behaviour — from constancy and dependability to volatility and flightiness — and only the Aquarians in question know just who they really are. Well, that's the theory at any rate!

Aquarius is an air sign, which means waterbearers 'think' their way through life. Their intellectual approach to everything can sometimes cause Aquarians to come across to others as somewhat cold and detached. Not that they don't have feelings — they're human after all — it's just that waterbearers prefer to solve their problems with their heads. And they'll rarely be swayed by any emotional arguments, either. Their powers of perception are usually second to none, but the Saturn side of their nature can sometimes weigh them down with depression. Whenever that happens, you should remember the Venus Principle — namely, that the best course of action for the "blues" is simply to have some fun! Take your bluesy waterbearers to lunch at their favourite cafe, or down to the fair and encourage them to forget their cares for a while. Or throw an impromptu tea- or dinner-party, or even just take them out for a drink. Aquarians are the most sociable creatures on earth, and there's nothing they like better than getting together with their friends. The food's no big deal — it can be veggie-burgers and fries, or sushi and salad for all they care: the walk and the talk are the things that really count.

Typical Aquarians spend a lot of time lost in thought: but to give credit where credit's due, a great deal of their thinking is concerned with other people. Aquarius is the sign of the humanitarian par excellence, and the world of politics and "causes" swarms with Aquarians who want to "make a difference." Think of Vanessa Redgrave, who used her Oscar-award speech to speak out for the PLO — or Germaine Greer, who transformed the women's movement. Both just happen to be Aquarians, and you'll frequently find that the females are more militant than the males! Even on a less spectacular scale, most Aquarians enjoy helping all kinds of people. You'll find many waterbearers raising money for charity, doing union work or helping out at a shelter for the homeless. The only problem here is, that Aquarians can sometimes neglect their own families, and they'd always do well to remember that "charity begins at home". Their social virtues are indisputable, though, for any kind of prejudice, such as racism, sexism or ageism, deeply and genuinely offends them. Indeed, Aquarian men are probably the only genuine male "feminists" you'll ever really meet.

Cool, brilliant and bewilderingly complex! If you think that sounds like Aquarius, you're beginning to get the picture. Remember, the air is quite rarefied way up there on the waterbearer's mountain, so if your mindpower isn't up to it, don't even think of attempting the climb. And once you *do* get up there, it's just like Everest and Wonderland all rolled into one. Aquarians are hard to fathom, it's true, but getting to know them could be the best fun you ever had. The waterbearer's an enigma, to be sure, but a thoroughly human one, too, and in the whole of the zodiac, not to mention the universe, you'll rarely find a better companion for the magical journey of life!

♒ Aquarius And Money

Aquarius is often billed as one of the least money-minded signs of the zodiac — which isn't to say that Aquarian millionaires don't exist! Far from it, in fact, as thanks to their creative genius and flair for innovation there are quite a few of them out there — notably those who finally got around to registering their inventions at the Patent Office! Most Aquarians get rich by accident, though, and usually whilst they're doing something else entirely. And even Aquarian billionaires don't really rate money as their Number One priority in life.

Unlike many other signs in the zodiac, Aquarians rarely see money as a symbol of security. To them, security lies in the mind, and the freedom to pursue their ideas. The "yuppie" ethics of the late 1980s left most Aquarians totally unmoved, for they never see money as an end in itself, but simply as a means to realise far more worthwhile goals, such as saving endangered species, say, or educating the Third World...

An Aquarian client of mine once told me, "Money means little to Aquarians because it has no intrinsic value. It's just the medium of exchange that society is using at the moment... So if you're writing about

Aquarians and money, it'll be a pretty slim volume indeed!" Not all Aquarians you'll meet are quite so laid back about money. But precious few, indeed, regard money as their primary goal in life. As the waterbearers see it, money's there to serve them, and definitely *not* the other way round...

Despite the brilliance of their airy intellect, the world of financial facts and figures is often totally alien to Aquarius. They simply can't get excited about it, and they only deal with it because they have to — and only then because money is their passport to the greater world of ideas. You see, money buys Aquarians the time and space to follow their thoughtforms, and this fact alone gives it value in their world.

Broadly speaking, Aquarians fall into two distinct camps when it comes to handling money, depending on which of their two ruling planets calls the shots in their own personal horoscope. Saturn-type Aquarians are rather like Capricorns in their money habits. These people often get off to a rather rocky start in life, which often serves to make them quite dutiful, frugal and thrifty. Saturn-style Aquarians can live quite happily on welfare, or on a truly meagre budget whilst studying for a Ph.D, and usually master the art of "living on less" to consummate perfection. These Aquarians deal with the Bank Manager and the Inland Revenue strictly by the book, and they're profoundly shocked at even the merest suggestion of fiddling their taxes. They often have lean times financially in the first half of life, but since they're quite good at both saving and planning, their finances often improve when they reach the age of forty and beyond ...rather like Capricorn, in fact.

Uranus-type Aquarians, on the other hand, run their money lives along completely different lines — or more accurately, just let it run by itself! Every sign of the zodiac usually reflects a hint of its opposite, and Uranian-style Aquarians often echo Leo's ways. These are the Aquarians who gamble and speculate and dream of "getting rich quick." Owing to their airy nature, many Aquarians find it hard to deal with the world of everyday financial reality, but Uranians find it harder than most. They'd far rather just be left alone to do the important things in life — like writing their thesis, or refining their inventions. So the nitty-gritty details of basic personal finance, like paying the rent, for instance, and saving money for their bills, can, to put it mildly, quite simply drive them to distraction. I've known Aquarians who find dealing with "all this financial stuff" so incredibly irksome, they spend their lives moving from place to place to avoid an endless string of angry creditors chasing unpaid bills. One waterbearer I know affectionately refers to his creditors as "the posse", and prides himself greatly on his repertoire of excuses for nonpayment! For this kind of Aquarian, financial peace of mind comes only when they can reconcile "mind and matter," and discover how to earn money in a genuinely Aquarian way, such as working with computers, for instance, or by running a therapy centre.

Saturn- and Uranian-style Aquarians, though, are two extremes of this sign, and financially speaking at least, most Aquarians fall somewhere in between. There are also certain money-traits that both types have in common, such as sudden changes in fortune. For example, a surprise windfall or an unexpected tax demand. Events such as these are very much the hallmark of Aquarian finances. But since change is their lifeblood, waterbearers quickly adapt to their changing circumstances, and soon get used to either having money or not. Those financial "ups and downs" just make life a bit more interesting! Rather like Geminis — their air sign cousins, Aquarians don't tend to think very much about money — even those Aquarians with a more Saturn-style disposition. But sooner or later, most waterbearers discover that if they pay more attention to the management of their money, the rewards can be great, indeed, since an improved cashflow can certainly help to make their dreams come true!

Notwithstanding their sudden changes of fortune, however, Aquarians also have many hidden assets that can help them to make more of their money. Waterbearers frequently have an innate ability to visualise the financial results they want, a gift they share with Librans. And when they put their minds to it, they can achieve just about anything they want to, by first picturing it as a "fait accompli" and by writing down their goals and reviewing them twice daily. Many Aquarians also have an unparalleled ability to nip a financial crisis in the bud by having a brainwave or an insight for moneyspinning idea, which opens up a whole new source of income.

Another great asset that Aquarians can use to their financial advantage is their extensive network of friends and contacts. Aquarians enjoy helping people, and people often enjoy helping them in return, if the need or occasion should arise. When Aquarians do have money, they'll *always* use it to help others, for they firmly believe that money is there to be used, not hoarded away in reserve. They also believe that their moneymaking activities should serve others, too, no matter *how* rich they become. Oprah Winfrey, one of the richest Aquarian women in America today, is quoted as saying , "Don't work just for the money: do it for the spirit", a statement that's Aquarian to the core.

Along with their open-handedness, Aquarians are usually open-minded, too, and they enjoy experimenting with new approaches to money. They're happy with the concept of bartering, which dispenses with money entirely, and will gladly trade their computing skills for a massage, or even a box of vegetables! The recession of the early 1990s saw a huge increase in the number of barter-based local exchange currency systems (known as LETS schemes), and, since these tend to short-circuit existing economic structures, they're a thoroughly Aquarian creation!

When it comes to managing their day-day-finances, most Aquarians are equality minded, and like to think in terms of "share and share alike". You may find the odd Aquarian male who insists on running the household in an old-fashioned Saturn-style way, but these kinds of Aquarians are few and far between. Indeed, many Aquarians find the financial responsibilities of marriage or cohabitation quite restrictive: they dislike the idea of financial dependents, and often reject the traditional "breadwinning" role. Aquarian women, too, will always expect to be equal financially, so partners who wish to be "kept" should definitely seek out another sign!

Most Aquarians have a frugal nature, which means they often live well within their income, and they can be thoroughly disapproving of family members who run up overdrafts or credit card bills. And although they may sometimes be vague or forgetful about paying bills on time, they never do so on purpose, since they hate to let people down. Debt's another thing that really bothers them, too, unless they're ultra-Uranian types — and they'll go to great lengths to avoid it. Their instinct is always to keep their money moving, so they'll happily lend money if they've got it, but they will get very upset if it's not repaid on time! Their high sense of Aquarian ethics means that they like to honour their word — and, in turn, they like others to honour theirs, too.

Aquarians have a great preference for working freelance, or for being self-employed, so very few waterbearers ever experience a regular cash-flow. Money tends to arrive in the Aquarian bank account in large, infrequent chunks, in a "feast or famine" mode, which highlights Aquarians' need to plan their money more carefully than most. Aquarians who work on contract or commission, say, may finish an assignment and then receive one large cheque, which they'll have to make last for months and months. But since Aquarians don't tend to be that focused on managing their finances, making their money last can sometimes present a bit of a problem. Aquarians' money problems tend to stem from their basic lack of interest — you see, they'd really rather be thinking about something far more important. But unless they give their budget bit of basic attention, they'll find themselves "in the red" with ever-increasing regularity.

Creating a financial blueprint will help all Aquarians immensely, and waterbearers who are set to go freelance, or who keep running into trouble, should consult a financial planner, who can help them to structure their funds. They need to get expert advice in setting up an accounts system, and then sign up for computerised home banking. They should then keep things as simple as possible by using a multi-function bank account, one that will issue standing orders, make deposits if desired and also pay their bills on time! Another useful strategy is to create a "cash cow" or financial buffer by building up adequate savings — always the very best protection against unforeseen expenses. As Aquarians are also creatures of habit, setting aside a regular day each month to review and update their accounts can also be a very helpful idea.

Although, as we've seen, many Aquarians find the nuts and bolts of money management somewhat irksome, the fixed nature of the sign means that most waterbearers can learn to steer their financial course quite equably, provided they establish some good, sound habits early on in life. Don't forget, too, that in common with the rest of us, the behaviour Aquarians saw in their early home environment is what they tend to model. Hopefully, they saw money handled in a healthy, conscious way. If not, they'll need to make a determined effort to change their early patterns by using creative visualization and other mental techniques.

♒ The Spending Style Of Aquarius

In keeping with their unpredictable, changeable nature, the spending style of Aquarius can be more than a touch erratic. Most waterbearers are generally quite frugal, but every once in a while, they're shockingly capable of the most thoroughly wild extravagances that place them right up there beside Leos in the champion spending stakes! It may sound paradoxical, but I've seen an Aquarian go into a video store to rent the cheapest line of VCR, and come out proudly clutching the latest top-of-the-range model, complete with every gadget and gizmo you could think of, plus a few more besides! Unlike Leos or Capricorns, though, Aquarians never spend to impress. "Keeping up with the Jones's" just doesn't figure in their way of thinking. They simply reason, with that impeccable logic of theirs, that if you buy the very best, it'll last a whole lot longer. Just like Capricorn, they believe in buying quality, and so they'll always spend as much as they can possibly afford. Hence their apparent extravagance, which they always justify as "saving money in the long run".

In keeping with the Saturn side of their nature, waterbearers will happily practise self-denial in order to afford the things they really want, and they'll happily cut down on food, say, if they want to buy a new computer. Mostly, though, their material wants are modest, depending, of course, on whatever else is in their chart — a Leo moon, for instance, might make those wants more lavish!

Unlike the other air signs, Gemini and Libra, most Aquarians don't rate shopping as a leisure pastime. They might get a mild frisson of enjoyment out of buying that state-of-the-art VCR, but the chances are they'd far rather stay at home and read a book. And since window-shopping makes their eyes glaze over with boredom, waterbearers often short-circuit the shopping process by buying goods by mail order, or scanning consumer surveys. The cautious influence of Saturn means that they prefer to buy goods that are "tried and tested", rather than browsing in the shops *ad nauseam,* or simply leaving the whole thing to chance.

The one great exception to the "anti-shopping" rule, though, is the whole area of technology and electronics, which Aquarians find endlessly appealing. Male and female Aquarians alike are often irresistibly drawn to machines and gadgets of all kinds, and this usually accounts for a major part of their spending. They like to keep abreast of the latest technical advances, too, and will spend a great deal of time — and money — on journals and magazines that tell them what the latest advances are...

Aquarius's passion for knowledge and learning means their bookshelves are usually full to bursting, and bookshops are a prime source of temptation. They adore science fiction — it satisfies that Aquarian urge to journey ever further into the far-distant future — and they also enjoy reading about all forms of transport. It's not sufficient for the waterbearer to simply read other people's accounts of the joys of hot-air ballooning, though. They need to share the experience, too, and that can get pretty expensive! Aviation is another of their favourite hobbies, and you'll find a higher than average percentage of Aquarians thronging the ranks of flying schools at weekends, in keen pursuit of their private pilot's license!

Being such unconventional souls at heart, Aquarians rarely spend money on the things that other people do — like their homes, for instance, or clothes, or even food! Waterbearers aren't much given to dining out, but when they do, they favour offbeat, wacky places, perhaps with live music or jazz. More usually, however, they prefer to entertain at home. If you've ever been invited to an Aquarian home, you'll know that your host rates comfort and utility far higher than showing off. The stereo and hi-fi will surely take pride of place, though once again, these will have been bought with quality in mind, rather than pure and simple good looks! If Aquarians are affluent, their homes will be filled with rare and unusual objects, collected perhaps on their travels, and the decor will be light and airy. Alternatively, you may be entertained in a dusty, cluttered apartment that bears the strangest resemblance to an electronics workroom. It may also look very much as though it hasn't been cleaned for a year! Aquarians favour buffet parties: their social gatherings may be somewhat light on food, but they're always rich in conversation....

One final area where Aquarians are willing to spend a great deal of money is on cars and transport in general. For few things matter more to them than getting from A to B. The Aquarian car could be an ancient Citroen, or perhaps a roomy Renault Espace. Or it could be a classic that they picked up for a song and restored to its former glory. There'll always be something noteworthy about it, though, and it'll probably be big enough to carry their friends around in, too!

♒ Aquarius: Saving and Investing

Precious few Aquarians have an overwhelming urge to accumulate and, unless they learn to save early, it's rarely a habit they spontaneously adopt. Waterbearers aren't usually the biggest earners in the zodiac, and their modest budgets often leave little over for savings and investment. Keeping a small balance on deposit for contingencies sounds sensible in their view, but unless they can be classified among the wealthier strata of society, few Aquarians think further ahead than that. Waterbearers see little point in having their money sitting around just earning more money . They'd far rather use it in a more constructive way — by investing it in a home, for instance, or financing a course or project. Paradoxically, though, Aquarius is one of the few signs that really needs to save, since waterbearers can so often be caught out financially by sudden, unexpected life changes. Losing a work contract or regular source of income won't be nearly so disruptive if there are backup deposits they can call on, and having substantial savings allows them to take some time off when they want.

Aquarians need to find a method of saving that requires little effort on their part, since they'll rarely be bothered to find out where their money will earn the highest interest. Building society accounts are a solid

Aquarian favourite, and a good approach is to have money transferred from their current account each month by standing order. Another equally painless savings strategy is to find a current account with a "sweep" facility that automatically transfers balances over a certain level into a separate savings account. Moving money around is something Aquarians find quite tedious and, as a rule, they favour savings schemes they can set up and then forget.

Aquarians who do have money to invest, though, take a very different line from their less well-endowed brothers. Astrologers have noted that Aquarians who are born into wealthy families, or who suddenly inherit wealth, are often extremely interested in finding good ways to grow their money.

Like their opposite sign, Leo, Aquarians are natural risk-takers, speculators and gamblers. Although their most profitable investments are often longer-term ones, like property and educational projects, they're also very drawn to the stock market, with its prospects of rapid returns. To succeed in the markets, however, they need to use a structured, long-term approach. "Get in quick, get out quick"-style manoeuvres may do the trick for Gemini, but they rarely work for the waterbearer! Open-minded Aquarians will often use astrology to help them play the markets.

Aquarians can also be drawn to invest in "get-rich-quick" schemes, too. Impatience is the bugbear here: Aquarius sees the potential of the idea, not whether or not it's realistic! Money may indeed fall into Aquarius's lap very suddenly, thanks to the influence of Uranus and, once in a blue moon, such schemes may pay off. More often than not, however, the Aquarian path to prosperity is a Saturn-style one, with returns on investments coming only after much hard work. Short-cuts may appeal to Aquarius, but they very, very rarely pay off.

Many Aquarians are also tempted in invest in the businesses of family and friends, and though this sounds like a good idea, it's usually a recipe for disaster. Aquarius is the sign of friendship, it's true, but business and friendship never mix; waterbearers who tangle up their finances with their friends may end up losing money rather than making it. Many Aquarians learn this lesson the hard way, and fail to realise until later in life that their most profitable investment is staring right back at them from the mirror! Since Aquarians have possibly the most creative, original minds in the zodiac, their *own* business ideas are always their best bet ...and the biggest profits are always be made in their very own backyard.

Aside from their self-styled businesses and inventions, Aquarians usually profit by investing in anything new and innovative, from hi-fi and radio, computers, video technology, hardware and software and multimedia publishing, to telecommunications, interactive programming and the Internet. Needless to say, they always have their finger on the pulse of the latest technical developments! Aquarians can also profit by investing in anything that's unusual — be it crystals, vintage cars or other rare commodities. New forms of management consultancy can also prove quite profitable, along with business support systems, translation and "occult" publishing. Transport ventures also make good investments for Aquarians, and you'll find them backing everything from airlines to new electric bus routes. Investments that help to conserve and protect the environment also feature strongly in the Aquarian portfolio, and many like investing in ethical funds. Interestingly, these funds are currently performing very well — thus proving "saving the planet" pays.

♒ The Earning Power Of Aquarius

Aquarius is generally regarded as one of the least materialistic signs in the zodiac and, incidentally, the least ambitious. But although you'll hardly ever find an Aquarian engaged in clawing their way to the top of the corporate ladder, it's also very true that waterbearers do want to make their mark on the world. The cartoon stereotype of Aquarius as the "absent-minded professor" type, happy as a sandboy conducting experiments in their science lab, far away from the rat race and all that goes with it, may contain a certain element of truth, but it doesn't tell the whole story, by any means...

Although Aquarians are rarely ambitious in a personal sense, scratch the surface of the least motivated-looking waterbearer and you'll discover that even they possess some pretty hefty ambitions. Ambitions for other people, though, more often than for themselves. Few Aquarians lie awake at night dreaming of fame and fortune: they're far more concerned with "changing the world". Most waterbearers are born with a deep need to serve humanity, and they generally view their work more as a means of improving society rather than a stepping-stone to personal glory. But it must be said that they're not averse to a little limelight either ...so if they can saunter into the public eye in the course of their chosen work, well, so very much the better!

Aquarians have this burning urge to change things, too, and history shows us that they're pretty good at it. Look behind any revolution or great invention you can think of and you're sure to find an Aquarian somewhere in the picture. Think of political visionaries like Abraham Lincoln and Harold MacMillan, and the impact they've had on the world. Incidentally, Ronald Reagan was an Aquarian, too, and although his politics may have lacked a reforming vision, he certainly showed his Uranian side by bringing astrology into the White House! Then there's Thomas Edison; he was ridiculed and mocked in his lifetime as a madman and eccentric, but if it hadn't been for him, we'd all still perhaps be living by gaslight.

Aquarians tend to have a very futuristic perspective, which they can't help but express through their lifestyle and their work. They're a bit like magicians or sorcerers, who've been given the great gift of seeing into the future. Their challenge is to try and translate what they've seen into workable ideas, or else to tear down old structures and create entirely new ones in their place. And the challenge of integrating the old and the new is one that often one that preoccupies them for the whole of their working lives.

Given their penchant for "time travelling" into the future, along with their independent nature, very few Aquarians seem to settle down in a career until they're well into their thirties. Their typical work pattern involves a considerable amount of travelling and roaming in youth, with a wide variety of freelance or "filler" jobs. Then comes a period of "apprenticeship", when waterbearers are building their skills and trying to turn their visions into reality. Later still, and often not until the age of forty or even fifty, those Aquarians who've succeeded in moulding their ideas into form, will finally make their mark. Like everything else in the life of Aquarians, their work is influenced in varying degrees by Saturn and Uranus, their two co-ruling planets. Uranus gives Aquarians the most amazing ideas and theories, while Saturn gives them the discipline and patience to see them right through to the end.

Regardless of the particular career that Aquarians choose — (politics, technology and teaching are special favourites), they generally prefer working with ideas and people, rather than things. They also love to keep moving, and their ideal working environment is a large, open-plan office, with lots of people milling around and a busy agenda of meetings. Aquarians thrive on discussion and exchanging ideas and they like nothing better than to talk things over. Indeed, it may sometimes seem as though they prefer to talk about things rather than ever *do* anything — but then they'll dash off a masterly report in a flurry of high-powered energy. For the typical Aquarian workstyle is just as erratic as their cash flow! And whenever you see them withdraw into silence, please just leave them alone. Those quiet times are quite essential to their work; that's when they do their very best work, in fact. Aquarians are the kind of people who'll sit in a meeting, say their piece, listen to everyone else, and then come up with an incredible way of reorganizing the whole system to make it a hundred times more efficient. That's the way the Aquarian mind works, and when it's functioning at its best, it's very impressive indeed...

The Aquarian mind can be compared to a highly-strung thoroughbred, since it needs constant stimulation and just the right environment to keep it working properly. Aquarians are enthusiastic souls — that's what makes them such brilliant salespeople, but their enthusiasm must be constantly fed to keep it burning brightly. Waterbearers need work that challenges them to keep learning, growing and thinking creatively, and they'll never be happy anywhere where they feel they're mentally stagnating. Just as Sagittarians need lots of physical space to roam around in, Aquarians need a great deal of mental space. Intellectual freedom, and the ability to think their own thoughts, are way up there on their list of priorities. You'll always find people with Aquarius strong in their charts doing unusual work of one kind or another, whether it's working as an astrologer (many do), or as a troubleshooting consultant, or stirring up controversy, like chat show supremo Oprah Winfrey.

Since Aquarians' natural bent is towards innovation, they're always happiest when they can design new systems, get them up and running, and then move on quickly to the next new project down the line. Change and variety are the Aquarians' lifeblood, and if their work should lack them, they'll soon become depressed. The need for constant change and challenge is why so many Aquarians work freelance, and end up becoming self-employed. Indeed, I can't recall ever having a single

Aquarian client with a steady, full-time job! Too much routine is anathema to the waterbearer's spirit and, provided they've put in the groundwork to establish themselves professionally, a freewheeling lifestyle is where their greatest happiness lies.

Since many Aquarians have great entrepreneurial flair, as well as the capacity for hard work and discipline, they can also do well when they start and run their own business. The only proviso here is that they acknowledge from the outset that their greatest talents lie in the "ideas" side of the enterprise — such as product design, marketing and selling, rather than administration and finance. Indeed, they often do best when they team up with an earth sign, like Virgo, Taurus or Capricorn, who can take care of the practical details that they tend to find so irksome.

Aquarians need to balance their need for change with a corresponding degree of focus, or else they run the risk of dissipating their considerable mindpower. Aquarians are easily distracted, and if they fail to concentrate on a single career calling at a time, they can wind up becoming "jack of all trades, master of none", thereby doing themselves and their talents a considerable disservice. By failing to consolidate, they can also miss career opportunities, since colleagues in their field will usually fail to take them seriously. Part of Aquarius' restlessness stems from their strong need for social contact; Aquarians are profoundly independent, but they're also deeply sociable, too. And the erratic nature of their working energy means that they're happy to work alone for shortish periods of time. But working totally solo is never a long-term option.

≈ The Aquarian Boss

Aquarius is the sign of the group, and waterbearers often like to work in groups, but, contrary to what many people think, I've noticed that Aquarians like to be in charge. Their attitude towards occupying positions of authority can be pretty ambivalent, though. For although they enjoy the feel of a fancy executive title and like nothing more than getting their way, they get pretty claustrophobic if they feel trapped and hemmed in by responsibility. Let's just say that Aquarians aren't among the zodiac's "natural" bosses, but they rise to the occasion admirably when they're called upon to do so! On the plus side, they're brilliant at negotiating, selling and dreaming up sure-fire solutions to even the trickiest of situations. But they can also be detached to the nth degree, and infuriatingly impassive. It's a sign of extremes, remember, and that goes for bosses, too!

≈ The Aquarian Employee

Although Aquarians can make good employees because they're basically quite cooperative by nature, there are certain factors that everyone who works with a waterbearer should always bear in mind. Firstly, Aquarians are extremely hardworking and diligent, but they'll only work hard at the things *they* want to do. Aquarians will always rebel against excessive routine, and they'll also kick against work they feel is too mundane. Rather like their opposite sign Leo, Aquarians love to work with the "big picture", and they get very bored and bogged down if they're faced with too many details. That's when they make mistakes and get sloppy and careless: it's also the point at which they become a liability rather than an asset. Never forget that Aquarians are great ideas people, the conceptual architects of the cosmos: they weren't born to work as administrators or accountants, so it's better for them to be where they belong! Finally, Aquarians aren't the kind of people to keep whining for pay-rises and bonuses: not that they'll take to being exploited either, but provided they're working on projects they believe in, they're rarely too hung up about the actual financial rewards.

♒ Aquarius & Career

Aquarians' first-class intellect and razor-sharp logic make them ideally suited to a scientific career. This is the sign of the "great inventor", and many of history's greatest experimenters and innovators have been born with the sun in this sign. If it weren't for Thomas Edison, we'd all still be reading this book by candlelight. Then there was Galileo, who startled the world with his famous telescope. The naturalist Charles Darwin was also an Aquarian, whose theories turned society totally upside down a century ago. Aquarians love to keep learning, too, so many find fulfilment in academic or university life.

One of the most popular career fields for Aquarians, and one to which they're uniquely suited, is that of information technology. With its unique mix of technology and communication, it's definitely a field where they can really come into their own. Modern business now depends so heavily on computer science that career opportunities have probably never been better for Aquarians of all ages. Aquarian IT experts work in fields as diverse as programming, networking and desktop publishing; and many freewheeling

Aquarians have successful careers as technology consultants.

Aquarians enjoy problem-solving, too, and relish finding ways of putting their talents to practical use. A great many builders are born under Aquarius, thus reflecting the influence of Saturn; and since Uranus is linked with electricity, there are many Aquarian electricians, too. Engineering careers of all kinds appeal to Aquarians, both male and female: their particular favourites, though, are telecommunications and transport. Your local garage repair man or mechanic may more than likely be an Aquarian, and have you also noticed how he loves to stop for a chat? Aquarians love working in radio, too, either as announcers or as technicians. Aquarius is also the sign of aviation, air transport and space travel. Every little Aquarian boy daydreams of becoming an astronaut and quite a few of them have succeed in making the grade. The first solo transatlantic pilot, Charles Lindbergh, was an Aquarian, and these days you'll find many Aquarians working as pilots, flight engineers and also in aircraft maintenance.

Another field of technology that draws Aquarians in droves is TV, film and video, and many rise to success both behind and in front of the camera. Aquarian director Ken Russell is renowned for his shocking masterpieces, as are fellow directors Francois Truffaut, John Schlesinger and the late Franco Zeffirelli. Many pioneers of the film industry were Aquarians, too, including Sergei Eisenstein and D.W. Griffith. Many leading actresses are also Aquarians, and they usually have a slightly offbeat image: Mia Farrow, for instance, or Zsa Zsa Gabor and Vanessa Redgrave.

Aquarian men are the "strong silent type" and many hearthrobs of yesteryear had the sun in this sign — there's James Dean, Humphrey Bogart, and the ultimate screen idol, Clark Gable. More recently, there's John Travolta, Tom Selleck and Paul Newman. Waterbearers love to shock people with their unconventional, outspoken viewpoints, and TV abounds with controversy-loving Aquarians: there's Oprah Winfrey, and the "agony aunt" Claire Rayner and the outspoken feminist Germaine Greer.

Aquarians love to get their thoughts down on paper, and they're well represented in the roll-call of unusual writers. The creator of Alice in Wonderland, Lewis Carroll, had the Sun in Aquarius, as did Virginia Woolf, Lord Byron and James Joyce, whose work literally revolutionised twentieth-century fiction. Latter-day Aquarians often excel as writers and journalists, or science-fiction authors and public speakers. Some Aquarians prefer using their communication skills to help others, finding job satisfaction as either teachers or business trainers. They usually prefer teaching from secondary level upwards, but with their gift for conveying ideas, most Aquarians can teach almost anyone.

Since Aquarius is the sign that lives to serve the greater good, environmental organizations like Greenpeace and Friends of the Earth are a natural magnet for them, even if only on a part-time, voluntary basis. With their gift for selling and persuading, Aquarians make excellent charity fund-raisers, too — whilst others strive to "change the world" by entering politics at a local or national level. Many Aquarians devote their working lives to building new kinds of social structures, and the whole New Age field is packed with Aquarians, all "doing their thing", and finding new ways of living and being. Lots of Aquarians are drawn to complementary medicine, for instance, and they make excellent hypnotists and healers. Many also practise mind-body medicine like the Alexander Technique and the Feldenkrais Method; others set up communities and centres. Uranus rules astrology, too: many astrologers are born under this sign, and can make the subject so fascinating and compelling that it holds their attention for a lifetime.

♒ Aquarius: Keys to Financial Success

- DO acknowledge and capitalise on the fact that your creative and innovative gifts are your greatest financial assets. Put your brainwaves to practical use and you'll be amazed at the results.

- DO invest in yourself — and not your friends. Build confidence in your ideas and back them up with your chequebook.

- DO make full use of your great ability to communicate. Develop your network of friends and contacts to the utmost, and remember to keep in touch: for you never really know when you might need their help.

- DO learn as much as you can about financial management and planning. Cultivate a long-term approach to your money rather than aiming to "get rich quick".

- DO remember to think positively at all times. Use the Saturn side of your nature to build self-discipline and structure, rather than making you pessimistic.

♒ Rich & Famous Aquarians

Galileo
Abraham Lincoln
Ronald Reagan
Charles Dickens
John McEnroe
Lewis Carroll
James Joyce
Django Reinhardt
Philip Glass
Mary Quant
Bob Marley
Alan Parker
Katharine Ross
Claire Bloom
Nastassjia Kinski
Elaine Stritch
James Dean
Clark Gable
Alan Alda
Telly Savalas
John Hurt
Cory Aquino
Libby Purves
Betty Friedan
Toni Morrison

WA Mozart
F.D. Roosevelt
Charles Lindbergh
Nikolai Tesla
Jackson Pollock
Virginia Woolf
Stephane Grappelli
Yoko Ono
Peter Gabriel
Placido Domingo
Vanessa Redgrave
Mia Farrow
Greta Schacchi
Jane Seymour
Charlotte Rampling
Jack Lemmon
Paul Newman
Gene Hackman
Robert Wagner
Ernst Borgnine
Barry Humphries
Lisa-Marie Presley
Oprah Winfrey
Germaine Greer
Helen Gurley Brown

Princess Stephanie of Monaco

⊬

PISCES
February 20th to March 20th

As our financial journey around the zodiac draws to a close, it's time to don your deep-sea diving gear and plumb the depths of Pisces the fish! Or should I say, "fishes", since the traditional symbol for Pisces is actually two fishes — swimming, somewhat confusingly, in totally opposite directions! Aptly enough, choosing their life's direction is often quite a problem for the fish, and many Pisceans find themselves thinking, "Which way should I swim? ...upstream or down?" And in the background, meanwhile, there's the equally pressing problem of money — or how to hold body and soul together during life's long and watery journey...

If the truth be told, Pisces is a pretty complex sign, since its shifting, mutable nature embraces aspects of all the other eleven — and there's usually no telling which of the twelve signs is likely to manifest next! Pisceans are subject to constantly changing, chameleon-like moods, which reflect their multifaceted role in the timeless tapestry of life. For although most fishes are generally kind and gentle, they'll be as aggressive as an Aries or sarcastic as a Scorpio, should the occasion truly demand. Catch them at a party, and they can be as witty as a Gemini or as charming as a Libra. In their workaday world, even the vaguest-looking fish may be as meticulous as a Virgo or as calculating as a Capricorn, and you'd be sensible not to forget it. And when it comes to affairs of the heart, they're confusingly changeable too — as detached as an Aquarius or as sensuous as a Taurus...

I'm sure you've got the picture by now, and you're probably beginning to wonder if there's anything at all about Pisces that's, well, really and truly Piscean? Yes, indeed there is. Think back to that gentleness and kindness, and there you'll find the answer, for the fish possesses both these qualities in rare and genuine abundance. Pisceans are wise and tolerant too — also rare qualities in this busy day and age. And then there's that other great gift, Piscean compassion, for few other signs have such deep-seated natural empathy for the suffering of their fellow men. When all's said and done, Pisces' virtues may not be that bankable, but the world we live in would nevertheless be far, far poorer without them...

As well as the fishes, another animal symbol that's linked to Pisces is the dolphin, a creature that's recently taken the spotlight in the world's imagination and consciousness. Dolphins have been revered for centuries for their wisdom and compassion, as well as for their unique ability empathise with the suffering of human beings. They have even been known to sacrifice their own lives when a human that they loved had passed away — a Piscean theme that recurs time and again in the legends surrounding this sign.

Astrologically, Pisces is ruled by the planet Neptune, named after the god of the watery ocean depths. Neptune ruled the seas, rivers and all the waters of the earth and, by all accounts, he was a pretty unpredictable soul. His moods were so volatile, they could change at a moment's notice; he could also be quite malicious too, wreaking havoc and disaster on unsuspecting sailors who ventured a little too far into the realms of his watery kingdom. Neptune was a shape-shifting god, who liked nothing better than to confuse the hell out of everybody by turning himself into a horse, or a rock, or even a mass of seaweed! In keeping with Neptune's mutable nature, most Pisceans are natural actors, who are sometimes better at "being someone else" than they are at living out their own lives...

Like many latter-day Pisceans, Neptune was sometimes afflicted with bouts of "divine discontent", or strange, insatiable longings for more than he already had. Neptune's restless nature is mirrored in the lives of countless Pisceans who've acquired more riches than they could ever want or need in a lifetime, but who are always searching for that elusive "something else" — that missing piece of the jigsaw that will make their lives fall magically into place. But Pisceans can only connect with this "magic" by developing their deeper, more spiritual side. For the serenity they're forever seeking can only be found by exploring their own inner depths!

Psychic powers and the gift of clairvoyance are also linked with Pisces, and it's interesting to note that the discovery of the planet Neptune, in 1846, coincided with a huge rise of interest in all things occult and psychic. The world spiritualist movement came into being at this time, thanks to the table-tappings and mediumistic exploits of the famous Fox sisters in the USA — although the sisters themselves were later exposed as frauds.

Recognising Pisceans isn't usually much of a problem, for Neptune's children often look quite vague and dreamy. If you're at a party, look out for medium-build people with pale, translucent skin. Fishes are often fair-haired, too, though you'll sometimes find dark ones with shiny, gypsy-like tresses. But as with their Scorpio cousins, the real giveaway here is the eyes. Piscean eyes are heartstoppingly lovely: they're generally pale, either delicate blue or pistachio green, and flecked with tiny ocean lights. The fish's eyes are often deep-set, and may even be slightly protruding. Pisceans often look as though they're about to burst into tears — and if they've been listening to a sad story, they may well do just that! Bump into fishes at a party or reception, and you'll invariably find that they have a glass in their hand, and it's unlikely to be straight soda, for the typical Piscean can sometimes be a bit of a lush. But drinking to excess is something all Pisceans should avoid, for it aggravates their tendency to "let themselves go" as the years roll by. Of course, not all

Pisceans turn out to be alcoholics, but it's a disease that they're particularly prone to.

Fishes can also have problems when it comes to coping with stress. Pisceans loathe pressure of any kind, and they really do need to swim in calm and tranquil waters. They're constitutionally incapable of living for very long in an atmosphere of conflict without it taking a toll on their health. When things get too "heavy" in Pisces' stretch of the river, they'll either take flight or simply drown their sorrows in drink. But peace and solitude are what they really need, along with a few quiet hours spent just mulling things over. Pisceans are so deeply sensitive to everyone else's "vibes", be they those of their mate, the cleaning-lady, or even just the postman, that every once in a while they need to withdraw from life completely, just to restore their vital energies and touch base with who they really are — and to remember that many of their "problems" belong to somebody else. Daily meditation can be a very helpful discipline, as it brings fishes back to their centre, and restores their peace and calm. It's also a useful outlet for their powerful spiritual energies, and stops them from overindulging in that "other kind of spirit"...

It's often said that Pisceans are born to "suffer or save", and the roots of this saying lie deep in the fish's watery nature. Just like the ocean, they absorb everything that's going on around them, and they're constantly getting involved in other people's "stuff". Pisces' sensitive, caring nature may well inspire them to go out and *do* something about the problems they see around them, in which case they'll naturally gravitate to the "saviour" end of the spectrum. These are the Pisceans who become social workers or politicians, in their efforts to change the world; they also flock in droves to the healing and helping professions.

But if a fish lacks discrimination, or a sense of personal identity, they can all too easily founder in the feelings of those they're trying to save. That's when Pisceans become "victims" and drift into a state of suffering. And whilst it's true that many Pisceans feign helplessness to manipulate their friends and family, ("Excuse me, (flutter, flutter) — could you just run down to the shops for me — my back is so stiff today"!), many fishes get genuinely stranded on the barren quicksands of life. You'll find countless Piscean wives who dreamed of "saving" their husbands trapped in truly hellish marriages to alcoholics and other kinds of addicts. Many do find the strength to leave eventually, but it's never an easy path. Happily, Pisceans usually get better at standing up for themselves when their Sun progresses into Aries. That's when they stop being doormats and acquire a bit of "backbone" — along with a healthy dollop of assertiveness, not to mention a sterner will!

Even as children, Pisceans are often unusually caring and gentle, and conscious parents will teach their young fishes the art of wise discrimination. Their instinct is always to relieve pain and suffering wherever they find it, but Pisceans also need to learn how to protect themselves, too... Another Piscean trait that's often observable in childhood is their psychic sensitivity. Piscean children will hold voluble conversations with their invisible "playmates", and may even discourse about past lives and tell you who they were "before".

Before you dismiss this as wild imagination, remember that Edgar Cayce, the US seer considered by many to be the greatest psychic of the twentieth century, was born under the sign of Pisces, and many fishes have followed in his footsteps. But the gift of second sight is often a hard one to carry amid the hubbub of contemporary life. The fact is, Pisceans see visions, and those visions are often quite mind-bending. It's as though they have the power to go off and visit other worlds, and then come back to tell us what they've seen. Sometimes, as with Einstein and Michelangelo — both of whom were Pisceans — their visions are so incredible, they really do change the world. But at other times, fishes just can't find the right words or images to express the things they've seen. And sometimes, having glimpsed the transcendent beauty of those other visionary worlds, they're loath to return to this one — and that gives rise to their habit of "escaping"...

Pisces is one of the most tolerant, easy-going signs in the zodiac, but when life gets too uncomfortable, Pisceans will simply refuse to join in. Piscean escapism can take many forms. On a basic level, many fishes refuse to watch the news or even read the newspapers, because they find everyday life too upsetting. They often prefer the rose-tinted world of daytime soap-operas and sherry at sundown! And when it comes to interpersonal relations, they can be equally slippery and evasive. The Piscean dislike of confrontation is equalled only by that of Libra, and they'll go to pretty extreme lengths to avoid it. When things get too hot for their liking, they often just "swim away", leaving no explanation for their friends, their family or the boss... If they choose to stay rather than leave, they'll often retreat into silence — or even an alcoholic haze, whichever works best at the time...

Pisceans are also credited with being indecisive, but their superficial air of vagueness can sometimes conceal a powerful will. Pisceans have trouble making decisions because they believe that everything in life is relative, and they can always manage to see things from the other person's point of view. They rarely stoop to argue, and very often they don't need to — for most fishes have mastered the art of passive resistance to an awe-inspiring degree. Most of them know that if you don't push too hard, but just wait patiently for people to "fall in", then life has a funny way of eventually giving you what you want!

Pisceans can be surprisingly strong-minded when they choose to be, and they're often idealistic, too. It may seem out of character for the mutable, daydreamy fish to take a stand on matters of principle. But don't forget, high-minded Jupiter was once the solitary ruler of this sign, which gives Pisces its faith in the future, as well as its willingness to speak out for a "cause". Prod a Pisces in their idealistic spot and you'll see a different person entirely. Suggest a trip to Macdonalds, say! You'll probably be treated to an ear-singeing diatribe on the destruction of the rainforests, not to mention the cruelty of meat-eating! People often make the mistake of thinking Pisceans are weak and inconsistent, till they've seen them defending their beliefs. Think of Piscean Mikhail Gorbachev, whose leadership helped to end the Cold War. Think of Einstein, too, or Michelangelo, and then you'll begin to see what

Pisceans can do when they put their minds to it ...pretty impressive, isn't it?

)(Pisces and Money

When it comes to money, Pisces is a sign that's full of surprises — and even the odd contradiction. Appearances might lead you to believe that Pisceans' generally vague and impractical air means that they'd dissolve into confusion at the merest glimpse of a calculator. But appearances can be deceptive, since the reverse is so often the case. For although it's true that Pisces is often more at home with "vibrations" and "feelings" than the sterner realities of a balance-sheet, the facts of their financial existence — if and when they choose to reveal them — are often far healthier than you might previously have supposed. The simple fact is, most fishes are actually quite good with their money and, one way or another, they always, but always, get by...

You'll also find, though, that money rarely ranks high on the fish's scale of priorities. The ruling passions of Pisces' life are always their dreams and creative visions, and although these may often need financing, moneymaking, pure and simple, is rarely seen as an end in itself. As Pisceans see it, money is just a means to helping people and to making everyone feel happy. Fishes are more turned on by what they can actually do with their money — not by just simply acquiring it, like a Taurus, say, or a Capricorn.

In addition, there's the fact that Pisceans often see money as just an illusion. Rather like the rest of us, they play the game of money because they've very little choice. Unlike many of us, though, they rarely get carried away by a feeling of material craving. "Money's just something that flows in and out of my life", says a Piscean client of mine, a children's nanny called Jackie. "It's good when I've got it, but it's not the end of the world when I don't. And when I've got it, I spend it — usually on having a good time with my friends. I don't feel it's particularly important to try and hang on to it, despite the fact that my work's irregular, because I know that there's always more coming. I trust that the universe will look after me, and it hasn't let me down yet!"

Jackie's relaxed approach to money is thoroughly Piscean. Fishes are great at trusting that there'll "always be enough", and it's a positive attitude that usually sees them through. And every now and then, of course, you'll bump into a millionaire fish. Rich fishes often get that way by accident, though, through marrying someone with money, or because they happened to inherit it. Or, rather like Aquarius, perhaps they found they'd made a stack of money whilst they were busy doing something else — like painting pictures, or writing a book, or recording a new piece of music. Please don't get the impression that fishes aren't fond of money, though. Most fishes are keenly aware of the pleasures it can buy, and how it serves to make life more comfortable. Pisceans have a profoundly hedonistic streak, and they like nothing better than indulging their appetites. But to their eternal credit, they always think of sharing their good fortune and doing all they can to help those less fortunate than themselves.

Best-selling authors Anthony Robbins and James Redfield were both born with the Sun in Pisces, and both have used their creative gifts to generate multi-million-dollar fortunes. Interestingly, though, both men have also made a point of sharing their wealth with the underprivileged, by setting up charitable foundations which receive a part of every dollar they earn. In line with this philanthropic approach, many Pisceans adhere to the ancient principle of tithing — giving a fixed percentage of your earnings, usually 10 per cent, to a charity or spiritual organization. Giving the "first fruits" of one's labours back to the universe in a gesture of gratitude also ensures that people don't forget that their wealth comes through them and not from them! It's also one of the oldest "prosperity principles" under the sun.

Certain Pisceans, though, set their course in life with the intention of making lots of money. But if you happen to inquire, you'll probably discover that they're doing x and y to finance their creative projects — or for some charity work, perhaps, that's also bound to benefit others.

In company with the other water signs, Cancer and Scorpio, Pisceans can be pretty shrewd with money. And if, by chance, they happen to harness their excellent intuition and almost psychic powers of judgement to their moneymaking ventures, they'll nearly always succeed in making considerable amounts of cash. But the urge to renounce the world and all its trappings is always present in the fish's consciousness. Sometimes they build themselves a pretty enviable lifestyle — a high-powered job, a lovely house and fancy car. But they may wake up one day with the feeling that they want to give it all away, and head off to live in a monastery. And although few fishes actually take such a drastic step, I've still seen many Piscean clients rebel against society's materialistic ways. Often, they may start to give away lots of their possessions — fine furniture, clothes and jewellery, etc. — in the pursuit of a simpler way of life. Pisceans know they don't really need that much to be happy — a bowl of lentil soup will taste like caviar if consumed in the right spirit, after all — and they sometimes find that, as far as they are concerned, the simple life is the happiest one of all.

In keeping with the fish's dual nature, Pisceans often veer between two extremes of financial behaviour, depending on whether Jupiter or Neptune is more powerfully emphasised in their chart. Jupiter is the ancient ruler of Pisces, and fishes who swim in this direction are the ones who've learned how to trust. Jupiter-type Pisceans have a deep-seated faith in the process of life and, no matter how black things look financially, they just *know* things are going to work out. Their intuitive powers are also second to none, and can often light the way through a dark financial jungle. More often than not, the fish's faith in life is fully repaid, too — for Jupiter often gives Pisceans considerable "money-luck", providing, of course, that they temper trust with prudence. This is the person who wakes up to find they've won the Lottery, or who, after years of financial hardship, writes a song that goes straight to Number One! Jupiter's influence means Pisceans can also be quite generous — and their generosity is usually returned to them many times over.

That's the good news. The bad news is that Jupiter sometimes makes Pisceans quite reckless with their money. Their boundless trust means that they're sometimes prone to great bouts of extravagance. And occasionally, you'll get the "Piscean drifter", who can be a terrible financial sponge. They'll regale you with endless stories of how much money their paintings are going to sell for, whilst they eat all your food and systematically work their way through your wine cellar! Sadly, some of the more creatively gifted Pisceans fall into this trap, and believe it's down to someone else to support them till their boat comes in. Go down to your local bar, and you may well hear someone wailing on about how they were born in the wrong day and age ...and whatever happened to artistic patronage ...and why doesn't anyone appreciate the arts these days — chances are, they're a Pisces!

Pisceans who are more attuned to Neptune, however, tend to manage their money in distinctly different ways. Neptune makes fishes worry about things a lot and, in particular, they about money, with the result that they pay more attention to money than would otherwise be the case. Neptunians feel that they don't know what the future holds, so they'd better be prepared. Fishes are often afflicted with strange, irrational fears. Paradoxically, though, this can lead to quite positive results! For though Neptunians may not lay their financial foundations as systematically or as thoroughly as a Virgo, say, they're still a lot more practical than most people would really suspect.

Neptune endows even the humblest-looking fish with a powerful psychic "radar" that they can use to generate wealth. Neptune-type Pisceans often have the knack of knowing just which products will top the sales league, or what colour the fashion world will want to wear next spring. Quite clearly, this is a tremendous asset in any field concerned with changing consumer trends, and that's why so many Pisceans work in fashion and product design.

Like the other water signs, Cancer and Scorpio, Pisceans will often invest in property. It's their retreat or sanctuary from the outside world, a buffer against inflation, and their investment in peace of mind. And although they enjoy spending money as much as the next sign, the influence of Neptune can make Pisceans pretty frugal. The Piscean passion for recycling is, very often, quite unsurpassed! Pisceans who are trying to cut themselves some financial slack in order to record their demo tape, say, or pen the first draft of a novel, will happily dress entirely from the charity shop, and live off toasted sandwiches made from yesterday's wholemeal bread. But since they're such romantics at heart, and so skilled at making poverty seem tasteful, those second-hand ensembles will probably look like designer outfits, and their toasted sandwiches will always be laced with exotic herbs. Neptunians rarely complain about living on a shoestring: they know how to make it fun and elegant, and they also know that "this too will pass"...

Neptune gives Pisces the gift of knowing how to batten down the hatches when a financial storm is blowing, but it can also make them somewhat materialistic, too. Pisceans who feel that their emotional needs weren't properly met in childhood may fall victims to "divine discontent", and lay up mountains of money in an attempt to boost their self-esteem. And although most fishes are generally fairly honest people, a less than promising start in life can make them prone to deceit and delusion. Neptunians who feel short-changed by life can be surprisingly ruthless in their financial dealings, not to mention self-centred and grasping. Happily for the rest of us, such "philandering fishes" are few and far between... But it's always a good idea to remember every sign's potential, for folly as well as virtue!

On a day-to-day financial level, most Pisceans manage their money quite efficiently – despite the fact that their approach can often be quite unorthodox! Piscean men often reject the classic "breadwinner" role, and though they're often adept at business, thanks to their excellent intuition, they can also be quite self-centred. Rather like Capricorn, in fact, Pisceans often choose a career or lifestyle, and just expect their families to "fall in." And since dreams and visions are the only currency that Pisceans really value, there's no point in arguing, either. Start a fight about money, and most Pisceans will simply swim away...

Piscean women sometimes adopt the role of a "starving artist", and live it out in a suitably stylish garret. Or perhaps they'll martyr themselves "for the family", taking on a humdrum, boring job, just to make the financial ends meet. Many a dutiful lady fish kicks over the traces, though, when her Sun moves into Aries, and she begins, at long last, to do "her own thing". But putting her own needs last is often a pretty tough habit to break.

Jupiter-type Pisceans often have serious difficulty in dealing with the mundane facts of financial reality, like paying the rent, for instance, and filling in their tax returns. It's something they'll need to master, though, unless they opt to take the easy way out and live off welfare handouts or their long-suffering partner instead. Jupiter's influence can also make Pisceans overly-optimistic about their present and future earnings, which means that they'll spend to the very last penny, without ever thinking of their budget.

Neptunian-style Pisceans, though, usually budget and save out of fear. But the watery influence of Neptune can make them prone to self-deception, too. A classic Piscean financial foible is that of "forgetting" to balance their chequebook. That way, they can carry on telling themselves that things are better than they really are. Nightmare scenarios can also ensue when Pisceans get caught up in their projects. That's when the paperwork really goes to hell and the fish is overwhelmed by a flood of unpaid bills! If terminal confusion is to be avoided, their partner needs to step in — or, if all else fails, a first-class accountant! Pisceans are often prone to irregular cash flow and income, so in times of financial plenty, it's important for them to build some reserves.

The one financial area where all Pisceans are really vulnerable, however, is their inability to say "No" whenever anyone asks them for a loan. Pisces is the classic "soft touch" of the zodiac, particularly where family and friends are concerned, and their open-handed manner can sometimes be a threat to their financial wellbeing. Pisceans will give money away freely, even when they really can't afford it, because they simply hate to say "No". They're vague about keeping tabs on their lendings, too, and will very often forget who they've lent to — and also, incidentally, how much! Sometimes they'll try and adopt a stonily unhelpful position, as a kind of token resistance, but they usually give in if someone asks them more than twice! The best course of action for open-handed Pisceans is often to set up a separate account for helping friends and family in need. That way, their urge to "come to the rescue" won't play havoc with their own domestic cash flow, and they'll always have sufficient to cover their monthly bills and expenses. Finally, do bear in mind that Pisces' vagueness about lending money also extends to their borrowings. Not that they don't have every intention of paying you back. It's just that they tend to forget...

⋊ The Spending Style of Pisces

When it comes to spending money, Pisceans are creatures of extremes and, generally speaking, it's a case of "all or nothing". Fishes can fluctuate between Jupiterian extravagance and Neptunian frugality with a speed that's really quite startling. And although cash sometimes slips through their fingers just like water through a sieve, their spending will instantly stop if they get seized by financial panic. There's an aspect of the Pisces personality that takes an almost masochistic delight in 'going without', and they can practice the art of self-denial to a degree that even Capricorn would admire. They'll live off split-pea soup for months, and comb the markets for bargain supplies. Their thrift-shop ensembles can be truly theatrical, and they'll buy everything second-hand, with the exception of their shoes — that's the one commodity they'll never, ever skimp on! At other times, it can be guilt rather than expediency that stops them from spending their money. Neptunians are capable of slashing their food bill almost to zero, or refusing to eat out, because of "the starving millions" elsewhere...

When Pisceans are feeling prosperous though, the Jupiterian side of their nature comes out to play, and this can make them surprisingly spendthrift. Typical Pisceans can be total impulse-buyers, who make spending decisions with their heart and rarely with their head. These are the people who set out with a shopping list, and then return home with a stack of different items! Much of their spending is emotionally-based,: they'll spend to cheer themselves up and they'll also spend to celebrate! They're also prone to spending freely on others. Piscean generosity is legendary — and, also, incidentally, quite genuine.

When they're feeling expansive, though , a fish won't bother waiting for the sales. If there's money in their bank account, that means they can afford it! Pisceans can sometimes indulge in spending sprees that would do credit to even a Leo — but unlike other signs, they also know just when to stop. When they feel they've spent enough, typical fishes will embark upon yet another cycle of self-denial, until the urge to indulge themselves strikes them yet again!

When it comes to spending money, Pisces' top priority is beauty. Fishes are generally hedonists at heart, and if a thing has beauty, it usually gives them pleasure, too. Much of their spending is lavished on their homes: the need to create a peaceful refuge from the world is a prime consideration for Pisces. And even when they're living on a shoestring budget, the fish's home is always a delight to visit. The lighting will be soft and shaded, the sofas draped with sensuous fabrics, and there'll be lots of lovely things to listen to, taste and smell. The walls will be hung with subtle, romantic paintings, and there'll be lots of objects and pictures that carry the theme of the sea. Piscean gardens are often exquisite, too, with many rare and unusual plants, flowing water and maybe a fishpond. Pisceans enjoy reading and their bookshelves are often stocked with escapist literature, like science fantasy or romances, rather than "How To" books or self-help guides! There won't be many gadgets around the fish's kitchen either. Pisceans don't spend money on the basis of "things being useful" — but your Piscean host will doubtless cook you a meal to remember, washed down with plenty of wine!

Pisceans are highly sociable, too, and like to keep up with the latest films and shows. Much of Pisces' "fun money" also gets spent on music, either by going to live concerts or adding to their own collection. Many Pisceans are keen musicians, while others collect old and unusual instruments, and sometimes learn to play them, too.

The need to escape at regular intervals also features in Pisces' budget, and when they leave town, they usually head for the water's edge. Many Pisceans have a second home or regular hideaway by the sea, and they also enjoy spending money on all kinds of watersports. Deep-sea diving, windsurfing and water-skiing are the fish's favourites, whilst well-heeled Pisceans will often opt for sailing. They're not the greatest athletes in the zodiac, though. You'll rarely find them spending money at the gym: try the local dance studio or yoga class instead!

Pisceans like to look good, too, and the typical fish's wardrobe will invariably be well-stocked. Wealthy Piscean ladies favour elegant, flowing garments in gentle, delicate shades, whilst less affluent fishes often opt for a "hippie" style. Whatever their budget-range, however, you'll never find a Pisces wearing tight or restrictive clothing: ease of movement and comfort are their Number One priorities. They'll also gladly cut down on their clothes budget to have more money to spend on shoes. Every Pisces lady has a footwear collection to envy — and even Piscean toddlers just love to shop for shoes!

Future-watching is another Piscean obsession, since "knowing what's going to happen" makes them feel more secure. Despite the fact that they're pretty psychic themselves, many fishes spend a small fortune on Tarot and astrology readings. Indeed, they often get so inspired by the seer's art that they enrol for psychic classes, too!

♓ Pisces: Saving and Investing

Despite their penchant for spending sprees, most Pisceans are quite adept at saving. Fear of the future is usually their primary motive, and setting money aside helps them feel a little more secure. Pisceans tend to be quite secretive about their saving habits, and they're more than likely to conceal their holdings from their family. You'll find Pisceans businessmen holding clandestine portfolios of stocks and shares that even their wives don't know about, and Pisces wives who save bank notes and silver in a teapot.

Neptunian fearfulness endows most Pisceans with the instinctive habit of "saving for a rainy day". Most fishes enjoy saving for specific projects, especially where these will enhance their self-expression or future security. Pisceans have little difficulty in saving for arts courses, for instance, or towards the cost of buying a home. But one trap they often fall into is that of casting their nets too wide. Fishes will take out a new insurance policy or savings plan on impulse — because they "like the look of the advert", and can end up with a huge range of savings they have genuine trouble keeping track of. Like Virgo, they often squirrel away lots of different funds, and then forget exactly where they've put what — which only exacerbates their financial confusion! Pisceans don't usually hide money under the floorboards, though, but they often can't remember just where they put their passbook! The fish's best savings strategy is to choose two or three schemes that offer good rates of interest, and to save by banker's order. It's also a good idea to have at least one savings account which can't be accessed instantly, to avoid any impulse spending.

When it comes to investment, most Pisceans do best with a longer-term approach, although their mutable, restless nature often draws them to high-risk speculation. Having a structured financial focus helps keep every Piscean on track and, as a general rule, investing in property are an ideal starting-point. Pisceans enjoy buying houses and apartments, and they're adept at finding unusual developments that they can restore and sell on at a profit. More business-minded Pisceans have established lucrative property holdings, often connected with the sea or with leisure. Whether it's seaside cottages in France, or bijoux town-houses in London, however, Piscean property will invariably be that "little bit different."

Shrewd and intuitive most fishes undoubtedly are, but there are certain investment pitfalls which they should all be well aware of. Their Neptunian nature makes them prone to deception, by both themselves and others. Pisceans have excellent powers of judgement, as well as a psychic "sixth sense", but they always need to check the facts and never do deals on hearsay. They can all too easily get swept away by the emotional charge of a "steal", and then find one day that they've simply been badly conned.

As a general rule, Pisceans also need to draw a firm line between business and pleasure. They'll often be drawn to invest in friends or acquaintances, but it's usually a classic route to letdowns. The supposition that Pisces is a "soft touch" is often grounded in reality, but fishes can protect themselves by following some simple ground-rules:

1. Don't invest in friends;
2. Don't do deals over dinner; and
3. Don't even think about doing business if you've been drinking.

These guidelines aren't a cure-all, but they'll certainly help considerably.

Investment-wise, one of the best fields for Pisces is the hospitality business, in all its many guises. Hotels, restaurants, wine bars, coffee shops and guest houses can all prove profitable, especially when the fish is involved in day-to-day operations. Businesses with a spiritual or religious connection may also be worth looking at: these include publishing, videos, and maybe even residential centres.

Pisces has a strong connection with the media and "image industry", too: advertising agencies, film and video, the record industry and entertainment promotion could all be potentially profitable – along with photographic laboratories and TV production companies. As well as marine property development, Piscean investors can consider other enterprises connected with the sea. These include yachting and chandlery, pearl-diving and salvage, fishing and seafood production. Finally, astrologers have traditionally linked Neptune to the gas and oil industry, as well as to chemicals. There's also a lucrative link to the wine and liquor trade – the only proviso being, take care not to drink the profits!

♓ The Earning Power Of Pisces

When it comes to competing in the career stakes, the simple truth is this: most Pisceans don't. The fish is one of the least ambitious signs in the zodiac, which isn't to say that you won't find lots of successful fishes out there! Pisces is one of the most creative signs of the zodiac, and the pinnacles of success are often crowded with fishes galore. It's just that Pisceans are generally far more focused on what they're actually doing — and the pleasure that it gives them, rather than where their career is going ...and more often than not, their work involves others, for Pisceans love people and frequently dream of saving the world.

But back to the vexed question of ambition... Although it's rarely a conscious kind of knowing on their part, Pisceans often see material ambition, along with making lots of money, as an intrinsically futile activity. Unlike some of the more "driven" signs, like Aries, say, or Capricorn, Pisceans are often born knowing that "all things must pass" — which also includes all successes and achievements. So all too often, they see very little point in trying. Armed with this knowledge, typical Pisceans will tend to approach their work in one of two different ways: either they'll decide that striving to build a career is a total waste of time and nail their colours firmly to the mast of the fishy "drifter", or else they'll harness their talents to the service of humanity. These latter are the more visionary fishes, who resolve to "swim upstream" and make their mark on the world. It's far from an easy path, and not every fish is up to the journey. But those that succeed often do change the world, and sometimes they also save it! For just like their Piscean brothers, Einstein, Cayce and Gorbachev, many Pisceans can and do succeed in making the world a better place.

Even the most motivated Pisceans can often come across as dreamy, vague and unfocused. But every now and then, you'll run into a fish who possesses real mettle, and who's bent on realising the higher potentials of their sign. These fishes are special people indeed, and their determination may take you thoroughly by surprise if you've only come across the more dreamy Pisceans before. But never forget that water will always dissolve any obstacles in its path, and fishes who've decided that they're "going places" are pretty well unstoppable.

That little word "decide" is what's crucial, though. For if fishes are to succeed, it's vital that they set their direction quite early on in life and focus all their subsequent efforts firmly to that end. Astrologers often say, somewhat cruelly, that if Pisceans haven't "made it" by their late twenties or early thirties, then they won't succeed at all, and it's this issue of "decision" that's totally crucial to the outcome. Pisces' first steps to success lie in finding out where their talents lie, for all fishes need to decide where they're headed, and then stick firmly with it! Otherwise, the temptation to simply drift and "go with the flow" can be well nigh overwhelming.

Experience shows that it's particularly important for fishes to have the very best start in life, including the best possible education . They need to start developing their gifts and abilities from the earliest possible age, along with the confidence to go out and use them. Shyness can sometimes be a crippling problem for Pisceans, and the sooner they overcome it, the better their prospects will be. Once Pisceans have fixed their course, and are willing to work hard to get there, they can scale the heights of success as adroitly as any Capricorn, though they personally haven't much of a head for "heights". In fact, you'll often find they have an earth or fire partner urging them on from the sidelines!

Pisceans can be incredibly compassionate and empathic, and they often find ways to put these virtues to practical use. Fishes are natural "caretakers", with a gift for nurturing people which often finds its perfect expression in the hospitality business. I have two Piscean clients who've each built up a first-class reputation running small, but exquisite hotels. Their aesthetic gifts have been brought into commission, too, for each hotel is rather like a gallery, with its tasteful decorations and arrays of objets d'art. Both establishments have a healthy level of bookings, made many months ahead, and even in the wake of recession, the owners can still command prime rates. Some Piscean hotels even put spiritual education on the menu, offering courses in meditation along with the hors d-oevres. Others offer dance or theatre, or even live music and jazz.

Pisces' second great career "asset" is their creativity, and a truly prodigious number of Piscean boys and girls grow up dreaming of becoming artists, ballet dancers or even film directors. Neptune's gifts can be used wisely in these fields, for many Pisceans have a rare ability to "tune in" to the collective unconscious and reflect it back in myriad shapes and forms. The road to creative success, however, can be paved with many pitfalls.

One problem would-be Piscean artists often encounter is that of building the staying power necessary to really hone their skills. Developing an art form needs dreams and visions, which Pisceans possesses in abundance. But it also requires discipline, craft and commitment, all qualities that Pisceans can sometimes find hard to muster. Musicians must practise their scales day after day if they're ever to reach professional standards, just as dancers must spend hours at the barre. The ease or difficulty with which a Piscean will "stick with it" depends on their individual chart and the amount of earth or Saturn aspects in their horoscope. Piscean artists will invariably find it helpful to cultivate the qualities of their opposing sign of Virgo, for little art of any lasting value can be fashioned without a modicum of craft! Routine may be anathema to Pisces' freewheeling spirits, but without it, they'll never produce the results they so passionately dream of. Some Pisceans baulk at the discipline required to reach artistic excellence, and soon swim back into the comfortable oblivion of daytime soap-operas, odd jobs and daydreams.

Pisces' creative genius is rarely called into question, but they often run into problems when dealing with the practical side of their work. Fishes loathe routine, and steer clear of red tape where possible. They're totally, utterly brilliant at seeing the "bigger picture", but not so good at dealing with the details. This means Pisceans are excellent at envisioning the future of a business, but can be quite a liability if let loose in the admin department! Picture the scene when all those "trivial" details, like tax returns and monthly accounts, get drowned beneath an ocean of paper on their desk! The Piscean hoteliers I mentioned earlier both had the good sense to go into business with earth-sign partners, who liked nothing better than balancing the books whilst the fish was playing "mine host". Failing the presence of a real-life earthy partner, though, all fishes need to connect with those qualities within themselves, and develop some practical realism to balance out their visions and dreams!

Like Gemini and Sagittarius, their fellow mutable signs, most Pisceans like their work to be constantly varied. In order to really appeal, it should also be slightly unpredictable, else life can become grey and lacklustre, like the ocean on a rainy afternoon. A little glamour and sophistication don't go amiss either, and if Pisceans have the opportunity to mingle with influential people whilst they're working, so much the better. Incidentally, fishes often have a gift for making powerful friends and allies who can help them in their work and provide financial support when it's needed!

The dual nature of Pisces, along with its restlessness and appetite for change, means that many Pisceans achieve excellence in more than one career in a lifetime. One Piscean hotelier I know enjoyed a highly successful career in advertising before opening an English-style pub on the fringes of San Francisco Bay. Best-selling writer James Redfield, author of "The Celestine Prophecy" — an epic spiritual adventure, had a prior career as a therapist and counsellor, before developing his gifts as a writer. The profoundly spiritual nature of "Celestine", which describes a hero's journey through the wilds of South America, is also typically Piscean, for it unites the triple themes of travel, religion and the spiritual quest.

♓ The Pisces Boss

Pisceans who have mastered the more practical side of life can and do make excellent bosses, but broadly speaking, few fishes were born to lead. They're happy to take command when they still feel free to move around, but few Pisceans will sacrifice their freedom for a fancy title on the door. Fluidity and flexibility are all-important to a Piscean, and they have a secret horror of life becoming either too ordered or routine. Decision-making isn't their strong suit, either, and most Pisceans get very bogged down by excessive responsibility. But if fate propels them into a position where executive power means dealing with people rather than "things", then it's a different matter entirely, and then Pisceans come into their own ...and when they have a vision to propound, then they're happy to leave their cosy backwaters and swim into the public eye.

⟩(The Pisces Employee

Since most Pisceans prefer to work behind the scenes, being a salaried employee often suits them better than running their own business. Freelance work in the arts or social services can also be a compromise option, provided, of course, the fish can summon the self-discipline that's needed to work without supervision. Pisceans must always beware, however, of taking on more than they can handle. A Pisces who gets overloaded may just swim off and leave the office to its fate! Pressure and deadlines don't suit the fish well, either. Pisceans prefer to come and go in a reasonably fluid manner, with plenty of time for coffee breaks and the odd extended lunch hour. Two things to be aware of though, if you're thinking of employing a fish: they don't have a great head for details, and their deeply sympathetic nature means that they invariably end up becoming the office's "agony aunt". A helpful strategy might be to place them in Personnel, where their friendly manner and skill at judging character will be assets, not liabilities!

♓ Pisces and Career

Whatever field of endeavour Pisceans find themselves drawn to, they'll never find satisfaction unless they feel that their work is of service. The desire to be useful is second nature to Pisceans, whether they fulfil it directly, by helping people in an immediate way, or indirectly, through creative work that enhances the lives of others.

The helping professions are an ideal niche for Pisceans who want to serve humanity "hands-on". Pisces rules the twelfth house of hospitals, prisons and institutions in the natural zodiac, and you'll find many fished working as nurses, doctors and prison officials, and also prison visitors. Pisceans are good at listening and counselling, so they're naturally drawn to becoming therapists. Many become analysts or spiritual healers; others, like counsellor Grace Goodman, a pioneer of family therapy, have devoted their lives to helping society's misfits. Some Pisceans combine their counselling skills with their psychic gifts, and an overwhelmingly high percentage of mediums, tarot readers and astrologers are born under this sign. Dreamwork, art therapy and reflexology are other therapies where they excel. Patient Pisceans enjoy working with children, too — like Lord Baden-Powell and the educator Rudolf Steiner.

Many Pisceans find happiness and fulfilment through working in the hotel business, as we've seen, but even here, there's often a highly spiritual dimension to their work. The fish is adept at creating a soothing, healing environment where guests can be looked after and leave their worries behind, and it's this atmospheric "magic" that's often the secret of their commercial success. The caring, sympathetic ethos works at every level of the establishment, for the Piscean barman, who listens to his customers' problems night after night, is also acting as an unpaid "counsellor". He's probably also the reason why those customers keep coming back!

Many Pisceans make their social contribution through working in the arts, in the widest imaginable variety of ways. Many, many painters and musicians are born with the sun in Pisces, and many of these performers feature strongly Piscean themes in their work. Flautist Chris Michell has been fascinated by dolphins all her life, and has found world success with her "Dolphin Love" album. Piscean Kiri Te Kanawa is another musical high-flyer, along with singer Nina Simone and the late Nat King Cole.

Many Pisceans combine their artistic flair with their ability to sense future trends, by working in the world of fashion. Gloria Vanderbilt is just one of the big name Piscean designers! Thanks to their skill at tracking down beautiful objects and their wonderful sense of colour, many Pisceans build excellent careers in the interior design. Fishes are good at handling "difficult customers", too — another working asset that's more than useful in this business.

Pisceans love to communicate, and some fishes combine their wordpower with their keen sense of visual imagery by working in the advertising trade. You'll find Pisceans by the dozen working in Madison Avenue and Soho, and it's one of the few areas of business where they do feel thoroughly at home. The other natural habitat of the more business-minded Piscean is the film and TV industry. Pisceans enjoy all aspects of the business, whether they're producing the movies, like David Puttnam and ex-Beatle George Harrison, operating the cameras — or simply setting up the lights. Film and TV deal in alternative realities, fantasy and ephemera, so they're a perfect environment for the fish. And needless to say, they love all the parties that go with the job!

Pisces is also the sign of the actor, and a great many fishes find fame — and fortune — in front of the camera's "eye". Pisces' talent stems from their brilliant gift of empathy, which allows them to penetrate the essence of each and every character they play. Indeed, some Piscean actors claim that they're often happier "playing their parts" than they are in being themselves! By a curious coincidence, Cybill Shepherd and Bruce Willis, of "Moonlighting", are both Pisceans, as are Liza Minnelli, Robert de Niro and Patsy Kensit. Traditionally, Pisceans are also said to feel very much at home in all occupations connected with the sea. I haven't run across a great many Piscean admirals in my time, but I do know many who've found their niche in the travel trade!

⯎ Pisces: Keys to Financial Success

- DO accept the fact that you've got to live in the real world, as well as the world of your imagination. Aim to put your dreams and visions to as practical a use as you can.

- DON'T let your emotions take over when you've got major financial decisions to make. Seek advice from outside professionals where possible before making important money moves.

- DO get in touch with your special creative gifts — and do all that you can to develop them. Never forget, your Piscean creativity is one of your greatest financial assets.

- DO strike a balance between fearfulness and trust: aim to take a balanced approach to your money and you won't go too far wrong.

- DO accept the fact that your cash flow may always be erratic — and be sure to put money aside during your times of prosperity and plenty.

♓ Rich & Famous Pisceans

Frederic Chopin
G.F. Handel
Michelangelo
George Washington
Edward Cayce
Lord Baden-Powell
Lawrence Durrell
Kenneth Grahame
Albert Einstein
Rudolph Steiner
David Niven
George Harrison
Elaine Page
Miranda Richardson
Elizabeth Taylor
Liza Minnelli
Kate Nelligan
Sylvie Guillem
Isabelle Huppert
Cybill Shepherd
Bruce Willis
Robert de Niro
William Hurt
Al Jarreau
Anthony Robbins

Elizabeth Barrett Browning
Auguste Renoir
Rimsky-Korsakov
Vaslav Nijinsky
Edward Kennedy
Victor Hugo
Jack Kerouac
Florence Nightingale
Mikahil Gorbachev
Rupert Murdoch
Bernardo Bertolucci
David Puttnam
Johnny Cash
HRH Prince Andrew
Glenn Close
Ornella Muti
Patsy Kensit
Wendy Dagworthy
Tyne Daly
Lyn Seymour
Michael Caine
Jilly Cooper
Kiri Te Kanawa
Sir James Goldsmith
James Redfield

MERCURY RETROGRADES

Mercury, the planet of trade, stations and then turns retrograde three and sometimes four times a year. Mercury then remains retrograde for around 20 days at a time. During these periods, it's inadvisable to make major financial commitments or enter into any legal agreements which involve the signing of documents. If you do go ahead with major commitments at this time — such as buying a house, signing a credit agreement or forming a business partnership — you may have to renegotiate the terms of the agreement at a later date.

So *don't* — buy a house, a car, make other major purchases, sign important documents or make legally binding agreements at this time. Wait until Mercury goes direct again if you possibly can!

In 1996...	Jan 9-Jan 30	May 3-May 27
	Sep 4-Sept 26	Dec 23 ⇒
In 1997...	⇒ Jan 12	Apr 15-May 8
	Aug 17-Sep 11	Dec 7-Dec 27
In 1998...	Feb 27-Mar 20	Jul 31-Aug 23
	Nov 21-Dec 11	
In 1999...	Mar 10-Apr2	July 12- Aug 6
	Nov 5-Nov25	
In 2000...	Feb 21-Mar 14	Jun 23-Jul 17
	Oct 18-Nov 8	

...Calling All Geminis & Virgos

Since Mercury is the ruler of these two signs, both Geminis and Virgos need to take *special* care at this time. Remember, any major purchases you make while Mercury is retrograde will be unlikely to bring you satisfaction. So resist the temptation to "impulse spend", and try to stay away from the shops until Mercury goes direct again.

MORE ABOUT ASTROLOGY

If you'd like to learn more about astrology and how you can use it to help gain more insight into your life issues and challenges, your best course of action is to start by reading as much as you can about it ...and then enrol for classes. Well, that's what I did!

In London, there's a specialist astrological bookshop that I thoroughly recommend, and it's open until 7 pm, as well: The Astrology Shop, 78 Neal Street, Covent Garden, London, WC2H 9PA.   Tel: 0171-497-1001

———

If you live outside London, or abroad, I recommend the following mail-order astrological bookshop: Midheaven Bookshop, 396 Caledonian Road, London, N1 1DN.   Tel: 0171-607-4133

———

For classes, including correspondence courses, contact: The Faculty of Astrological Studies, 396 Caledonian Road, London, N1 1DN.   Tel: 0171-700-3556

...this is the main teaching body for astrology in the UK, and runs both introductory and advanced classes, either in London or by correspondence worldwide.

———

If you're interested in a more psychological approach to astrology, contact:
The Centre for Psychological Astrology, BCM Box 1815, London, WC1N 3XX.   Tel/fax: 0181-749-2330

———

For general information on astrology, contact:
The Astrological Association of Great Britain,
396 Caledonian Road,
London, N1 1DN.   Tel 0171-700-3746

...the Association publishes a Journal six times a year, and organises a comprehensive programme of public lectures and meetings, as well as an annual Conference.

RECOMMENDED READING

If you're serious about improving your relationship with money (and I'm sure you are, or else you wouldn't be reading this book), then it's good to cultivate the habit of reading literature of an inspiring and uplifting nature which can help you to create more prosperity in your life. The books recommended below are the ones that I've found most to be most useful...

Creative Visualization by Shakti Gawain
Bantam Books £4.99

Awaken The Giant Within by Anthony Robbins
Fireside Books £10.99

How To Think Like A Millionaire by C.A.Poissant
Thorsons £6.99

The Instant Millionaire by Mark Fisher
Hammond £4.99

The Trick to Money is Having Some by Stuart Wilde
White Dove Int £9.99

How To Attract Money by Robert Griswold
Piatkus Books £6.99

Money Magnetism by J Donald Walters
Crystal Clarity £6.99

What Colour Is Your Parachute?	by Richard N Bolles
A Manual For Job Hunters	Ten Speed Press £11.99
Money and The Markets:	by G Bates & J Bowles
An Astrological Guide	Thorsons £9.99

———

All the books in this recommended reading list can be ordered by mail-order direct from:
Barton House, PO Box 6, Dartmouth, TQ6 9YE, UK.
Credit card orders welcome — call 01803-835593 anytime ▧ ▣ ▭

Order three or more of the above titles and p&p is completely FREE! Otherwise please add £2.50 per order.

Overseas customers: please add an additional £2 <u>FOR EVERY BOOK ORDERED</u> to cover the additional cost of airmail postage. Please make cheques payable to 'Barton House' in UK pounds sterling.

The easiest way to order from abroad is by credit card: call (+44) 803-835593 anytime or fax (+44) 803-833464. email address: 100620.3604@compuserve.co

STOCK MARKET ASTROLOGY

If you'd like to find out more about how astrology can help you to improve your chances of making money on the stock market, then you need to speak to the leading expert in this complex field — Daniel Pallant, of *Treasury Consultants Ltd.*

Formerly a very successful property developer, Daniel began devising a financial forecasting system based on astrological principles, in the late 1970s. Over the years, this has proved to be remarkably accurate in its predictions.

Working closely with two computer experts, Dan has created a forecasting system based on the statistical correlation between astrological factors and FTSE 100 Share Index. Pallant publishes daily stock market forecasts through his *Trendfinder* service, and has predicted stock market movements with a consistent 60 – 65% accuracy!

Trendfinder is a valuable financial tool for any stock market investor or financial professional, and is one of the most reliable forecasting services available today.

To contact Daniel Pallant or to find out more about *Trendfinder*, please call or write to:

Treasury Consultants Ltd., PO Box 10,
Godalming, Surrey, GU8 4YW.
Call 01428-684325 or Fax 01428-684325
Email: treasury@dial.pipex.com

...and don't forget to mention that you read about *Trendfinder* in *Money Signs!*

ABOUT THE AUTHOR

Jane Bowles is an award-winning journalist, author and TV personality. After reading Philosophy, Politics and Economics at Oxford University, she began her media career in 1980, initially as a TV writer and reporter for Channel 4 documentaries. Around the same time she began studying astrology in depth. After qualifying with the Faculty of Astrological Studies in London, she went on to study for a Diploma in Psychological Astrology with Liz Greene, who is regarded by many as the world's leading astrologer.

In recent years, Jane has established her reputation as the UK's foremost writer on astrology and personal finance. She writes extensively on this subject in the national press.

In 1993, she was commissioned to co-write the book *Money And The Markets: An Astrological Guide,* published by Aquarian/HarperCollins. This groundbreaking work attracted widespread praise in the business press and was described as 'the definitive work on financial astrology' by Charles Harvey, former President of the Astrological Association of Great Britain.

Jane lives in Devon with her husband David and young daughter.

Jane Bowles has been hailed as "The Linda Goodman of the 1990s"...

HOW TO JOIN
OUR _FREE_ MAILING LIST

Join the Barton House mailing list and we will keep you informed of new books, audio-tapes, astrological services (including consultations and computer horoscopes) from Barton House!

A FREE Gift For You...

Simply send us your name and address to add to our mailing list and we will send you a _FREE_ booklet of Jane Bowles' _Moneysigns_ Financial Predictions for 1996.

**Please help us to network
this book by telling
your friends...**

...TO ORDER MORE COPIES
OF *MONEY SIGNS*...

Additional copies of *Money Signs* can be purchased
by mail-order priced at £8.99 each.

UK p&p is *FREE*: overseas please add an additional
£2.00 extra <u>per book</u> to cover airmail postage.

Credit card orders welcome: call our order line anytime
on 01803-835593 (or fax 01803-833464). ◼ ▦ ▭

Please make your cheque/PO/bank draft payable to
'Barton House' in UK pounds sterling.

Please post your order to: Barton House
PO Box 6, Dartmouth, Devon, TQ6 9YE, UK
or call 01803-835593 or fax 01803-833464
outside UK call (+44) 803-835593 or fax (+44) 803-833464

Compuserve email address: 100620,3604
Internet email address: 100620.3604@compuserve.co